Richard L. Ward

dead ends to
somewhere

The story of a vaccine to save

500,000 children worldwide and the

reluctant student who invented it

**Christopher
Matthews**
Publishing

www.christopherm

Bozeman, Montar

Dead Ends to Somewhere

Copyright © 2011 by Richard L. Ward

ISBN: 978-0-9833164-2-8

Published by Christopher Matthews Publishing
Bozeman, Montana
Printed in the United States of America

ACKNOWLEDGEMENTS

I am beholden to several of my siblings for their encouragement during the writing of this story. I am also indebted to my lifetime friend Frank Seitz who started me on the path to write my story and encouraged me throughout the writing. Finally, I am grateful to my children, Christopher and Stephanie, my daughter-in-law Mary, and my wife Shirley for their careful review of the manuscript, insightful comments, and bearing with me during the writing. This story, much of which you experienced first-hand, is dedicated to you.

Prologue

She had made the trip before, three times with her first child and twice with her second. The clinic hadn't gotten closer, and the normal four hour bus ride over the treacherous Jamaican mountain terrain on rutted dirt roads would be extended by the ceaseless rain, if she could reach her destination in Kingston at all. But she knew she had to try. There were no health care providers on which she could rely in either her remote village or others that dotted the mountainside which she called home. Her husband would not be returning from his custodial job at the resort near Montego Bay on the opposite end of the island for at least another month, so the decision was hers alone to make. She was just fortunate her mother had recovered from the dysentery that swept through her village several months earlier and killed many of its older inhabitants, including her father. At least her mother would be there to care for her two older children while she was gone.

Her youngest child had just turned eight months old on the previous day when his latest bout of diarrhea began. Diarrheal illnesses, like respiratory diseases, were commonplace in all three of her children's lives. She handled most with self-taught anecdotal treatments, but for those she deemed life-threatening, she bundled up the afflicted child for the torturous journey to the clinic. The two days of explosive diarrhea experienced by her youngest child, coupled with extensive vomiting, now warned the young mother that another trip was urgently needed. In spite of the weather, she couldn't afford to wait any longer; the bus came only once a day.

The trip became the nightmare she had anticipated. The pain she experienced from the constant jostling and penetrating heat was exceeded only by the inner pain elicited by the equally constant wailing of her very ill child. Several times in the steeper terrain, the dilapidated bus slid sideways, nearly pitching into the unguarded canyons below. With each slide, the panic in the other passengers escalated, but the young mother was so engrossed in the misery of her child that their screams did not even register in her brain.

By late in the afternoon, the bus finally arrived in the outskirts of Kingston, leaving the young mother at a stop within walking distance of her destination. She arrived through the still driving rain at the clinic just minutes before it closed for the day. There were no physicians present, and the nurse's assistant who examined her child provided only a bottle of liquid to be fed to the child as rehydration therapy. The young mother protested, attempting to explain that her child could not keep anything in his stomach and, therefore, could not hope to retain this new concoction. But her protests were to no avail, and she was turned out again into the early evening, just in time to catch the bus for the return trip home.

During this second bus ride of the day, the young mother tried multiple times to force drops of the new liquid past her child's throat, but her few successes were met with renewed vomiting, and the diarrhea was endless.

When she reached home around midnight after her excruciating journey, the child was already showing signs of serious distress. His skin was drying up and his eyes and stomach seemed to be sinking into his tiny body. She had never witnessed this before with any of her children, but knew something had to change soon or this son would be gone. All night she continued her attempts to force liquid into her child's stomach, but by early morning he was no longer able to swallow even a drop. When the time finally arrived for her to board the bus with him for another trip to the clinic later that morning, her baby had stopped crying and his breathing was irregular and faint. She knew she would never reach her destination with a living child, but she had to try. Her fears were not unfounded; her youngest child died in her arms before she was gone an hour. Rotavirus had claimed another victim.

It would be another 14 years before a vaccine that could have saved this child's life would become available on the island that had been his home.

Table of Contents

1 The Awakening

It seemed inconsequential. It was just another sixth grade assignment. Sister Mercedes' only instructions were "write a paragraph about something you like to do." Neither the nun nor I had a clue that this assignment would permanently alter the course of my life, let alone start me on a path to discover a vaccine that is being used to save the lives of children across the globe. Fortunately, for both the children and me, it did just that.

There are countries in the world, such as Germany and Switzerland, where a child's educational possibilities are etched in stone when they reach 12 years of age. In those places it has been assumed that by the time children reach that milestone, they will have demonstrated, through the assistance of fail-safe testing systems, both their interest in and capacity for learning. Once this has been determined, courses of study are devised based on each child's qualifications. Fortunately for me, the pigeon-holing of children into educational pathways was not part of the system in Montana when I was 12 years old. If it were, my career choices would have shriveled to those requiring little by way of book learning. Certainly, the nuns who attempted to teach me during my first six grades had little doubt about my intelligence and capacity for learning. Based on their observations, both were somewhere between miniscule and non-existent.

I reached the conclusion early in my scholastic life that the lack of formal kindergarten was the missing link that stymied my ability to learn. This seemed obvious since the students who received the highest marks in my class seemed to have all attended kindergarten, and those of us that had not were bottom feeders. Thus, I had missed the most important opportunity of my lifetime, an irreplaceable loss. There were several exceptions to this rule that I conveniently chose to ignore.

This discussion about missing kindergarten and thereby being doomed to illiteracy makes it sound like I really cared. Frankly, I didn't. This attitude may have had some effect on my performance. To me, school had three good parts that consisted of two 15 minute recesses and one noon hour period used for lunch and playtime. The rest was filler – and my scholastic accomplishments directly reflected those perceptions.

Although I struggled to stay afloat during my first four grades, the teachers I had in that span instilled me with sufficient fear to at least remain within hearing distance of the class average. That motivator dissipated when I entered the realm of Sister Mercedes in the fifth grade. I suppose it didn't help that this nun had been a classmate with Noah. Old is not necessarily bad, but it also is not necessarily good, and the pendulum seemed to swing toward the latter alternative in her case. In addition to the age difference relative to my previous teachers, Sister Mercedes was also height challenged. Since I had been growing, the reduced height differential significantly lessened the fear factor. Her advanced age and lack of a size were accompanied by a third physical trait that made her even less fearful: her tear ducts were chronically over-stimulated. One only had to mention the sufferings of Christ or the lack of spiritual understanding of a pagan child or a serious transgression of one of her male students, such as urinating on the toilet seat, and her eyes would well up with tears sufficient to require the dredging up of the same well-used handkerchief buried somewhere deep in the recesses of her habit. How can you truly fear a cry-baby?

Besides her physical liabilities, it was also apparent that Sister Mercedes had a small group of special students to whom she directed her attention. I don't think the rest of us were purposely ignored; we were just not going to amount to much, so why should she waste her time trying to teach us? We were just lucky that Sister Mercedes was not the determinant of our career choices. Mine would have been pounding sand down rat holes. All told, this was not the perfect scenario for a student who was already suffering from attitude deficit disorder.

Although my interactions with Sister Mercedes appeared to have little positive effect on either of our lives, my aspirations as a student were in perfect rhythm with this woman's expectations. In fact, her lack of interest in me had some clear advantages. For example, she would assign homework every afternoon just before we closed down for the day. I think I sort of heard her, but I never really connected with what she said. My mind was invariably already out the door. Besides, I knew that only the chosen few would be expected to respond to her assigned tasks. That almost always took me off the hook. On the few occasions when this calculated risk proved to be wrong and I was asked about the homework assignment, I would just stare down at my desk and look stupid. This merely confirmed the nun's opinion of me. So ignoring homework really worked to both of our advantages. It saved me the effort and allowed the good sister to verify her judgment about my abilities. It was a win-win situation.

This lack of attention to homework and other scholastic activities did have a downside, however, as portrayed by my numbingly slow progress, particularly my reading skills. Due to factors such as lack of kindergarten, any semblance of a library at home, growing up with old parents who were very tired of child rearing, personal disinterest, or any of a myriad of other contrived or verifiable excuses, my reading abilities were clearly underwhelming even before I encountered Sister Mercedes. This situation may have been foretold as early as the first grade. My teacher initially assigned me to the "C" reading group as she did all first graders that had not attended kindergarten. Within several weeks, however, my ability to comprehend the written word had progressed so little that I was demoted to the "D" reading group with two other non-performers, both of whom were eventually designated as retarded.

In the second grade I was far more interested in eating my book than reading it, something I routinely did while standing with the other underperformers during our time in reading line. During those periods of unending torture, each of us in turn was able to choke up only about three short sentences. There is nothing more boring to a second grader than listening to other lousy students trying to sound out words that had no meaning to any of the parties involved. Keeping track of where we were in the book under these circumstances was essentially impossible, especially when the book kept shutting as I was consuming it. Since I couldn't read, I had no chance of finding the correct place in the book when my name was eventually called.

One fateful day, Sister Iona finally noticed that I had ingested a large fraction of the non-print portion of my reading book; I had purposely eaten around most of the print, so I really couldn't see what harm I had done. For this infraction, I was assigned after school eraser-pounding and under-desk sweeping duties. Sister Iona patiently explained that my parents were too poor to pay for the book, so working it off was the only feasible method of repayment. I was not previously aware of my parents' destitute state and felt very badly for them and for me, especially since it meant that I had to be associated with school for extra minutes every day during the remainder of the school year. A more with-it child might have used this experience to inspire life-long attitude improvement. In my case, such a change would have required a brain transplant.

My lack of reading skills "surprisingly" remained evident in the third grade. A desperate Sister Iona, who was fortunate enough to have the opportunity to share a second year with me, began to call in reinforcements. Within days after school started, I was assigned to sit with Jenny Lou, a cute but literate classmate. She would patiently listen each day as I attempted to plow through several sentences. I was much more taken with the idea of sitting cheek-to-cheek with this lovely creature in a tiny seat than learning to read, so the experiment was probably doomed before it started.

After several weeks with my new instructor, a shocking development occurred that forever clouded my image of my substitute teacher's qualifications. The scenario was this. After taking one of our many standardized exams (which were rarely graded), Sister Iona quizzed everyone in my class about whom each thought got the worst grade on this particular test. This one, to my dismay, had been graded. There was no scarcity of names to be selected from amongst the lesser students and, of course, my name was near the top of the list. In fact, it was suggested twice. I personally volunteered no names but merely sat frozen in shock. Based on the mirrored looks of terror in the eyes of other students sharing my credentials, my emotions had companions. The relief I experienced upon learning that this time I was not the designee was almost surpassed by my surprise at learning that my tutor was the one being honored. From that day forward, I knew that Jenny Lou could add nothing to my reading skills because she knew even less than me, thus putting the last nail in the coffin of our experiment in reading.

It was never clear why Sister Iona performed this drill. Perhaps she had an angry day or perhaps it was a day she set aside to provide an instruction in humility. If the latter was the case, the lesson was a total failure because Jenny Lou rebounded and was more confident than ever. Perhaps this drill was performed as a lesson intended for the whole class, making us aware that the other shoe could fall on our collective throats at any time. I was desperate when taking these tests for several weeks thereafter, always assuming my name would be next in the roll call. At one point, I became so obsessed with doing well that I used one of these tests to verify the existence of God. I didn't promise God anything. I just pointed out that if He existed He would correctly answer a series of questions to which I had no clue regarding the answers. He proved He existed and did me one better. The test went ungraded. I didn't risk that challenge again. You don't test God twice.

My pedantic development as a student paralleled my lack of progress in personal hygiene. For example, in the second and third grades, I routinely wet my pants. It may have been out of the fear and embarrassment associated with requesting a trip to our unisex bathroom in front of my classmates. However, it may also have been just a habit that I developed. I normally would not let go with a gusher, and since my pants were mostly thick, highly absorbent cords that my mother had sewn, I never produced a visible puddle below my seat, something that occasionally happened with other kids. My cords were always dark in color, so that helped disguise the wet area. I also learned to turn my back to people and hold my legs together if approached during the drying phase. Interestingly, even though I must have had a seamy odor, especially since I typically wore the same pants for at least a week between wash periods, my little habit was never, to my knowledge, detected. That cannot be said of everyone.

One particular close call occurred on a confession day. This event would take place before every first Friday of the month, during which time our entire classroom would march in double file to our church a block away and, after lining up, would one-by-one confess our sins to a totally bored and sometimes snoring priest. We all had a lot to confess in the third grade. Those of us who failed to put our fingers in our ears during the confessions of our louder classmates learned, in fact, just how boring sins could be. The good news was that the sin of "listening to the confessions of others" provided us with something to confess ourselves during our own turns in the confessional.

During these confessional marathons, we remained in the church until every one of us was finished before we were ordered to march back to our classroom. Since only one priest was there to hear our confessions, this process was not a two-minute exercise. The church had no bathroom, and we were not allowed to go back to school, located less than one-half block away, no matter how critical the need. This had the foreshadowing of a bad situation, especially for a kid who regularly used his pants as a reservoir for urine anyway.

The "close call" occurred on a confession day when I either had an unusually full bladder or the time in church extended beyond the usual two hours. Whatever the reason, I released more into my pants that day than they could absorb. I carefully tried to spread out the puddle with my foot, but was still convinced it would be detected. I never knew whether the boy behind me in line just got blamed for my puddle or whether he produced one of his own, but the word got out that he had wet his pants. Perhaps because I had just gone to confession or because I was still in my own personal Hell from fear of detection, I was not an enthusiastic participant in that day's crucifixion of the other pants-wetter.

Because of Jenny Lou's failure to teach me to read in grade three, my deficiency remained evident into the fourth grade. That year we were blessed to be taught by Sister Evangeline, a young and very strong nun, who routinely pounded my desk with her ruler during my daily oral reading sessions. I think she was trying to create a rhythm to my reading pattern, but one can readily guess how successful that was. Fortunately, I had stopped peeing in my pants by then because she, either by mistake or on purpose, would often catch my fingers when establishing her rhythm. When really frustrated by my lack of performance, she would also attempt to elongate my ears which were already oversized for my head. "Persuasion via the ear" was a common method of teaching for Sister Evangeline.

Sister Evangeline also destroyed my faith in saints. Catholics are taught to pray to saints, just like they would pray to Mary the Mother of Jesus, because these folks are housed closer to God and He can hear what they are saying better than He can our petitions, or at least their words carry more weight. In addition to praying to saints in general, each of us had our own special saint for whom we were named and who was expected to provide us special protection. My special saint was Saint Richard de la Wyche, the Bishop of Chichester, who died on April 3, 1253. So the 3rd of April was my special day, or at least it was until Sister Evangeline came into my life. Because Saint Richard would look out for me, at least on April 3rd, I felt pretty much invulnerable that one day of the year.

On returning from afternoon recess on the April 3rd under the tutelage of Sister Evangeline, I tested my invulnerability. Sister Evangeline was stationed by the drinking fountain which we were not allowed to touch on our way back into the classroom. Her philosophy was that if you wanted a drink, you should have cut out of recess early to get it. There was a fat chance of that happening, at least for me. Anyhow, on that afternoon, some brainless, dehydrated kid attempted to slip around the good nun to wet his lips, just before being crushed. And crushed he was, just as I arrived. Since I felt I was invulnerable that day, it was my duty to step in and defend this helpless child. I wasn't obnoxious about it. I merely inquired, "Sister, why are you being so mean to him? He is just thirsty." That was all that was needed. I had questioned the authority of God Almighty. The offending child was dropped to the floor and the hand of God was instantly at my face and neck. Within seconds I was sharing the floor, even before the original culprit had time to vacate the space. The remainder of the recess group filed silently around my prone body as Sister Evangeline was making her final pronouncement which had something to do with, "Don't you ever question the authority of God." That was the last time I put an ounce of faith in the protective powers of good ol' Saint Richard.

With a fine set of reading skills acquired over the first four years of grade school, I was fully prepared to be a star reader in the fifth grade. Our first report card arrived six weeks into the year and, as was predestined, I received a "D" in reading. Even though my scholastic record was less than fantastic before this time, my grades had managed to stay in the "C" zone. The fact that I had never heard of a child who had actually received an "F", a "D" meant that I had successfully reached the bedrock of grades. Not surprisingly, the importance of this event did not register with me, that is, until after the subsequent Parents/Teachers Meeting.

Even though my parents were used up as child raisers after dealing with my eight older siblings, they were still social butterflies, which was usually played out by going either to the grocery store, church on Sunday, or Farm Bureau meetings. Thus, the pleasure of attending a Parents/Teachers meeting was a special event on their social calendar. The ultimatum delivered by Sister Mercedes at this particular meeting was that "Richard is to read aloud at home every night until he improves." The fact that we had very little that I could understand by way of reading material at home seemed a likely excuse to stay my execution from improvement. However, all our grade school classrooms had small libraries, and I became briefly familiar with the one in the back of our fifth grade classroom. I toted home a new book every day for a whole week, and my mother would semi-patiently sit with me every night until I finished it. Of course, I made sure I selected one of the shortest books. Even so, it was a grueling experience, especially for my mother who had already put in over 14 hours of hard labor before our evening sessions even began.

Perhaps my reading skills did briefly improve, or perhaps my mother just got more tired than usual, but the evening reading sessions evaporated after the first week. From my mother's viewpoint, the exercise was a huge success because I never received another "D", even in reading. What she didn't realize was that this remarkable outcome was due less to a new found reading proficiency than to an improvement in my skill of remaining outside of the awareness zone of Sister Mercedes during the remainder of our time together. Some kids can stay hidden during their entire school careers; fortunately for me and my future, I was less talented and was only able to carry this off on a regular basis during my two years with Sister Mercedes.

Either by chance or through my own lack of caution, awareness of my presence still occasionally registered with Sister Mercedes, but only for brief interludes and invariably with unpleasant outcomes. Most of these encounters were associated with something other than my sub-par classroom performance. I seemed to have a real knack for ticking off this nun. One of the surefire methods centered on snow and what could be done with it. Keep in mind that I lived in Montana and the school year spanned from Labor Day to Memorial Day. That gave me at least eight out of nine months of the school year to utilize snow, even in a mild year. The biggest single snowfall I remember totaled four feet, and it occurred on the 10th of May. So snowball chucking was a way of life, even if it was forbidden on the school grounds.

On one occasion, the windows of the high school science room located three stories up in our ancient brick schoolhouse were opened for a brief period to release hydrogen sulfide fumes generated by one of the aspiring sophomore scientists. Since open windows were almost as rare as alligators during Montana winters, these offered an irresistible challenge to my colleagues and me. So up popped the snowballs and out popped the head of Sister Roseanne, the high school principal. The four culprits were easy to spot, even from three stories up. We were the ones with the cocked arms containing the snowballs. Dear Sister Roseanne was very kind; she even met us half way in the deal. That is, we met half way up the stairs to the high school floor in the fifth/sixth grade classroom. Better than that, both Sisters Roseanne and Mercedes were there to welcome us. A lot was said in the first five minutes; after that I lost track. Our punishment was standard: 500 sentences on the blackboard saying something about not throwing snowballs.

Repetition is the mother of learning, so that day I at least learned a few words very well.

The living targets selected to receive the snowballs I threw were generally ones that could reciprocate. Sometimes, however, I was less discriminatory, but only because I was a bad shot. On one occasion, my third grade tutor Jenny Lou harassed me to the point of letting her have one in the teeth. There were at least two reasons why taking this course of action was profoundly stupid. The first was I knew that even forming a snowball would get reported to Sister Mercedes, but I did it anyway. Secondly, when I threw the snowball, I failed to notice that Judy was standing directly between Jenny Lou and me at the time of release. I knew Judy was half blind since her glasses were as thick as coke bottles, but I didn't know she was also deaf. She totally ignored my clear warning, and in the next instant -- pow -- the snowball was lodged between Judy's glasses and her eyeball. I guess it must have hurt. At least that was what she and Jenny Lou collectively reported to Sister Mercedes. So, another 500 sentences was the order of the day.

Having observed the everlasting kiss-up techniques of my nemesis Jenny Lou, another classmate and I finally shouldered the responsibility for the entire fifth grade to let her know she was not fooling anyone, or at least not us. The reaction to our subtle suggestions that she might possibly be construed as a teacher's pet was predictable. Once the message was delivered to Jenny Lou during a quiet period of class workbook exercise, the target of our attention haughtily marched to the front of the room to transfer the information to Sister Mercedes. Jenny Lou could weave a great tale, so the one she whispered into Sister Mercedes' ear that day must have been a whopper. Of course, her story may have merely tweaked Sister Mercedes' anger button due to our recognition of the inequities being promulgated in her classroom. Regardless of the reasons, the nun's transition from being in a deep sleep to being completely enraged required less than five seconds. Her transformation was remarkable, especially since I had previously viewed this unassuming lady as relatively innocuous. She rose at least two feet above her normal diminutive height and moved with astonishing speed to escort my accomplice and me by our collars to the cloakroom. There she expended what appeared to be a lifetime's worth of pent-up rage with enough vehemence to be heard in the high school classrooms one floor up. She was frightful to watch, especially since her tirade was buffered by only my one partner in crime.

Because of the exuberance with which it was delivered, little of the actual substance of Sister Mercedes' speech reached my memory bank. However, its meaning did not escape me. It also did not escape my companion because when the report of the incident was delivered to his home that evening, he was immediately transferred to the public school across the street. Having witnessed that potentially favorable outcome, I considered the same course of action. However, I decided that things could be worse, and if I delivered this story to my home, no matter how I enhanced it in my favor, they would get worse. I think that was the last time I called Jenny Lou a teacher's pet, at least to her knowledge.

There is probably some cerebral connection between possessing the ability to read and the ability to write. I was equally poor in both categories. Thus, on one fateful day during the latter part of my sixth year in school, and second year with Sister Mercedes, our class was assigned its first creative writing exercise on the aforementioned topic of "something we like to do." At least it was the first attempt at creative writing to make my radar screen. During this exercise, I gave my full and undivided attention to explaining my love of baseball and interest in being a professional pitcher for somewhat less than six minutes. Unfortunately, Sister Mercedes had neglected to tell us we were also expected to proofread what we wrote. Of course, it is also a remote possibility that I had not listened to that part of the assignment. Missing this detail was a fatal flaw.

After having fully enveloped herself in our finished masterpieces between evening prayer periods, Sister Mercedes arrived the next day filled with enthusiasm, and primed to deliver endless compliments to her aspiring authors. At least one could dream. What she had really decided between prayer sessions was to read the best and worst stories to the class, possibly to provide dual lessons in pride and humility. You can guess whose essay she selected to provide the lesson for the latter. She not only read my masterpiece, but every grammatical error was emphasized and every misspelled word was graphically displayed on the blackboard. In addition, and to my utter horror, she announced my name as the author when she had finished. It was an experience to be remembered, and it certainly was.

This incident was the turning point in my life. It could have gone either way. I might have been so deflated that I just gave up entirely, dropping out of school as quickly as legally possible. However, the outcome was a bit different, certainly something that Sister Mercedes would not have foreseen in her desire to punish me for my ineptitude. It may have been a combination of shock, anger, and humiliation that got my attention. However, in retrospect, I have concluded that the lasting change in attitude stimulated by this incident came from something much deeper. This "something" was an aroused spirit of competition instilled by my father in each of his nine children. Based on his training, I was already fully mature as a competitor in playtime activities before I even started the first grade, but this spirit remained latent when applied to scholastics. Sister Mercedes unwittingly, but fortuitously, forced me to shift my competitive spirit to something other than games. In addition to my father's training in competitiveness, both of my parents provided training in resiliency in the face of overwhelming adversity, something I would only come to fully understand as I grew older. So armed with these two guides, I resolved that on the day of my humiliation this type of classroom experience would never happen to me again.

The actual formulation of a plan to become scholastically competitive took several months to develop, but was eventually designed during the subsequent summer. One evening in late August, I was sitting with my mother on the porch of our farmhouse watching the blackbirds mass together before their annual migration south, steeling myself for another go at school. During this time of reflection, I pledged to her that I was going to get at least one "A" in something in the seventh grade. Amazingly, it happened. However, it was not in reading. By that time in my educational career, I could not even see the dust trail left by the proficient readers in my class.

Throughout my seventh and eighth grade years, we had 20 minutes of story reading to look forward to after each noon hour, and the reading was done by the students. I loved the stories but lived in dread of being called on to perform. Of course, it never happened. If I had offered my classmates a choice of buying the book from me or listening to me read it, I could have paid for the school year with my earnings in book sales. Both of my teachers during those two years were painfully aware of that fact, and since this reading period was supposed to inspire pleasure and not pain, my worries were for naught.

Although becoming a proficient reader was destined to be a multi-year project, the fuse that was ignited in me that fateful day with Sister Mercedes continued to be fueled by the spirit of competition. My family was poor but it was also proud. I was often reminded by several of my eight siblings how special it was to be a "Ward." Not unrelated to family pride was my father's urging not only to compete, but to win. Thus, the ball that was pushed during my sixth grade awakening was kept rolling by this need to compete and win. So, in spite of the fact that I was still a sub-standard reader in the eighth grade, I finished that year fourth overall in a class of 26. This was a dramatic improvement after being near the bottom only two years earlier.

As the years with Sister Mercedes were left behind, my struggles with reading gradually dissipated. However, it was not until the latter part of high school when, after several years of employing the art of reading to acquire actual information, I became aware that I could truly read. As it turned out, it was a good thing I could. It was a skill I would need.

2 Early Lessons

As graphically portrayed to me by Sister Iona when I was a second-grader, my family was poor, something inherited from my father's side of the family. Both sets of his grandparents fled Ireland with the masses during the Potato Famine in the mid-1800's carrying little more than the clothing on their backs. They eventually settled in the almost 100% Irish Catholic community of Melrose, Iowa. There my dad's parents attempted to raise a family of five boys and two girls on an unprofitable hillside farm of sun-baked clay. With only an eighth grade education, my dad's vision of professional opportunities was restricted to farming, farming, or farming. His parents were so destitute that when his mother died in 1921, my dad's inheritance was to pay for her burial. The cost was not great but was still substantial by his standards, and this obligation delayed his own marriage by two years. Even this extra time did little to prepare him financially for the subsequent depression and era of the Midwest Dust Bowl, especially since he had fathered four children by the time he lost his own farm to creditors in 1930. My father was an Old World Catholic and viewed even the rhythm method of birth control as sinful and against the laws of the Catholic Church. Thus, to compound the situation, he added four more dependents in the next five years while attempting to survive as a sharecropper.

It also did not enhance the family fortune that my dad had been inflicted with a debilitating chronic illness designated as severe asthma by the local physician. The symptoms of his disease unrelentingly progressed with each stress-filled year. His inability to draw a full breath coupled with the sticky-hot, endless summers of southern Iowa in the 1930's, permitted sleep only after total exhaustion. The downward spiral of my father's health severely restricted his ability to work the farm, thus adding more financial stress to his already poverty stricken family.

But the Irish are known for both their resilience and expectations of suffering, otherwise known as God's will. My dad was the traditional Irish family patriarch and, therefore, was expected to be the example of resilience. This necessitated that he blindly plod on according to his established beliefs regardless of what was happening around him. And things were definitely happening, right on his doorstep.

Hardship and poverty were a way of life for my dad, but not for my mother. Her own mother died, after ten successful births, when my mom was only eight years old. This had the making of a tragic life for my mother who was next to the youngest in this horde of children. However, her father ran a lucrative brick factory whose earnings were shared with his many children. Fortunately, his spirit for family was inherited by his children who, each in their own way and in their own turn, replaced the lost mother.

Springing from this loving and dedicated family, my mother became a confident teacher. Her first assignment was a one-room country schoolhouse near the Irish community of Melrose. She chose this post to be near her sister Gertrude who lived in Melrose and held the respected title of Postmistress. However, Gertrude had detractors who did not take kindly to her perceived overbearing attitude. This, coupled with her shortage of Irish heritage, stimulated the bestowal of less complimentary titles. By default, my mother Loraine was guilty until proven innocent by a substantial segment of the local population.

Gertrude's saving grace was that she was married to Jim Ward who was 100% Irish. One positive for my mother was that Jim had a younger brother Tom who was just as Irish and happened to be available. Although not accustomed to being steeped in poverty as was Tom's lot in life, my mother learned to ignore it, or fell in love in spite of it. Their engagement came quickly, but the period of engagement seemed unending to my mother. She often repeated the story, always concluding with "I truly thought we would never be married, even though I loved Tom more because of the concern he showed for his family." Finally, on a sunny June day in 1923, Tom and Loraine recited their wedding vows.

Be careful what you wish for, it may come true. The extent of their honeymoon consisted of a walk to a local pond to blissfully watch the sunset, topped off with a one-way buggy ride to their four-room farmhouse. When the sun rose the next morning, so did Loraine, but unlike the sun's day, hers never set. She was a city girl who knew how to work, but never like this.

The division of labor was clearly defined, and my mother's allotment was everything except the farming. This line was rarely crossed from either side no matter how inequitable. My mother quickly learned practical survival skills, like soap production from pig fat, squeezing off chicken heads between her foot and a log, and canning of every conceivable plant and animal body part. Indoor plumbing was not a consideration, and the water pump was located next to the barn, a two minute hike from the house. Electricity was only a distant dream. Naturally, child rearing and its associated functions were strictly women's work, and for my mother there would soon be an abundance of both. Within ten months of her honeymoon, she became pregnant, nearly the longest dry period she would experience in the next 11 years. So the cycle of work and pregnancy became her life, a cycle as certain as the motion of the earth.

Shortly after the birth of her fifth child in 6 1/2 years, my mother experienced her first of many "nervous breakdowns" from depression. During these periods, the younger children would be lent out to neighbors or relatives and my mother would take extended "vacations" with one of her seven sisters, usually Sister Lillian who was a caregiver in Chicago's Mercy Hospital. On one of these vacations, my mother was administered shock treatment which did not stop the breakdowns but did dull her senses sufficiently that by the time of my birth in 1942, she had become a shell of her former self.

Things so deteriorated with my dad's health that by late in 1937, his physician issued the pronouncement, "you will be dead by the end of next summer if you remain in Iowa." The following March, he boarded a train for the cleaner, dryer air of the West. His lungs continuously hacked up crud until he reached the Montana border where it all miraculously stopped. Thus, it was only natural that Montana would become known as "the promised land." The train he was on continued across the state, and each day my dad gained strength. He eventually alighted in Spokane, Washington, where during one month of serious eating, he regained full health and 30 pounds on his emaciated frame.

My dad's recovery, however, was not being duplicated on the home front. Once leaving Melrose, my dad's focus was strictly personal. He never communicated with my unstable mother during his entire absence. She waited in vain for any information that would clarify whether he was dead or alive, or even had intentions of returning to her and his eight children.

Just before his departure, my dad had moved his family into a tiny, bedbug-infested shack on the outskirts of Melrose where, in addition to being riddled with bedbug bites, the bodies of all inhabitants were besieged with rashes of boils, over and over again. As my mother was sleep walking through her 24-hour shifts, she began to slowly crack, fueled daily by her growing belief that she was to be left alone with the full family responsibility but without any means of support. During this time, her confidant became my oldest brother Joe who was 13 at the time. Joe was highly sensitive, and even though he was a child that loved to hear his own voice, he also had the capacity to listen. And listen he did, day after day, night after night. Thus, in my mother's darkest moments, she laid it on Joe how she planned to stab to death all the children and herself if my dad did not return. Each night when bedtime was finally permitted, Joe would lie awake with his ears tuned for the slightest suggestion of my mother's approach. My father did finally return, but by then Joe's trust and optimism were permanently lost along with his childhood; the experience disallowed him another fully restful night before his death in 2003.

The return of my re-energized father did, however, stimulate a rapid superficial healing for my mother. No time could be lost. His asthma would zap him again if they delayed. They had to leave immediately. Within a month, the belongings accumulated during 15 years of marriage were sold, given away, or packed onto two contraptions that loosely qualified as a truck and a car. My dad drove the car and a 17-year old neighbor boy was induced to drive the truck on the promise of snow-capped, green mountains and perhaps even a job at the end of the line. They became the northern equivalent of the "Grapes of Wrath;" two destitute parents, eight dependent children aged 2-13, a driver and two overloaded vehicles crawling toward the sunset.

In spite of its appearance as a formula for disaster, the tedious journey was remembered as a long camping trip by the children old enough to retain the experience. The only major happening occurred about 100 miles into Montana when the truck's engine blew a rod. Fortunately, my parents had managed to retrieve nearly $300 for the items they had sold. This was sufficient to replace the engine with a used model installed by a local mechanic in the metropolis of Broadus, population 74. After a week's delay, the migrants began the final push which took them over and into the Rocky Mountains, finally landing them in the lush June paradise of Montana's Gallatin Valley.

It may have seemed like heaven, but it was still the depression and even this remote section of the country felt the heavy influence of a nation in distress. Jobs were difficult to land and harder to keep. My dad's only experience was farming but, fortuitously, one of his more affluent ex-neighbors from Iowa owned a large spread on which my father was employed for the grand sum of $25 per month. The primary reason he was selected for the job from the multitude of applicants was that he was a first cousin of his new employer's wife.

Included in the deal was the use of a bunkhouse for this family of ten. It contained four rooms, two of which qualified as bedrooms. In summertime it was livable because most sleeping was done outdoors, and the rain that spilled through open holes in the roof could be collected in assorted buckets rather than flood the house. However, when the winds of winter arrived in October along with several feet of snow and temperatures below -30 degrees, any remnants of euphoria with the pioneer life evaporated. For my mother, appreciation for Montana and its snow-capped mountains was slow to develop anyway. These same gorgeous peaks personified prison walls that blocked any hope of return to her childhood home and security in Iowa -- no matter how bad it had been before they left. Thus, for Loraine all was not roses, even in the delightfully warm days of summer, and the flowers along with her hope froze solidly in the winter.

At the end of the first summer, my dad's employer dealt him another blow, saying he no longer had a paying job for him. He added, however, that if he wanted to feed his cattle for the winter, he could remain in the bunkhouse. My dad somehow found temporary employment at a hardware store in Bozeman that allowed him, with family still living in the hovel, to survive the winter. Their lot in life was not unusual for families during this latter Depression period, but their experiences were still lessons in resilience of which I have reminded myself during my own subsequent times of crisis.

Luxuries were nonexistent during my family's first winter in Montana, but the physical, mental and spiritual growth of all eight children was kept on course by my parents. There was enough food, the older kids attended the local school, and Sunday Mass was never missed, no matter how high the snowdrifts. This was the Sunday morning scene: a family of ten in a dilapidated car stacked floor to ceiling, plowing through snow drifts over a frozen dirt road to keep their chances of salvation intact.

By springtime, my dad had managed to rent a farm of his own with an on-site, five-room dwelling containing an intact roof that affectionately became known as "the little brown house." This was where my family was living when I was born in 1942 and where I spent the first four years of my life. The accommodations consisted of three small bedrooms, a functional kitchen, a small living room, and a three-holer outhouse. This house provided my family their first opportunity to live with the miracle of electricity, but still without indoor plumbing. The living arrangement was simple: one bedroom was taken by my parents, and the other two, each with two double beds and little else, were sleeping quarters for either my four brothers or four sisters. My arrival three years later was like the straw that broke the camel's back. Somehow I had to be assimilated, and since my sisters were smaller, the final squeeze was resentfully theirs to make.

One stereotype of big families is that they have deep, protective relationships nurtured by repetitive expression of love. A second stereotype is that they fight all the time, competing for recognition, space and food. My mother proclaimed that "none of my children ever fought" so, by default, my family must have been the former. I will reiterate, she was never quite right after receiving shock treatment, so much of what my mother believed was strictly wishful thinking. The majority of the interactions between my siblings were based on competition, fueled by my father who pitted one child against the other in essentially every activity, possibly to get the maximum output from each. His litany included "I'll bet Legs (his name for my sister Gen) can beat you all across the road." "Are you sick today John? Bob is pitching the hay higher (never mind that he is three years older than you)." "Louis could have harnessed that team in three minutes. What's taking you so long Joe?" And it went on.

My salvation was that I was much younger and posed no intellectual or athletic threat to any of my brothers or sisters. By the time I was old enough to offer respectable competition, almost all my siblings had left home. However, this did not shield me from my father's mission to make all his children competitive. Since he had only an eighth grade education, little of his attention was directed at my scholastic achievements. That department was under my mother's supervision if it was anywhere. My dad's competitive fixations were directed toward my physical accomplishments, both manual labor and sports. Even when I was doing well in either of these activities, however, I felt I never measured up to my dad's expectations. He never gave me a compliment face-to-face but certainly did not withhold his critiques. He did succeed in molding me into an earnest competitor and, in so doing, probably did me a favor. However, I have never forsaken the possibility that there is still a compliment hiding out there somewhere, even though my dad has been dead for nearly 40 years.

Aside from the competition, subtle bonds of dependency and affection linked my siblings that could not be extended to me. I was a late-phase anomaly, almost an only child in a family of nine kids. Being seven years in age behind my nearest sibling did have one advantage. My mother finally had the luxury to again be a mother. This activity had largely been on hold when the numbers of children slid past four and the nervous breakdowns kicked into gear. I relished sitting on her lap absorbed in her tales of Indians, animals, and faraway places, stories she had memorized from childhood. My biggest dread was reaching my fourth birthday because on that fateful day I was no longer allowed to sit on my mother's lap in church.

My father and I did not have the same bonding experience. He never ventured to pick me up as a child let alone cuddle me. My first remembered awareness of this hands-off relationship was on the day the first and only formal portrait of our family was taken when I was four years old. There in the picture is my brother Joe in his seminarian cassock, my brother Louis in his Navy uniform, and the rest of us wearing the best we had. I was, of all things, sitting on my father's lap having a foreign body reaction. I have no memory more poignant than the distaste I had for being required to be in that position, even for only a few snaps of the camera. This sentiment improved with age, but even at the time of my dad's death when I was 30 years old, my reaction was more of sorrow due to missed opportunities than remembered shared experiences.

They say you have to be tough to survive in the West and those that aren't don't. By the time I came along, this cliché had mostly become just that. However, there is a reason the population of Montana has never exceeded one million, even though it is massive and its scenery is unsurpassed. Population control in Montana is mostly due to the fact that the average person doesn't relish eight months of winter. Therefore, most newcomers disappear south as soon as the September snows hit, then they don't return until the ice breaks in late April or, more often than not, don't return at all. Those who stay the winter have to be tough...or stupid.

My first recollection of personally needing to be tough came when I was three years old and was not weather-related. My family owned several varieties of wagons used for transporting livestock, hay and other farm commodities. Some were of ancient vintage with iron wheels, and only the most recent acquisitions had new-fangled rubber tires. The means used to convey these wagons also altered between the old and the new, consisting of either a team of horses or a tractor. On one occasion, I witnessed my sister Clo, who was nine years my senior, bounce under a wagon and ride on its axle as it was conveyed across a field. I knew this had to be the greatest fun in the world and was just waiting my chance. The opportunity came when a full load of hay was being delivered from field to barn via the gravel road immediately in front of the little brown house. I scrambled to the roadside where my presence was formally acknowledged by my brother Bob who was driving the team of horses pulling the wagon. He misunderstood my intentions and instructed me to wait until he reached the gate if I wanted to ride in the wagon seat. I was not as nimble as my sister, and tripped on my passage to the axle. A wagon wheel was on my head and dragging it through the gravel within a heartbeat.

At least two circumstances contributed to the fact that I am telling this story. One was that it was a wagon with rubber wheels; a wagon with iron wheels would have just run over my head and smashed it like a watermelon. The other was that the team pulling the wagon did not have the consistent power of a tractor, and the extra pressure of pulling my head was quickly noted by my brother. Because of these factors, damage was minimal. There was merely gushing blood followed by a frantic trip to the family doctor in Bozeman who extracted a small bucket of gravel from my face and closed the wounds with multiple stitches. There weren't many plastic surgeons on call that day in Bozeman, so the scars were permanent. That had its good points because the scars were later deemed to be a visible demonstration of my toughness, and permanent evidence of the same gave me a special place in Ward folklore.

"Where were you when Dick got his head run over?" My sister Gen inquired of my sister Rose Marie.

"Why, I was hanging up the wash. Where were you, sunbathing? Certainly not helping Mom," was the retort.

"Well I got to him first and probably saved his life," uttered the sunbather in her defense.

There was even serious competition in my rescue. So it went and sometimes still does. I personally capitalized on this "heady" experience multiple times in the coming years to excuse my inability to learn to read.

My dad had lived without amenities his entire life and my mother had learned to do the same after their marriage. My dad enforced the latter by being in complete control of the checkbook. Because of their frugality and the fact that farming was relatively lucrative during the years of the Second World War, they were able to save enough after seven years in the little brown house to make a down payment on another farm of their own. Thus, before I turned five, our family moved to a 264-acre farm within walking distance of Gallatin Gateway, a tiny village composed mostly of lumberjacks and located 11 miles from Bozeman.

To me, neither the farm nor its ownership was important. What was important was the fact that the little brown house was finally to be replaced by what I perceived as a mansion with actual indoor plumbing and a bathroom. It wasn't the bathroom's toilet that impressed me; I normally continued to use the accompanying outdoor three-holer anyway. The most awesome feature of the bathroom was the bathtub. Now we no longer had to tote water from the outdoor pump to the stove, then after it was heated, transport it to a washtub placed somewhere in or outside the house and, one after another, crawl through it in an attempt to attain some semblance of cleanliness.

In addition to the greatly appreciated bathroom, the "Gateway house" had what appeared to be a myriad of other rooms. There were four bedrooms, a spacious eat-in kitchen, a large dining room with a table used for homework by someone other than me, and a living room actually large enough to comfortably seat our entire massive family and several guests... all at the same time. It also had a front foyer whose cast-iron stove served for both cooking and heating. It was my daily duty to stock it with chopped wood before going to school. Although I never appreciated the humor, there had to be at least something funny about watching the futility of a six-year old boy chopping armloads of wood with a dull axe in the morning darkness at 20 degrees below zero. I said you had to be tough to survive in Montana.

Since this was the first respectable house in which any family member except my mother had lived, Montana was finally fulfilling its original promise. Even for my mother, that house provided a temporary respite from her demons; no extended "vacations" were required during her seven years in the Gateway house. These were the good years.

A few months after moving to the Gateway house, we acquired a dog. Our family had had dogs before, but not during my tenure. Most importantly, this dog was to be my birthday present and I was to pick it out from our neighbor's litter. Of course, the dog's parents were mutts. I never knew a farm dog that hadn't descended from mutts. Almost everyone is familiar with the breed. Their most defining trait is to balance their front paws on the sideboards or cabs of pickups and flap their tongues in the wind with expressions of total bliss. The faster the pickup travels, the more permanently fixed becomes the expression.

Selection of my puppy was simple; it was the tiny ball of fur that tottered to me and tugged at my trouser leg. This creature soon wished he had not made that move. My birthday is in mid-November and by then Montana is already deep in winter. This eventuality, coupled with the fact that in our house no animals were allowed, was setting up to be a rude and cold awakening for this newly-weaned puppy. None of my pleas or childlike insults, such as "he is going to freeze, it's 20 below" or "why are you so mean," had an ounce of impact. At that moment I had lost my stomach for a dog and would have gladly returned him to his mom to survive the night, but that was not an option. My mother did put a cardboard box containing some old coats onto the back porch as his makeshift dog house. The puppy was not stupid, and as I peered through the window in desperation, he had already burrowed into the coats.

My parents were right. A puppy could live outdoors in a Montana winter; at least one night. With this experience under his belt, the puppy's own coat quickly thickened, preparing him for Arctic living (which was probably warmer than Montana), and he was able to survive as long as he had the box. The barn across the road would have provided accommodations preferable to that of the unprotected porch, but the house was where the humans lived. His instinct for that association overruled the one for comfort. Somehow he made it through the entire winter in his box.

He was a dandy dog and was so-named. He was my ever present companion, at least when outside the house. Dandy became an expert dog-stroke swimmer and gave me the confidence during the few warm summer days to venture into the swift current of a glacial canal that weaved through our farm. I taught him elaborate tricks, like putting his front paws on my chest when I patted it, or walking a narrow plank to climb to the roof of a low shed. However, Dandy was no fighter, even though when cars pulled into our driveway he sounded and looked sufficiently vicious that those unacquainted with him remained glued in their seats until rescued. This is a constant for farm dogs whose primary duty is to look vicious and bark, an art form of primordial origin intended especially for visitors. Once the visitor has been released from their vehicle, the dog's final act of defiance is to lift his legs and pee on all four tires, at least if the dog is male. Dandy was a pro at this.

Our neighbors had a dog that, unlike Dandy, did qualify as a fighter. This blackish-grayish-yellowish demon with glassy white eyes would tear at my pant legs, and occasionally my leg, every time I set foot in his yard. Since the two Henry boys that owned Bingo were my only potential playmates that lived within a one mile radius, and since my siblings did not view playing with me as entertainment, I became well-acquainted with that hound from Hell.

All my outdoor experiences were shared with Dandy, so visiting the Henry boys was no exception. My pacifist dog would apprehensively follow me into the Kingdom of Bingo, attempting to be invisible. But the same scene was inevitably played out. Bingo would first bite me, after which he would charge Dandy who would roll onto his back and look as pathetic as possible. At those times, I would have sacrificed my dream of a BB gun of my own if Dandy could have been transformed into a German Shepherd. Once both Dandy and I had sufficiently acknowledged Bingo's territorial rights during these visits, the damnable creature would become metamorphosed into a normal dog. When the Henry boys visited me, they were inevitably accompanied by my buddy who ignored me since it was my territory, but never extended Dandy the same favor. I yearned to tell them to leave their dog at home, but then I was afraid if I did, they would not come themselves and then who would I have? This act was seemingly played out forever until Bingo mercifully disappeared one winter night. Both Dandy and I were finally given a reprieve.

One unusually warm summer when Dandy was just over seven years old, he developed a chronic hack that racked his body and stifled his energy. He still trailed me everywhere, but with less enthusiasm. As a twelve year old, my veterinary skills were limited, and it appeared both my dad and brother Louis, who by then was managing the farm, were equally impaired, at least when it came to treating dogs. Unfortunately, dogs had no intrinsic value as farm stock, so when one showed signs of distress, you either shot it or had it put away. Having a dog seen by a veterinarian for actual care was not part of the equation. That costs money and you don't pay money for a worthless dog. I had no money myself so that option was out.

I often wondered if anyone in my family was aware of my love for Dandy. Would they have paid to have him at least looked at if they had been? All I could do was cry, and that didn't help Dandy. The option exercised for Dandy was the lesser of the two evils. The last I saw of him was in Louis's arms as he carried Dandy into the vet clinic for extermination. At least I was not required to carry him.

Lack of personal involvement was not always the case in the demise of my pets. For someone who has not grown up with cattle as pets, bonding with these animals may seem difficult to comprehend. However, if the reality of this is questionable, one need only visit the auctions that accompany the many 4-H fairs held around the country each year. There one can witness the spectacular payment the 12-year old just received from the local slaughter house for the pet bull he has fed, trained, and shown from birth suddenly undergo metamorphosis into "30 pieces of silver" in his hands. The tears shed in those auctions could drown the next eruption of Mount St. Helens.

I never had this life experience since we lived on a dairy farm and my 4-H projects were raised to supply milk and not steak. When I turned ten years old and joined 4-H, I was given a calf that was to be both mine and my 4-H project. This heifer was born during the same moon as a young bull that after a few weeks into his life was de-bulled. These two, the little heifer and little steer, grew up together as my pets. Dandy and I would frolic with them each day with me often astride one or the other as they raced through the creek and across the field. They grew quickly and just as quickly lost their interest in horseplay. However, their backs were always available as great places to sit and contemplate as they munched grass.

The purpose of a steer on a farm is not for decoration. This was our source of meat and my brother Louis did the butchering. He would shoot the animal, attach its hind legs to the loader on the tractor, then lift it and bleed it out before skinning and slicing it into hunks of meat for freezing. He was very efficient. I watched, but was never asked to participate, that is, until the day of reckoning arrived for my pet.

"Hey, it's time for you to take one of them down" said Louis as he handed me our single shot .22 rifle.

He was not aware that the subject of his request was my pet, but I was too proud to refuse this demonstration of manhood. Somehow through the tears I sighted the rifle toward my pet's head and fired. I guess I did well enough since it did not require a second shot. That day I did not witness the butchering. However, I also did not become a vegetarian.

When I was ten years old, my brother Louis got married and assumed responsibility for the everyday farm activities while my dad moved semi-retired to Bozeman, nine miles from our farm. Although the reasons for his sudden change of life were well-disguised, my father clearly disliked milking cows and jumped at the opportunity to pass the torch to one of his children, even though his general health was fine and he was only 58 years old, far below retirement age for a farmer. He would never admit his aversion to milking cows because work had been his whole life and he vociferously proclaimed his love for useful farm animals, especially cows. In addition, his personal ambition to remain in charge would normally have stifled any temptation to retire, even if the pain in his knees became excruciating every time he got under a cow to milk it. After retirement, my father continued to drive the nine miles to the farm each day, arriving just when the milking was being finished in the morning. He would then put in a hard day of work, but would make tracks just before the milking began at night. His timing was obvious.

The move to town may have fit into my dad's life pattern, but within weeks after this event, my mother's "vacation" cycle was resurrected and off she went again to visit her sister Lillian in Chicago. One could attribute this to many things, including menopause, but from my objective viewpoint it had one clear cause. I call it "bad house selection."

My dad not only controlled the check book, but also made all the major decisions in the family. He viewed that as part of his patriarchal duties. When he decided it was time to leave the farm and move to town, we moved. When a house was chosen to move to, he chose the house. Even at 10 years old, I cared greatly about that decision. I think my mother did as well, especially since she was about to vacate the one decent place in which she had lived during 30 years of marriage. But the choice of a house was not her decision to make. Prior to selecting his final choice, my dad provided a short list of possible houses. Disappointment was evident amongst the three of us that would be accompanying my father in this move, i.e., my mother, my sister Marg, and me. This did not impress my father who had decided not to spend more than $5,500. Even in the Bozeman of 1953, that bought you very little.

His final selection was the lesser of the evils we had been shown, but it still resembled the shacks of old. It contained two miniature bedrooms with an unimpressive eat-in kitchen, big enough to fit only a small table against one wall with a single chair slipped under each of the three exposed sides. In addition to a bathroom only big enough to fit one small person between the toilet, sink and tub, the main floor was rounded out with a combination living/dining room, but much of its floor space was occupied by a massive open grate through which hot air was vented from a gas-burning furnace housed in the basement. I mention the latter because my parents lived in that house 20 years until my dad's death in 1973, during which time numerous grandchildren experienced a taste of the fires of Hell as they crawled across this inferno. Every time a wee one would arrive in the winter months, a fortress of chairs would be erected. But these little people were sneaky and eventually found a way to squeeze through for their branding.

The house also had a tiny basement, part of which contained a dirt floor. My sister Marg, who was in her last year of high school, was given the bedroom. This meant I was relegated to the basement. The house had a clothes washer packed into one corner of the kitchen, but the room was too small to fit a dryer. As a result, clothes washed in the winter were hung to dry in the basement where they sometimes dripped on my head like water torture throughout the night. The smell of mildew on my clothing during the winter months never fazed me much, but it was a bit of a turn off for some of my more elitist companions, especially those of the female variety. Dear God, if my dad had just spent another $100 on a house with a clothes dryer, I could have been popular.

So the rights to the family farm had been passed. Based on Irish tradition, this inheritance should have gone to the eldest son, but Joe was a college professor by then and had zero interest in being a farmer. By the fact that my father had cut back in his involvement, at least as concerned the milking, meant my brother Louis would need help, thus launching the "Era of the Hired Man" to further my early education.

The first of these characters arrived before the dust had settled behind my dad's tires. It was an interesting swap since the new hire was 68 years old and had seen some rough times. This old geezer didn't care much for cow milking either (60 cows, five o'clock morning and evening, no exceptions allowed), so he took his leave in a month. This made him a trend setter as many of his successors also departed almost at the moment they arrived. The record stay was two years, the average was six months, and one fellow lasted only as long as his ride from town.

Although the farm had a semi-respectable bunkhouse, the single hired hands seemed incapable of either cooking or cleaning for themselves. Instead they opted to bunk with my brother and Maureen, his 20-year old San Francisco bride. The amazing thing was that they let them. Maureen had majored in music at Belmont College and planned to be an opera singer, that is, before being swept off her feet by my gallant brother. This had occurred during Maureen's 1952 summer visit with her aunt who lived on a neighboring farm. Their six week tryst provided few clues of the life she was about to choose or, if it did, Maureen's receiver was turned off. Probably the most shocking revelation upon permanent arrival in Montana the next summer was that her honeymoon home was to be shared with persons whose most complimentary description would be "colorful."

Since I continued to spend my summers on the farm where I had full exposure to these characters, they had the opportunity to teach me the real meaning of life. The best lessons probably came from a young drifter named Slick who stayed with us a few months in the summer of 1955. Within his repertoire of stories was his description of the greatest vacation ever in which he was on the road for two weeks during which time he was never sober. He became aware of his route during the interlude only from postcards he later received from female companions with whom he had promised to share his future. If nothing else, this fellow and the many others that came before and after him, taught me what not to do with my life.

Even though my dad had officially retired by his move from farm to town, his presence on the farm was still not to be taken lightly. Louis was forever being given exhaustive lectures on farm management which, surprisingly, he seemed to more appreciate than resent. I was cut from a different cloth and generally had the opposite reaction to my dad's lectures. One particular lecture stands out in my mind.

On a very hot summer day in my 12th year, my dad was mowing hay in a field far from the house. Louis was concerned about my dad's past health issues, and feeling he needed relief from the heat, sent me as his reinforcement. I trudged the mile through the blistering heat and arrived to inform my dad of my mission. The conversation went like this.

"Louis thought you would be getting hot and tired, and asked me to come and take your place."

"That's fine. Have you ever used a mower before?"

"Not really, but I have watched others mow," was my response.

"Then come up and show me what you can do."

When I had seen others make the 90 degree turn at a corner, they would lift the mower blade, hit the foot brake, make the short spin, then quickly lower the blade and continue mowing. My first and only attempt at this maneuver on that auspicious day was dramatic. I lifted the blade and hit the brake as planned, but kept my foot planted, thus causing the tractor to spin directly into the middle of the field. I, of course, panicked and lowered the blade some distance into the field. Thus, I not only crushed the un-mowed alfalfa but also created a swath reminiscent of something left by aliens. After a scathing reprimand, my dad's final comment was, "Go back to the house. You don't know how to mow hay." Off I trudged through the steaming field with my tail between my legs.

My dad was right. I did not know how to mow hay even though I'm sure I could have been taught. Perhaps he thought humiliation was the best teacher. This experience certainly did not kill me, so it must have made me stronger. Over time, I realized my dad really liked mowing hay and was not about to be displaced by a young punk, even if it was his own son and even if he himself was about to have a heat stroke. This was a competition he could win, and he did.

Lessons on a farm can come from almost any source, even from a horse. However, Pat was not just any horse. It is unclear whether he was immortal because he was full grown by the time I first remember him when I was three and he was still going strong when I last saw him 19 years later. I have verification of his size in a family portrait taken in 1945. Spread across his roan-colored back in an approximate order of size and chronology are me, Clo, Marg, Gen and John. There was still sufficient space for my four oldest siblings; they just weren't around when the picture was taken. The eternal patience portrayed in that one snapshot captured the essence of this massive animal. When Pat was parked by a fence post, even a four year old could land and stick on his substantial frame. He never moved; he didn't even wince.

Pat was a homebody, sometimes too much so. During an overnight visit by a first grade classmate, he begged to ride a horse, and Pat was the logical choice. Since I had proven rapport with this colossal animal, I was placed up front to provide direction. It was simple. I could hang onto the reins and Pat's mane, and my classmate could hang onto me. The trip away from the barn was without incident. Pat just walked with his usual steady, bumpy gait. However, when the turn for home was made, Pat's gait accelerated. I was too little to stop him. Within a few seconds, both my classmate and I went off the side, me on the bottom and my left elbow on the bottom of me, broken and dislocated. Even though this all started with Pat's primordial rush to return to the barn, he stopped instantly where we were shed and waited to be led home by two bawling boys. I never thought to blame Pat for my injury, and my confidence in him remained unshaken. Besides, my broken arm released me from the last week of first grade. My elbow never quite healed properly, but since I broke the same arm another five times before reaching the age of 20, it probably didn't have much chance anyway.

My introduction to steady work also came under the tutelage of Pat, this time at the age of eight. I was just beginning to get serious enjoyment out of childhood when suddenly, on what was otherwise a delightful July day, my dad issued the edict "Okay, play time is over. It's time you learn to work." My first job was to run a buck rake which was powered by a team of horses. One was the idiot horse of the century called Bird. She fit the name perfectly. Fortunately, the other was Pat, who kept both Bird and me in line. He also kept the rake in line and out of ditches and away from fences, and even out of the canal that snaked through our farm. When he knew we needed a rest he would stop, but only when we needed the rest. Pat never considered his own needs. Rest stops were also energy renewal periods accomplished by the consumption of mouthfuls of fresh hay, at least until Pat's water tank started running low. Then the stops would increase and the eating would cease. These combined behaviors would insure that Pat had sufficient reserve left in his tank at quitting time to make the gallop home. Actually it was a fast trot; he rarely wasted the energy required to reach a full gallop.

Pat also had a surefire method to insure a steady food supply. When the pasture in which he happened to be housed became, in his mind, depleted of nutrients, he would simply jump the fence into the next. The size of the fence was of little consequence. He would merely face the intended barrier, rise up on his back legs, and release them like coiled springs. He sometimes miscalculated and ended his leap astraddle the fence. No panic here. He knew someone would eventually show up to help him return to his appointed rounds. Even if the fence was barbed wire he never bled a drop. Some family member would eventually see him and say, "Hey, Pat has been in that same spot for three days. He must have tried to jump the fence again." Sure, one gets a bit thirsty and hungry in three days, but the wait usually beats getting cut up or breaking a leg.

As the months moved into years, and the years became decades, our farm was finally worked strictly with tractors; there was nothing left for Pat to do except eat. My dad loved Pat as much as I did but feared that he would be found frozen in the field some winter morning. Rather than suggesting he himself might be becoming soft, my dad instead exclaimed, "It's time to sell Pat. We don't need to fund the retirement of a useless hay burner." I never saw Pat again, but he and the lessons he taught have never been forgotten.

The rapport I had with farm animals such as Pat and Dandy was not a universal phenomenon. A case in point concerned a Holstein bull we had for nearly a century. I still have nightmares about this brute. There I am in my dream, moving my legs in a corral but seemingly not going anywhere and the bull is hot on my heels. I somehow make it to the fence and am desperately ascending when I wake, just before reaching the top. Thus, the outcome is never decided.

Our real-life bull, respectfully named Smiley based on his sterling disposition, weighed exactly one ton, had a full set of horns, and was meaner than sin. This was not a great combination. He usually resided in a small pen that was half inside and half outside our barn. When Smiley hung out in his latter quarters, my friends and I had free access to him. The outside fence was built like a rock which provided us with the confidence to harass him regularly. He would bellow and bang against the fence when pegged with pebbles, but what really ticked him off was being shot with the Henry boys' BB gun. That aroused the ire of this docile creature about 20-fold, something we really enjoyed witnessing.

The purpose of a bull is, of course, to breed cows. To accomplish this, it was necessary to allow Smiley access to the animal in question. His pen had a massive door that was both bolted and barred. To release him, one would surreptitiously unlock or remove all components on this door without him being aware. If he hit the door when it was half unlocked he would have flattened anyone on the other side. Fortunately, that never happened. Once the door was unlocked, one would swing it wide open with a single motion and remain hidden behind. Smiley would then roar out and claim his prize. That was the easy part.

Once the deed was done, Smiley had to somehow be coaxed back into his cubby, and everyone around was enlisted to participate in this exercise in order to block potential escape routes. That group even included me. We all carried large clubs to feign our dominance, but Smiley could, of course, have taken any of us out in a heartbeat. Apparently he didn't know that. I guess that's what gives humans the upper hand in these situations.

I suppose Smiley was meaner because of the gregarious acts of my friends and me, but on a scale of one to ten, he was already on nine without our help. At least I like to think that. He was one potentially dangerous animal, but he had great pedigree and produced marvelous offspring. It was one happy day, however, when he was transported to another needy farm to work his wonders, all 2,000 pounds of him.

Although the struggles of my parents as well as my own personal experiences as a farm child in Montana were not unusual for the time, they are a heritage that belongs only to me, and the lessons they taught have been used for support as the roadblocks in my life were later encountered.

3 Three Coaches

Our development during the first years of life is directed primarily by our parents, grandparents and siblings. In the next phase, teachers become a major force. However, for boys being educated in small schools in Montana during the 1950's, no one was more important than the coaches, and their impacts, at least in my case, can endure for a lifetime. How did they acquire this power? During basketball season from November through March, these individuals determined whether the sun of our emotional lives would even rise, solely by controlling our playing time on the basketball court. The acute effects of this interplay, associated primarily with peer recognition or our perception thereof, usually lasted only until the next basketball season. The chronic remnants of these experiences can persist, as in my case, for a lifetime.

So why was basketball so important? Because in Montana there are eight months of winter and basketball was the only sport associated with cheering fans that was played indoors in the 1950's. Shortly after most Montana boys born during that period could walk, they began throwing a ball toward some basket. By the time they reached school age, the outcomes of pick-up games of basketball were already a matter of life and death, especially if the participants were nursed from the bottle of competitiveness like me. Organized basketball began as early as the fourth grade and was well entrenched by the sixth. In middle school years, your identity was determined by whether you were one of the starting five, the players who received the majority of the playing time. Then it was on to high school where you were either one of the "first five" or your life was meaningless, and the coach was the sole decider of that outcome.

I now realize the our high school coaches were pawns of the system, and were only doing what they perceived as their jobs. "Win at any cost" was the prevailing motto. Sadly, most of these individuals had no understanding of their power to enhance or annihilate a kid's sense of self-worth. We gave them that power, but we were just kids and had no control over what we relinquished. Our parents and teachers stood by helplessly as we handed our psychological status to these individuals, most of whom had never themselves taken a single course in psychology.

So who were these all-powerful beings to whom my classmates and I handed control of our personal happiness? The main things they had in common were that they were white, Catholic, male, and recent college graduates that needed jobs.

Moving from the eighth grade to high school was not a confidence builder, but confronting Coach Curran, whose mission in life appeared to be to shred any vestige of residual confidence in incoming freshman, set the stage for a difficult year. This man had aspirations of much higher things for himself than teaching and coaching high school students. After all, he had been Mr. Everything in basketball at a small Montana college, and even during his high school days had acquired the title of "Jumping Jim." I never saw him jump except at my throat, but I was told he was one white man that could. He probably had many redeeming qualities, but the only one obvious to me was that he had a very pretty and ingratiating wife, a first class lady who volunteered to direct our school play. I hope she appreciated her husband more than I did.

Within minutes of the opening bell in freshman English class, Coach Curran was relating the story of his harsh upbringing in the all-boys Butte Central High School. Butte was the largest city in Montana at that time, but that was not saying much. It was the home of the Anaconda Copper Company and the entire city was constructed over 1,000 ft deep copper mines. The majority of the inhabitants were Irish Catholic miners who lived hard but generally not very long. Kids from Butte seemed to think their town was special. Few other Montanans shared this sentiment.

This was the town from whence Jumping Jim Curran had sprung. A portion of his harsh upbringing, which he bragged about with animated pride to us fully-impressionable high school freshmen, was the method of crowd control employed by the Christian Brothers who taught at Butte Central High. Apparently, whether they deserved it or not, students were routinely called to the front of the room during class and asked to stand with their backs to the instructor. He would place his hands on the student's shoulder and simultaneously whack him on both sides of his neck with both open palms, using sufficient force to create instant eye watering. Depending on the instructor's mood on a given day, the neck lashes could be few or many.

Coach Curran considered this a necessary ingredient of a boy's education, and transferred the practice fully intact to Holy Rosary High School, but only to freshman boys. Probably because Coach Curran perceived older male students to be less tolerant, they were spared his lashes, and he wouldn't have lowered himself to touch a girl. I was one of the lucky few to be at the right place at the right time. There were 12 boys in my class and none displayed even a hint of juvenile delinquency, but that didn't curtail Coach Curran. It is unclear what criteria he used, but I seemed to be the most in need of his daily attacks. He had to hit someone and I was probably the least likely to report his actions at home. Sooner or later, however, this he-man eventually brought tears to the eyes of all 12 of us. No one, to my knowledge, took the tales of his beatings outside of the classroom, so there were no repercussions. It is difficult to remember whether the lashings actually subsided as the year wore on, but it seems that Coach Curran's craving to display his dominance by physically humiliating us was generally satisfied by early springtime.

The beatings were only one of several ways that Coach Curran attempted to destroy our confidence. He was not only the English teacher but was also the coach, and the high school basketball teams were under his command. The 1957 Rosary High seniors were generally good athletes, so the "A" squad had a respectable year under Coach Curran. However, there were no superstars. Even so, Coach Curran reminded us "B" squad members throughout the season that none of us was of sufficient quality to even hold the coats of the A squad players. Another classmate and I were perceived to be the best of the freshman basketball players, so Coach Curran gave us special encouragement by saying that, if we both worked very hard, we might eventually attain the skills of his two senior guards. One of these was a steady player and a relatively good shot. He was to be my classmate's ideal. My best hope was to attain the basketball prowess of a scrappy but erratic player who couldn't score more than four points in a game if no one guarded him. This pronouncement provided me with real inspiration.

Montana high schools in 1956 had only three sports in which boys could participate. We were fortunate since girls didn't have any sport unless one included cheerleading. These three were football, basketball and track. Because we didn't have football at Holy Rosary High School until my sophomore year, that left only basketball and track during the tenure of Coach Curran. Basketball was "the sport," but in spite of this, I knew even as a freshman that I had more ability in track and felt I could be competitive in the running events. At least I had that vision before Coach Curran came into my life. His wife directed the school play that spring and I had been selected for a minor role. Play practices were daily events after school, as were track practices. With this situation at hand, I approached Coach Curran with my solution.

"Coach" I said, "I know I have agreed to be in this play and that I have to be at practice every afternoon until it is over, but I also want to be on the track team. Since the practices are at the same time, could I do the workouts after play practice and still participate in the track meets?"

This should have been no burden to Coach Curran because he disliked track and did little to direct or even monitor the practices. I think his response was more devastating to my ego than the slaps he delivered in the classroom.

"Ward, that is just dumb. This play is your opportunity to shine. Why screw around wasting your time trying to compete in track. Based on my observations, you aren't much good in track anyway so why would you want to sacrifice your talent as an actor?"

Who knows, maybe Coach Curran was just supporting his wife's program. As always, I just grinned and bore it, knowing he would be leaving soon and there would be another time. That time did come the next year with the arrival of Coach Joe Doohan.

Joe Doohan, a 140-pound, freckle-faced dynamo with flaming red hair, hit Holy Rosary High School like a bolt of lightning. This man blew into my life with flashing eyes, a full head of steam, and an absolute "can do" attitude. He came the year the Holy Rosary Athletic Board instituted a football program in the high school. None of us had ever played organized football, so Coach Doohan had his hands full. No problem! After the first day of school it was time for the first football practice, at least that was what we expected. However, there were no footballs that day and very few during the next week. What there was were two hours of daily calisthenics and wind sprints followed by strength- and agility-building drills. We had all been in organized sports programs for several years, and we all knew what it was to be in shape. I spent my summers doing strenuous farm work so I knew there was no way I wasn't in top condition. Coach Doohan figured otherwise, and soon proved his point.

During that first week of football practice, my muscles were so stiff that it took the first 30 minutes of calisthenics each day before I could reach my ankles with a full swing. I found a whole series of muscles that I had never used before and possibly would never use again. Our entire football team shuffled around from class to class like cripples. Then, after that first week, it all magically passed. We kept up the same drills; we just no longer experienced the side effects. That year we were not a great football team, but if the games would have been extended to six quarters, we would have crushed everyone.

Coach Doohan took on every aspect of life with his same "can do" approach. His attitude was "there is nothing that can prevent success if you prepare yourself and want it enough." He himself was much too small to be an effective football player, but he wanted to play. Ergo: he went to a small college where he could use the talents he was given and play football. But that isn't all he did. How many football players have led debate teams in college? I knew of one. Based on his debating experience, he felt compelled to provide the same opportunities for his students. Thus, in addition to his other teaching duties, he introduced a forensics program into Holy Rosary High School together with a debate team, challenging anyone with enough gumption to join both.

The forensics class was full, but only four of us took the complete challenge. So most nights after football practice, and then after basketball practice, and then after track practice, we were debating. Anyone who would listen was confronted with affirmative and negative arguments regarding why the "USA should substantially increase its expenditures of foreign aid."

I never liked to debate because I was typically exhausted by the time our evening sessions began, but had zero interest in even suggesting this to Coach Doohan. This was something I had begun, and there was no room for anything but to finish, and finish well. I started as a totally lousy debater. After one particularly poor performance in a practice debate with a team from Bozeman High School, Coach Doohan held a special meeting with just me for an entire evening, explaining the use of the English language and some of its words like "Soviet Union" which I had always pronounced as "Solviet Union." I never got it wrong again. In fact, I never got any of what he told me that night wrong again. I wouldn't have dared. I thought the man was God, or at least was afraid he might be, and certainly was not going to risk otherwise.

This story is mostly about basketball and Mr. Doohan coached that too. In the process, he restored the confidence I had lost under Coach Curran. I viewed myself as a blue collar basketball player. I worked very hard, was good on defense, shot very seldom, and tried to set up good shots for my teammates. I think Coach Doohan liked this approach; at least he certainly gave that impression. I was on the first five immediately and stayed there until the last game before Christmas when an opposing player extended his leg and sent me into freefall, stopping abruptly on my left elbow. When I explained to Coach Doohan the next day that my arm was broken, I will never forget his expressed disappointment. This response replenished much of the confidence that Coach Curran had taken from me the previous year. Within two weeks, Coach Doohan had me playing again full time, initially on the B squad with essentially one usable arm. He never permitted me to miss a beat, and by early February, I was back on the first five of the A squad. What our team lacked that year in the win column we made up for in acquired life lessons, most of which centered around "you will get only what you earn, and that will take time and effort."

After basketball season came track which most boys in our high school viewed as a means of torture rather than as a sport. Prior to my time with Coach Curran, however, I had considered my athletic abilities best suited to track, so the time had come to test this theory.

I viewed myself as a potential decathlon type, being able to do reasonably well in every aspect of track from throwing to jumping to running short distances. The emphasis on the latter is the word "short." I hated running any event of more than 220 yards. After the first week of track practice, Coach Doohan suggested I was not a decathlon man after all and, in fact, was not even a sprinter, but could be competitive in the 880-yard run. I didn't want to listen, but agreed to at least run races of half that distance. I also continued in my vain attempts at jumping and sprinting. As the season progressed, it became more and more apparent that I was ill suited for both; however, I was having some success in the 440-yard run. Finally, Coach Doohan, to my dismay, entered me in an 880-yard race in a rather large meet involving schools from throughout southwest Montana and parts of Idaho. I was shocked when I won the event rather easily. Since one had to qualify at the District Meet in order to move on, and this meet had already passed, there was to be no more 880's for me that year. I honestly didn't know whether to laugh or cry. Strangely, I had found the 880 to be much less strenuous than the 440 because the pace was slower and my legs didn't transform into flaming knots as inevitably occurred during the last 50 yards of the 440. I made it to the State finals in the 440 that year but did not place, fully realizing it was not my best event. Coach Doohan gave me the opportunity, but did not force it until he knew it was necessary. Needless to say, I ran the 880 the next year, even when Joe Doohan was nowhere around.

The "Doohan moment" I remember best occurred in springtime several days before the District Speech Meet. Our little group of debaters was still going strong but so was our track team, and a track meet was scheduled on the Montana State College campus the same day as the District Speech Meet. I knew I couldn't be in both places at once and approached Coach Doohan with the dilemma.

"Coach" I began, "you know I have a bit of a conflict coming up this Saturday. I'm supposed to be racing at the same time I am scheduled to be debating."

"Actually, Dick, you need to read the schedule more carefully. Your debate times are all staggered nicely with your running events."

"But coach, its more than a half mile between the two places, and even I would be a little embarrassed to run in a suit or debate in running shorts."

"Hey kid, I'll be coaching both events, so I have faith that you'll find a way to work it out too."

I started the day in a suit but changed in and out of it three times. Timing was everything. I really didn't know whether I was supposed to be preparing a rebuttal or sprinting to the head of the pack. However, I did both. During the course of the day, my debate partner and I won all four of our debates; I won my preliminary heat in the 440, and then placed third in the finals. Yes, Coach Doohan was right again. You can do a lot if you put your mind to it.

Joe Doohan left at the end of that year to continue his education. It took years for me to even partially understand what he had given me in only a few months. Had he stayed, he would have had me on a course to be a Rhodes Scholar or one of us would have died trying. Very recently, I attempted to locate him in order to express my appreciation for what he had done for me. I eventually resorted to calling the small college he had attended with only a faint hope that they might know his whereabouts. They knew, but I had waited too long; Joe Doohan had been dead for 11 years.

With the departure of Coach Doohan, in marched Coach Nick Iverson, fresh out of two years of military duty. He had been my coach on the eighth grade basketball team when he was a senior at Montana State College, and with his re-arrival, I knew I had it made. I had been a stalwart on his eighth grade team and he was returning to coach that same team. Sure, there were a few seniors to compete with, but I had already proven I was better than them the previous year, and this man's allegiances were to me, not them. I was also the quarterback on the football team and that was something no one would change.

Was I in for a shock! Actually, make that several shocks. After two weeks into football season, Coach Iverson determined that I had a weak and inaccurate arm, and definitely did not belong at quarterback. I was demoted to play an end position. After adjusting to the personal ego hit this move engendered, I grew to like the new position. I even eventually accepted the fact that I wasn't much of a quarterback.

We had a mediocre football season but then it was time for the important sport – basketball. I now had only two more years in high school to gain eternal recognition as the superb basketball jock I knew I must be. Coach Doohan had restored the confidence Coach Curran had attempted to demolish and I was on a roll. Besides, our new coach had already acknowledged that I had outstanding basketball talent in the eighth grade, hadn't he? Well, maybe not.

The season started well and I found myself in my rightful place on the starting five during the first two games. All was going according to plan. Then it was time for the game with our arch rivals. I was recognized as a defensive specialist and was assigned to guard their best player and top scorer. It didn't matter what position he played. Therein was the rub. I was 5 '10" on tiptoes, a typical height for a high school guard in the 1950's. And that was what I played – guard. This was on both offense and defense. I had no clue how to guard someone who played in the key or under the basket, especially someone that was four inches taller than me.

Our opponent's strategy was to position my assigned player on the free throw line with his back to the basket. From there he could receive passes from any angle and do what he wanted with the ball. My job was to either prevent him from receiving the passes or, if that failed, prevent him from doing anything serious with the ball. The first time our opponents had the ball, I thought it prudent just to let my assigned player get the pass and I would stop the action after that. He got the ball, faked left with me following, and then went right for an easy lay-up. Okay, that didn't work! The next time I planned to just prevent him from getting the ball. The point guard bringing the ball up the court faked a pass to my man, I took the fake and went around him to block the non-existent entry pass, and then he dropped behind me for the real pass and, bingo, another lay-up. That was it! I was taken out of the game and replaced by one of the seniors that I had easily beaten out the previous year. That also ended my role on the starting five.

I did everything I knew to demonstrate to Coach Iverson that he was making a horrible mistake. I behaved like a tiger in all practices and routinely stole the ball from anyone and everyone. When I got into games in the last two to three minutes, I was a wild man with explosive pent-up energy and rage. Sometimes I was even effective. Did Coach Iverson notice? No, I had clearly demonstrated to him my lack of talent in a one-minute defensive breakdown playing a position I knew nothing about and for which I was given no instructions by anyone. It was clear I either had to figure these things out by myself ahead of time or it was all over; there was no margin for error.

That was the season I received my instructions for living. Week after week I continued in my futile attempts to be noticed by the coach. If I could have poured out my heart and shared this with someone, it may have blunted the disappointment and slowed the rising despair. However, there was no one. Teammates that were experiencing the same crisis were not approachable. Who could even suggest that we were being mistreated by a coach? Besides, during the next week you might get bumped up, and then how could you even look at your confidants who were not? Other by-passed teammates may have had family members who could provide some measure of reassurance, but not me. I felt my brothers would view me as a loser, and my sisters were unaware I even played basketball. My parents were unapproachable since I never discussed anything personal with either of them. This was my battle to win or lose; there were no crutches.

As demoralizing as it was to get little playing time, the worst disappointment came late in the season during a tight game with Townsend, one of the best teams in our District that year. I waited and waited, biting my tongue until I got the chance to show I could make a difference in the outcome of the game, but that opportunity never came. We won by two points and Coach Iverson was off-the-board elated. He whacked me on the back, asking me if this wasn't the greatest win ever. I remember my response as if it was yesterday. I simply muttered, "I wish I could have played." To me it was clear. I came first and the team came second.

After showering, which was unnecessary since I hadn't broken a sweat, I wandered out into the gently falling snow, taking several hours to walk the normal ten minutes to my home. I cried and then I screamed at the falling snowflakes, and then I cried some more. Then it passed, and life moved on. My only consolation that year came in our final game of the District Tournament, which if we had won, we would have moved on into the Regional Tournament. I entered in the last two minutes when we were behind by 15 points. During that time, I stole the ball twice and scored six points. The radio announcer commented "where was this kid the whole game?" I had been wondering that for the whole season.

Basketball season was finally over and track season was beginning. For this one I knew what to do – Joe Doohan had shown me. I won every race in the 880-yard run that year, including the State Championship where I set a new State Class C record. I also placed fifth in the 440-yard run. Did Coach Iverson care or even notice? Not really. He hated track and spent practice time playing ping-pong in the gym with my teammates that felt as he did. Not surprisingly, I was the only representative from our high school to qualify for State that year.

Then came my senior year, which was literally my last shot at high school fame. Coach Iverson was back and this time I was less than elated by the fact. However, as Joe Doohan would have said, "you take what you are given and make it work."

Our overall athletic talent that year was well above average for a tiny school. We got second in the District in football and lost only one game by one touchdown to the team that later became State champions. That, however, was of little importance; in our high school, basketball was still king.

With the previous year's seniors gone, Nick finally realized I was alive and basketball was again a joy for me. We were a short, fast team. Coach Iverson figured that this meant we could win only by running everyone to death. Thus, it was a fast break and full court press every game, the entire game. Coach Doohan had gotten us in shape and it carried over. This strategy worked through the regular season, through the District and Regional tournaments, and even through the State Tournament and into the final game, a position well past anything experienced by a Holy Rosary team anytime previously. Then the strategy didn't work. Our opponents in the State Championship game had a team much like our own, except they had one big guy who controlled the backboard. He would get almost every rebound off our basket and wing the ball to any one of his four midget teammates dashing down the court. Somehow a full court press just wasn't going to be effective when two of us were trying to slow down four of them. The fast break attack belonged to them, not us.

At half time we found ourselves down nine points, a difficult but not insurmountable position with a reasonable strategy adjustment. So where was Coach Iverson at half time? He was pacing, pacing, saying nothing, but just pacing. We had only a few minutes left when I realized nothing was going to change. Coach Iverson had never faced this situation before as a coach and had no other plan. Our team was a one trick pony. It was full court press/fast break or nothing. I was the team captain and felt it was time to use my rank.

"Coach, they are killing us with their fast break and we have no way to stop them. Can't we switch to a sagging zone defense and block off the big guy from the basket, then slow everything down and play a half court offense?"

"No, by golly, we got here with the running game, and we are sticking with it. We just have to try harder."

Then there was silence. I don't know whether my suggestions would have helped, but they couldn't have made things much worse, and we certainly needed to change the pace of the game. By the end of the third quarter we were down 11 points. Then our hotshot shooter decided to take the game under his wing. Every time he touched the ball he fired it at the basket whether he could see it or not. We lost by 30 points. In the end, however, we had a great year based strictly on talent, and the luck that it took until the last game before we encountered another running team. It was a nearly perfect way to finish high school basketball.

One last track season remained, and the urgings of Coach Doohan were still ringing in my ears.

"You are a distance runner, Ward, not a sprinter. Go with what you've been given."

Based on his admonitions, I moved up to run both long races that year, the 880-yard and mile runs. I finished with another State record in the former and a second place finish in the latter.

Track constituted my last official activity with Coach Iverson. I know he was a man who thought he was giving all he had to help his players. Thanks at least partially to him, my last year did wonders for my ego; probably too much, since my combined sports successes were well beyond anything I could ever hope to repeat. This experience also set the stage for serious insecurities that materialized when reality hit after I stepped into bigger arenas.

Now, 50 years later, I have had time to reflect on the real impact these three coaches had on my life. Coach Curran probably felt he provided lessons in toughness for which I should be forever grateful. At least, I would like to think that is what he had in mind. In spite of his rather primitive approach, he may have accomplished his goal. I do not remember him fondly, but based on the course my life has taken, some extra toughness probably helped.

With Coach Iverson, I found that if I hung in there, life could have its rewards, information that has been resurrected during the downturns in my life. I will always recall when he wrote a recommendation letter for me during my last months under his tutelage, saying "when I have a son, I want him to be just like Dick Ward." Those words became his lasting heritage for me.

In the end, the coach and teacher for whom I have had unending gratitude is Coach Joe Doohan. He provided a spark that gradually ignited a flame to do something meaningful and lasting with my life. I just wish I could have told him.

4 The First Stop on the Road to Freedom

I graduated from high school in 1960, one year before the words of JFK were to inspire a nation. "Ask not what your country can do for you, but what you can do for your country." It was a new decade, one that at least started with a dream that each of us could make the world a better place. Armed with idealism and the certainty that I too could make a difference, it was time to start the quest. The first order of business, before ascending that mountain, was to establish my independence, and that could not be done under the watchful eyes of very old parents. Thus, I needed to leave town, at least for one summer. I needed to spread my wings. I needed freedom.

Although I equated freedom with leaving home, I wasn't a complete fool. I even realized this might require a little planning. Also, I was too insecure to risk this venture alone, so about three months before graduating from high school I began trying to convince my classmates, Tim and Tommy, to come along. Initially, at least, they were easily seduced.

Our first task was to agree on a destination. After much deliberation, we settled on San Francisco. My sister Clo and her husband Bruce lived there, and if all else failed, I could rely on them to save us from ourselves, a definite case of intricate planning. The big picture was quite clear. We would simply arrive in San Francisco, rent an apartment for the summer, get jobs and be free. The fact that we didn't have $300 between us presented no problem.

Our second act was to purchase a reliable automobile to get us to our destination. Tommy already had one in his possession, but we all agreed that his fine machine wouldn't get us out of Montana let alone to San Francisco. After much deliberation, we concurred that spending about $50 each should set us up fine. Not unexpectedly, none of the three used car salesmen in Bozeman were enamored with our budget. This only slightly discouraged us. There had to be someone who knew somebody that needed to replace a reliable automobile with $150. After casting our nets, the only catch was a church member whose mother had just passed. He assured us she had owned a great machine with almost no mileage. He was right on both counts. Twenty years earlier it had been a great machine and it had very low mileage. In fact, it hadn't been moved from its storage shed in nearly 10 years. It was a toss-up whether the shed or car was in the worse condition.

With this disappointment, our next act was to revert to Plan B, i.e. take a bus to SF. Never mind where we might stay when we got there or how much it would cost. It would all work out. Of course, my sister Clo was still in the wings. This well-designed plan remained viable until about a month before our anticipated departure date by which time Tim finally worked up enough courage to lay out the basics of our impending voyage to his parents. It was immediately obvious to them that we were totally naive about what we would be facing. They didn't want to stifle our spirit of independence by suggesting we were crazy -- but they did anyway. At least they stifled Tim's. They didn't refuse to let him go; they just made him an offer he couldn't refuse – a new 18-foot outboard boat and water skis. In our most recent planning sessions, it was already evident that Tim had begun to waffle about the plan anyway, so this offer just provided his final excuse to bail. It looked like freedom's road would be traveled only by Tommy and me. My parents had seemingly conceded that I had full freedom to go wherever I wanted as long as it didn't cost them anything. Tommy's parents didn't say a word. I guess they felt I would keep him safe. Man, was that ever a reach.

One week before our launch date, Plan B was ditched in favor of Plan C. Our classmate Ike, who had a car of sorts, decided the planned trip sounded groovy. Besides, he had an uncle in SF that had actually invited him to spend the summer. He just needed companions for the trip which could be translated as "someone to pay for the gas." Ike always needed someone to pay for gas. He and

Tommy were my only classmates who had cars of their own and, being attuned with the ways of the world, Ike knew how to use this to his advantage. He would haul any of us if we were going where he wanted to go, but would invariably stop at the A&W Drive In for a hamburger and root beer. Often he never had money, so since he was hauling us, we could pay for it. The next stop was inevitably the gas station. Ike never bought gas. He would just make sure he was hauling someone when he got low and, voila, his gas bill didn't exist. We were all familiar with the routine. However, riding with Ike, even with gas and food and motel bills, still seemed preferable to the bus.

About three days before we were scheduled to blast off, my dad finally came to the realization that I was serious about this adventure. I had kept him informed from the beginning, but I guess he thought the idea would blow over. Once he finally understood the gravity of the situation, it was time for his day in court. His opposition started with low grumblings which were soon scaled up to chastisements and threats.

His first volley was "you are just lazy and are trying to get out of real work on the farm."

When he didn't get the expected result, he followed this up with "you won't find jobs and will turn into bums."

His closing remarks were "don't ask me for money to get home; just remember I warned you."

If he had made his points three months sooner, I probably would have caved in, but by the time they were expressed I had graduated from high school, knew almost everything, and was committed to the task at hand. So, on a bright Monday morning in early June, three sheltered neophytes from the backwaters of Montana each traded in 17-plus years of security for their first shot at real freedom, and headed south toward the City by the Bay.

Up to this point, I had only ridden with Ike in his present car for short trips around town. Thus, I was not aware that when this fine automobile got revved up over 40 mph, it would shake like it was in its final stages of pneumonia, just before the arrival of the Grim Reaper. Ike claimed the car had been recently aligned, and this had not stopped the shuttering. I doubted his story since it was not in Ike's nature to fork out cash for an alignment. In addition to the vibration problem, Ike noted that he had brought along a six-pack of oil because his fine car needed a quart refresher every 75 miles. I'll admit I had ignored the black cloud that trailed Ike's car up to this moment. Now it mentally evolved into a sickly tornado that we couldn't shake. Man, the bus was sounding better and better.

Fortunately, there weren't many cars occupying the two-lane highways of the American West in 1960. Otherwise, we would have felt compelled to pull over every five minutes to allow traffic to pass. Of course, we had to add oil almost that often anyway. When cars did pull around us as we were chugging along, it was typically accompanied with much honking followed by shouted threats and innuendos concerning our heritage. During his turn at the wheel, Tommy's typical reaction to this abuse was to retaliate by flooring the gas pedal which sometimes resulted in speeds in excess of 50 mph if we were heading downhill. The car would shake uncontrollably, but somehow Tommy kept it on the road. At these times, Ike would repeatedly begin to sing verses to the hit tune "It takes a worried man to sing a worried song."

After two endless days and 11 quarts of oil, we finally arrived in Reno. None of us had been inside a real casino, but had been watching them drift by as we urged the car through the state of Nevada, the only place in the country with legalized gambling. After a full day's discussion on how we would exploit our opportunity in the "Biggest Little City in the World," we were hot-to trot. On our first pass through Reno, the city was more little than big, and we were in California before we realized we had completely passed it. I voted to continue on, but was vehemently overridden by the other two. I was ready for Reno, but I didn't want to push our automobile an extra mile which was necessitated by our turning around.

We returned to Reno and checked into a motel. The lady at the front desk offered us coupons for free drinks at several casinos saying "you boys are all 21 aren't you?" At least the other two were 18. I was seven months short of that mark and could have passed for 14. I guess the lady was blind. So we got ourselves slicked up and, with coupons in hand, headed out for a big night on the town.

The first casino we hit was Harrah's, a major one on our list of free coupons. Fortunately, no one checked our identification at the door. If they had, we would have flunked our first test since none of us was sophisticated enough to have a fake ID. We immediately bellied up to the bar and, with full trepidation, ordered our first round of the only drink we knew, a Tom Collins. After a quick observation over the top of his spectacles, the bartender made the drinks, but without rum. I guess he was familiar with our type. We moved on, but in the next casino we were carded. Before we mumbled something about leaving our I.D.'s at home, the lady making the request suggested that I could check her I.D. later. After recovering from the shock of being turned away, it took several minutes for her words to register. Then we had a ten minute debate analyzing what she might have meant. After deciding that I didn't hear her right, we moved on again.

Most of the casinos we passed through that night didn't card us even though persons less that 21 were not legally allowed inside. If they had followed the rules, it would have been a short night. As it was, we got served everywhere we were permitted in, and most bartenders even put alcohol in our drinks. It took several casinos before we realized that drinks were free if we were gambling. Did that ever open up our horizons. With that bit of knowledge, we would sit almost anywhere pretending we were engaged in gambling, just waiting to order the next round of drinks. It turned out to be one fun night for three kids from Montana, and a fine introduction to a summer of freedom.

Back on the road the next day with our first hangovers, we were facing Donner Pass. This was a time before the interstate system eliminated those endless switchbacks and somehow reduced the altitude of mountains by about 50 percent. Up to this moment in our trip, we had avoided any serious climbing in our oil eating machine, but now we had no choice. All we had to do was get up and over this mountain, and the car could almost coast the rest of the way to San Francisco. It was not to be. We chugged through the first seven sets of switchbacks, but as we were gunning for the eighth, wham-mo, the engine exploded and our last four quarts of oil splattered across both sides of the highway. Ike's dear red machine was dead.

After pushing the car far enough off the road where we had hope it wouldn't be hit, we hiked three miles to a campground where there was a phone and a phonebook, praying that all our worldly possessions would not be lifted from the abandoned car in our absence. We didn't have enough sense to post one of us as a guard; we just trusted that everything would be there on our return, something that even slow thinking kids would never do today. Ike located a garage mechanic with a tow truck 30 miles away who, for a sweet price, would rescue us. The price had to be shared since Ike was again short on cash as expected. After leaving the defunct automobile for an engine replacement, it was back to Plan B and the bus for the last 130 miles. That would have been the better option from the beginning, but then think of the fun we would have missed.

Shortly after the bus left the foothills of the Sierra's and descended into the flatlands of Central California, I began to understand the meaning of the signs reading "Keep California Green and Golden." In Montana they skipped the Golden part. By early June in California, there had been no rain for at least three months, and the temperature outside our air-conditioned bus hovered around 115 degrees. Unless water was poured onto whatever could grow other than desert plants, they were "golden." This would not change until at least the late fall when the rains returned. For well-traveled folks or California residents, this is not news, but for three travel-stunted kids from Montana, it was a real shock. I had always thought the deserts were further south.

As we were leaving the desert-in-the-making, California's Sacramento Valley, the bus passed through some low hills, the temperature dropped 60 degrees, and we had our first vision of the glorious Bay Area. With endless water on the right and green splashing the hills of the East Bay on the left, the bus approached the Bay Bridge. There was the Golden Gate Bridge superimposed behind Alcatraz Island and the expansive San Francisco Bay, all fronting the distant setting sun. We then knew for certain that the location selected for our summer interlude was going to be "the greatest."

We had finally arrived, but what was going to be our next move once we alighted at the SF bus station with almost no money in our pockets? It was simple. I merely called my sister Clo and she sent her husband Bruce to pick Tommy and me up and take care of us at her house. Our original plan for full freedom was to live on our own, but the execution of that plan seemed to already be getting scuttled. This had been the fallback position anyway, and it worked for me. Within an hour of our arrival, Ike was picked up by his uncle, and my brother-in-law welcomed Tommy and me and our four borrowed suitcases into his home. Maybe this was the way it was supposed to be after all.

Mass building by a single developer resulting in the overnight creation of huge subdivisions composed of nearly identical houses came into vogue during the late 1950's. Daly City, which butted up against the Pacific coast immediately south of San Francisco, was one of the first to be accorded the honor of this novel form of housing. When Tommy and I arrived in 1960, this new form of suburban sprawl was laid out in a labyrinth of intertwining streets stretching over several square miles of hillside above the Pacific Ocean. The homes were all very new and very nice, but they were also very nearly identical. During the summer months, fog from the ocean rolls into Daly City by mid-afternoon and blankets the streets until mid-morning. That leaves homeowners only a few hours each day to locate their houses. Coming home at night in the fog is a real challenge and has been associated with fabricated stories of husbands getting in bed with someone else's wife – accidentally.

Somewhere in the middle of this suburban sprawl was where Bruce and Clo chose to make their first home. They had been married less than three years before our unexpected arrival and already had two babies who were 1 1/2 years and six months old, respectively. Combined with Bruce's new job as a nuclear physicist, they didn't have a lot of free time. Entertaining two young bums for an unspecified period was certainly not on their agenda. Even so, they were surprisingly gracious, and provided us with a large room and shared bed in their basement where I struggled to sleep each night through the roar of Tommy's walrus-level snoring.

My goal on arrival was still to live independently as planned. To make this happen, our first order of business was to land respectable jobs. Where should we start? The building trade seemed reasonable based on the massive number of new houses surrounding us. So early on the morning after our arrival, Tommy and I headed for a site near downtown San Francisco identified as the "Builders Union," transported by a nearly new Buick loaned to us by my brother-in-law. He must have been smoking something to provide two kids, neither of whom had ever driven in a city of more than 40,000 inhabitants, with the one and only family vehicle, even for one day. Before our departure, I diligently checked maps to plan our route. Unfortunately, they provided little data on how to get onto the freeways or on which side to exit after we finally were on them. After multiple tours of the same six block area, I finally found a way to enter the one we needed, but when it came time to exit, the ramp was on the left rather than the right as expected. Bang! I shot straight across four lanes of heavy traffic. A lot of rubber was deposited on the highway in my wake, but no one was killed and Bruce's car was still intact. I did better after that.

Within minutes of our arrival at the Union Hall, it was clear this was going to be a waste of time. The few stragglers hanging around waiting for jobs all looked like they should have been parked on corners with cups and signs. We didn't look like them, but our chances of getting jobs were even slimmer. The clerk managing the facility wondered if we were lost, and when told otherwise, explained that we would have to join the union and wait at least three months before there was any possibility of employment. Since we didn't have three months to wait, we headed for downtown and Market Street, assuming that in all those humongous stores someone had to be looking for reliable, willing, but very inexperienced young helpers.

My next shock, after finally negotiating the route and locating a parking spot, was learning the cost of leaving the car for a couple of hours as we patrolled the stores. When you live in a city you grow accustomed to this sort of thing, but I had never paid for parking in my life, let alone $2.50 per hour. At that rate, the car would cost us more not moving than I could ever hope to make running my butt off in some job. After biting the bullet, the car was abandoned and we set off on foot down Market Street, hitting the employment offices of every retailer in downtown San Francisco. I had never filled out an employment application in my life, but that day I felt I filled out a million without even a glimmer of a successful outcome. Somehow, no one viewed us as valuable additions to their staff. Totally discouraged and exhausted, we put our tails between our legs and headed home, trying to stay sufficiently alert to not smash the car in the rush hour traffic.

Early the next morning we set out again, but his time without a car. Bruce and Clo lived five miles from the edge of SF where the city bus routes began and ended. Daly City had their own buses but they were few and far between. By luck and persistence, we eventually located one of these tiny vehicles traveling somewhere. As it turned out, it was on its way out of SF rather than into town, but the extra 30 minutes riding to the end of the route and back didn't cost extra. We also got the opportunity to see more of Daly City, even if it did all look exactly the same.

After reaching the drop-off point, we eventually located the city bus that would take us to the next bus that would take us to the next bus that would take us to Market Street. After paying for each bus at each point on the route, someone finally educated us on the meaning of transfer tickets. With this newfound knowledge and a surprisingly positive attitude, we renewed our attack on SF employment offices.

After a fruitless morning, we decided to split up for the afternoon so that we could cover more ground. I'm not sure where Tommy went or if he even found an employment office. He did, however, attempt to buy a coke at some point for which he presented a $20 bill. Tommy knew that $4.80 in change couldn't be right but, when he inquired, he was told to move it along or he would be arrested for vagrancy. It would have been interesting to see the outcome of that. Tommy didn't know what vagrancy was but knew it couldn't be good, and decided his only recourse was to follow the advice. He did find his way back to our planned rendezvous site, actually two hours early since he didn't make any actual attempts to locate a job, and we retraced our steps to Daly City in time to catch the local bus before it shut down for the day at 6 PM.

The sun rose the next day, though you would never know it in the Daly City fog, and off we went again, knowing the third time had to be the charm. From the previous day's experience, at least we knew how to get downtown. On arrival, we again split up and I continued on with my quest, hitting one employment office after another. I did get one nibble that day, this being the possibility of employment as a busboy in an all-night restaurant. You can guess which shift I was slated for. I at least had enough sense to put that one on hold. It's not clear whether Tommy's luck was better or worse than mine. He certainly didn't waste his time seeking employment. However, since he was infatuated with buses, he boarded another as soon as he was out of my sight. By this time he fully understood the meaning of a transfer ticket, so he was able to move from bus to bus around the city without additional charge. He didn't know where he was at any time, and he didn't really care. I suggested his luck may have been better than mine because he saw the entire city of San Francisco, had a great time doing so, and miraculously found his way back to where he had started, all for the price of one bus ticket. Don't worry, be happy!

The next day we split up again at Market Street and Tommy set off immediately for a second go at the buses. I, in the meantime, quickly located potential employment. The job I was offered seemed a bit shady even to me, but it was explained as "network marketing." I really had no clue what was expected, but was told to report at 8 AM sharp the next morning looking professional. I also had no idea what that meant.

My new potential employers reeked of sufficient sleaze to warn me that I still needed to continue my job search. Later that day I finally was offered a real job; a stock boy at Macy's for which I would be paid the outstanding wage of $1.56/hour. This translated into $62.40/week before taxes. That low salary clearly eliminated the apartment Tommy and I were going to rent for the summer.

Since I had agreed to report for duty the next day at the marketing job, and since Tommy decided he had seen enough buses for the moment, we agreed that he would be my replacement. I was quite sure they wouldn't know the difference anyway. So both of us had actual jobs the next day, or so it seemed. I spent the day moving cheap Japanese hibachis and salt and pepper shakers from the storeroom to the display counters on the fifth floor of the downtown Macy's store while Tommy was loaded into a van with 12 other prospective "marketers" before they all headed for the suburbs. On the way, he and the others were handed a list of magazines they were to market door-to-door. About an hour later, they were dropped off at various points in the suburbs and told to return to these sites at 5:50 PM sharp or they would be left.

It was not a great day for Tommy. In Bozeman, Tommy was known as the superstar of door-to-door salesmen, and magazine sales had been his specialty. Somehow he had a knack for this type of activity, at least on his home turf. This was not the case in the suburbs of SF. He diligently went from house-to-house ringing doorbells which were seldom answered. When they were, his conversations rarely lasted more than several seconds. No sales were made and Tommy had no access to food or water the entire day. His ride back to Market Street did eventually show up an hour late, and when Tommy reported his lack of success, he was told he need not come back the next day. He should have stayed on the buses, but if he had, he would have missed this opportunity of exposure to the real world.

Tommy spent another week looking for a job. However, he really didn't know how to do it and spent most of his time on the buses. That was his comfort level. Bruce tried to coach him on job searching, but Tommy never recovered from the day spent marketing. His heart was out of it and he was ready to go home. Life was more predictable in Bozeman, and that was where he wanted to be. Enough of this adventure crap! He had his old job as a stocker in a food store waiting for him at home. So two weeks after arriving in the big city with high hopes and major expectations, Tommy boarded the bus that brought him into San Francisco and headed home.

One evening before Tommy fled, however, we visited a couple that were family friends and lived in an apartment in the Mission District of San Francisco. Their back balcony hung out over a wooded hillside with the panoramic view of downtown San Francisco laid out in the distance. It was a gorgeous night without fog, and the scene below was truly surreal. Tommy took one look and his excitement level immediately went off scale.

"Man," he blurted, "there must be some fine carnival in town. Let's get going."

I really hated to disappoint him, especially in light of his recent setbacks, by explaining that what he was seeing was where he had been riding buses each day, but was just camouflaged at night. However, it had to be done.

"Oh crap," he replied in the most disappointed voice possible, "I knew it was too good to be true."

On another evening before Tommy's departure, Bruce, Clo, kids, Tommy, and I took a 40-mile car ride across the Bay to visit some of my cousins in Oakland. Within an hour of our arrival, Clo had the fabulous idea that I should take this opportunity to become better acquainted with several of my younger relatives without her interference. So off Tommy and I went with three newly-introduced cousins for a night of serious bonding. Since it was already after 9 PM when we left the house, only minutes before Clo and Bruce did the same, a ride home with them was eliminated. We hadn't gone more than a mile when one of my hospitable cousins alerted us to the fact that the last bus across the Bay Bridge would be leaving within the next 45 minutes. They weren't about to bring us all the way back to Daly City. The best they would offer was to drop us outside the Oakland Bus Terminal and wave good-by. It had been an enchanting 20 minutes; we all got well-acquainted. If first impressions are informative, I learned I didn't care to see them again anytime soon.

I knew before we set off on this expedition that Clo had pushed me into a ludicrous situation, but I didn't have the courage to object to her momentary loss of brain function. She was still my big sister and I was the little brother, a guest in her house. So, as a result, Tommy and I were again heading back into San Francisco on a bus, but this time with full cognizance that it would be many hours before we would reach our destination. We made our connections through the city fine; the city buses were still operating and by then we knew the way home. When we were finally deposited at the Daly City limits, it was nearly midnight. Neither of us had ever ridden in a taxi and had no idea how to get one. In fact, the thought of taking a taxi never even entered our minds. I also couldn't call my sister and ask for a ride since we had no access to a telephone. We were only about five miles from home and we were young. Even in the fog we knew we could find our way.

Somehow, it wasn't as easy to navigate through the fog at night as it had been in daylight. We wandered bewilderingly through the streets of sidewalk-level fog, occasionally shinnying up street signs to reveal where we were. Even at that, we got majorly off course several times. Once we had finally located the correct street, we were forced to approach the front doors of the houses in order to decipher their numbers. That fog was a real bummer. Shortly after 3 AM, the two exhausted travelers finally located the house with the correct number on the correct street. We had survived another day (and night) in the big city.

Tommy left for home two days later, and with him departed my last chance to live the summer independently. I guess I knew my original plan wouldn't materialize from the very beginning, but now I was finally forced to admit it. However, all that was really damaged was my pride, and that needed an adjustment anyway. I had a great place to live for a summer and even had a job of sorts. What more could I ask? San Francisco was perched before me like a low-lying fruit, ready to be plucked.

Exposure to ethnic diversity, whether racial or religious, was not a secondary benefit of growing up in Montana and being educated in a small Catholic school. I don't think I knew anyone that was Jewish; since I didn't recognize typical Jewish names, this group would not have had identifiable markers. In contrast, black people were easily recognized, but there weren't any. I take that back. There was one black family in Bozeman when I was a child. I remember seeing the mother in the Dime Store when I was about five years old. I was able to recall this because I had never seen anyone that color before, and would not again for several years. This was before the civil rights movement, so black athletes were not even in vogue as yet at Montana State College. Therefore, San Francisco presented me with a whole new world in ethnic diversity.

One of the buyers in my department at Macy's was black – a man about 15 years my senior named Alan. He had been a track star in college and, as a result, showed an immediate interest in me because of my own self-proclaimed skills in the sport. Surprisingly, even though my upbringing had instilled me with distrust for persons of other religions, this did not carry over to racial differences.

Alan was single and invited me to go with him on multiple outings during the course of the summer. Bruce and Clo immediately concluded he was gay and that Alan was interested in me for that reason only. He could have been and I might not have known the difference. However, in retrospect, he wasn't. Within days of our introduction, he took me to dinner at Fisherman's Wharf. I hated fish! We were force-fed trout when I was growing up since it was the only edible fish coming out of the streams of Western Montana. My mother always fried them in lard, using no added ingredients to disguise their fishiness, and I was required to eat them. Man, I hated fish! Alan informed me that it wasn't acceptable to order anything but fish at Fisherman's Wharf, and assured me it would taste nothing like the trout that I had previously been compelled to eat. He was right. I also had sourdough bread for the first time. I ate it because I thought it was expected, sensing with every bite that I was chewing sour milk. I got over that too, but it took several years. The evening turned out to be a true gastronomic awakening.

By the time I got home that night, I was experiencing a strange itching in my extremities. Then all parts of my body began to itch and swell. The only way I could relieve the urge to scratch myself to death was to go under steaming hot water in the bathtub. I think my sister cared, but figured I would either survive or I wouldn't, and her involvement was not going to affect the outcome. Besides, we were all leaving for a weekend in the Sierras at dawn and she had far heavier concerns than my survival, number one being her sleep. It was a long night. At 2 AM, I thought I might die, but decided it would be better to do that than awaken Clo. By 4 AM, the symptoms began to subside and I began to think I might not die after all. By 6 AM, when everyone who had actually slept that night was showing signs of life, I knew I was going to live too. Who knows which of the variety of novel cuisines I consumed that night had brought on the response. The only food to which I have a known allergy is lobster, and that took several later exposures to develop.

At the break of dawn, Clo's family and I headed out through the early morning Daly City fog, me bolstered by the fact that I had survived and the others by the anticipated adventure in the mountains. Our destination was a small resort in the low Sierra Mountain gold country that was managed by the relatives we had visited earlier in the summer, whose benevolent children had abandoned Tommy and me at the Oakland Bus Terminal. I was really looking forward to bonding with that group again. In an attempt to be optimistic, I envisioned that they might be kinder this time. They weren't. They seemed to think that since we were relatives, we would expect the weekend to be provided gratis, and treated us that way. Perhaps we should have paid when we arrived; that way they might have recognized we were not free-loaders. Maybe I overreacted to the lack of civility by the group that had dropped me off in downtown Oakland; maybe they simply didn't like me and their behavior had nothing to do with the money.

It was setting up to be a long weekend when I encountered my savior at the group lunch. Her name was Carrie. She was just another guest and, on second blush, appeared much more attractive than her looks deserved. Perhaps it had something to do with the fact that she was going to be a junior in college and was light years ahead of me in sophistication, but still gave me some measure of attention. She was probably a typical California girl for the time, something that I had not previously encountered face-to-face. But for me, she was a weekend goddess. During several hikes into the mountains, she excitedly related to me her spell-binding college adventures, with all their trials and tribulations, and endured my attempts to interest her in my athletic prowess and worldliness. She never gave even a remote impression that she had any personal interest in me, but did agree that she would arrange for us to double-date with someone of her choosing in the near future. The future came the following weekend.

Carrie lived with her parents in Sausalito, just over the Golden Gate Bridge from San Francisco and only about 15 miles from my summer abode. She related that she had a guy friend about her age that had a younger sister about my age, so it looked like an ideal arrangement. I would merely pick up the threesome and we would make a night of it in San Francisco. Surprisingly, Bruce and Clo agreed to loan me their car for the evening, so with $44 in my pocket,

I began my Friday night on the town. $44 then was like $500 today, so I knew this was overkill. Also, it was all I had.

My first stop was the gas station where I filled 'er up for $3. This seems incidental, but as the evening wore on, it became important. I met my companions at Carrie's house as I was told to do, and also met my first disappointment for the evening. To put it mildly, my first blind date, introduced as Maggie, was less than attractive. Not that orange-tinged hair, a face filled with pimples, and a mouth full of braces can't be attractive. It's just that in her case it didn't come together well. My first thought, before even giving the girl a chance to say hello, was to feign sudden stomach cramps and take my remaining $41 home, hoping for better luck next time. However, I still had this thing for Carrie, hoping somehow she would see me a bit more in the light that I viewed myself.

We started the evening early, so our first stop was dinner. This may come as a shock, but that was the first time I had taken anyone to dinner. That was just not done in high school in Montana in the 1950's, at least not in my circle of friends. Dinner, as planned by Carrie, was to be in Chinatown. She was the guide; the rest of us were tourists. This may come as another shock, but I also had never had Chinese food. Carrie was not only a guide but also a licensed educator. Maggie's brother and I split the costs so I was out a mere $14 for dinner, including the parking.

Our second stop was the "Top of the Mark" Hotel for a performance by Lena Horne. I, of course, had never heard of her, but Carrie assured me she would be terrific. She was, and as it turned out, would be for many years. However, the $18 charge for two diverted my viewing pleasure. Throughout the performance I distracted myself with multiple scenarios, all involving math. I knew the evening would not end here and knew that it would involve at least one more parking garage. Doing the math, I figured I had just enough money to get the group home but would not have enough to pay the 25 cents to get back across the Golden Gate Bridge. Panic began to set in.

Upon returning to the car, I was given a bit of a reprieve when Carrie ordered her date to pay for the parking. I immediately began recalculating, and realized there might be a bit of light at the end of the tunnel. But where would this tunnel lead next? Dancing of course! Carrie had it well planned. Our next stop was a hot spot on North Beach. The cover charge was only $2 each, so I still had a faint hope that if Carrie's date would again pay for the parking, I might yet have enough money left in my pocket at the end of the evening to get back across that damnable bridge. By now, however, I was cursing myself for buying gas. That $3 seemed like a lost fortune.

I know I wasn't much fun to dance with or even be around. However, I had only one thing on my mind, and that was getting home. By then, my affection for Carrie had evaporated. My only cost associated with this last stop was to purchase some soft drinks which were more than the cover charge. I knew this was outrageous, but there I was one more time, at the mercy of my pride and Carrie's will. I still had hope that the evening would not be a total embarrassment when I ran out of money. All I needed was for Carrie's date to pay for parking again and that this would be our last stop. Miraculously it happened and I somehow arrived home with $1.25. What was I worried about anyway?

By this time in the summer, I had been transferred to the Macy's warehouse. It really was intended as some sort of promotion, but for me it was being sent to Siberia. The building had no windows, so I never saw daylight during week days from 8:30 to 5:00. Initially I had a mountain of work. There had been a major backlog of items not sent to the seven branch stores in our department, so my job was to correct that situation. The stockers in the branch stores wished that I never existed. I loaded every truck leaving the warehouse with accumulated crap which inundated the workers on the other end. However, I did not see that as my problem. Unfortunately, after a week of furious activity, I was done for the summer. There was essentially nothing else I could do. Sticking price labels on packages, which was the only other significant activity being performed in my department, was carried out by union workers of which I was not one. When I offered to help move items in other departments, I was resented as an over-achiever. My only resort, other than doing multiple sets of push-ups each day, was to bury myself in the storage shelves and sleep. I did get a lot of rest.

The only good thing about the Macy's warehouse was that I had my own phone, also a novelty in my life. I didn't have any real use for it since one could only use the phone for local calls. However, it was there. At 8:45 AM on the Monday morning following my tryst with Carrie and company, she called to inquire about our pleasure-filled evening and whether I was ready for another the next weekend. My spontaneous reply was "I can't hear you very well. Could you repeat what you just said?"

"We all had a great time and want to go out again. Where would you like to go?"

I responded with, "I still can't hear what you are saying. Please run it by me again."

"I said, we had this great time and want to do it again. Can you hear me now?"

I concluded the conversation with, "No I can't. Maybe you should call again next week. I think they will have the phones repaired by then."

My last response was followed by a sharp click on the other end. Carrie didn't call back the next week. I forgot her phone number, so couldn't call her either. Of course, I wouldn't have anyway.

My weekdays at work that summer were boring as hell, but the weekends always held a new adventure. On the one following the Carrie fiasco, Alan took me to the USA Olympic trials at Stanford Stadium. Since track was our main connection, it was a fine time, a sharp contrast to what I had experienced the previous weekend. The night we were there, John Thomas broke the world record in the high jump. To me, this was like getting a glimpse of Heaven. Alan continued to provide adventures throughout the summer but none measured up to this.

On another weekend, Bruce and Clo and family went to Santa Cruz with me in tow. This experience might not have been much for folks from California, but this country bumpkin had previously been exposed only to traveling carnivals whose highlight was generally riding the Ferris wheel. Thus, the amusement park at Santa Cruz was a fairyland. There are persons who keep records for the most rides on particular roller coasters, and I must have set the single day record for the monster in Santa Cruz.

That weekend I also put my feet in the ocean for the first time. The lakes and rivers in Montana are mostly just ice water, but everyone knew enough to not attempt to swim in them until they got above 60 degrees in late summer. However, Santa Cruz had an ocean beach with breaking waves and all, and in spite of the frigid temperature, people were actually in the water without wet suits. Even though the ocean there was as cold as the mountain lakes in Montana in June, I knew I couldn't let California wimps show me up. It was "go in to knee level for one minute, then retreat for one minute, then go in to waist level for one minute, then retreat for one minute, then go to chest level for one minute, then retreat for one minute." By then I was sufficiently numb to remain in the water, fully immersed, for five minutes. I got out just before hypothermia set in. I guess people who live there eventually get used to it or they don't know any better.

One weekend in late July, I took the bus to Davis to visit my high school classmate Frank who was literally sweating though a six-week introductory summer college course in biology at the University of California. He must have had a screw loose to waste time in the summer going to school, but he did, and to make matters worse, he did it in the inferno of the Sacramento Valley. The daytime temperatures in that place averaged at least 110 degrees and the nights were not much cooler. I was there only long enough to become half fried, and to convince Frank to visit Daly City and readjust his thermostat. He showed up a week later when my sister and her family were visiting Yosemite for several days, so we had the house to ourselves. This was a first for both of us. Perhaps it offered that bit of freedom I went to San Francisco for in the first place, only this time we had all the conveniences of a real home. Most impressive was the liquor cabinet. Bruce and Clo were great party animals as judged by the selection of beverages stored there. So what do a couple of protected 17 year-olds do when exposed to this situation for the first time? They experiment, of course.

My only previous exposure to serious alcohol consumption was during our one night stand in Reno a couple months earlier, and Frank didn't even have that experience to draw on. Neither of us liked beer as it turned out, so we were compelled to resort to the harder stuff. I had no idea there was such a difference between rum, gin, vodka, scotch, and brandy. When it was dessert time, I blended a very sweet concoction Bruce sometimes sipped called a Pink Squirrel. The first glass was great but the second stimulated us both to unload our stomach contents, which was overdue anyway. It was another novel California weekend, and Frank left with the remark that it compensated for his six weeks of "institutionalized learning in the fires of Hell."

All good things have to end. By late-August both Ike and I had had enough of this good thing and headed north as the birds in Montana were gathering to go south. His red bomb of a car was up and running again. I don't know what miracle had been performed on this beast, but this time it didn't vibrate at even 60 mph.

My first voluntary action on arriving in Bozeman was to call Tim to relate in colorful detail what he had missed. He had just come off his two weeks of summer water-skiing, and had met a new sweet-heart. Tim could never juggle a girlfriend and any other thought process, so my florid description of a summer in San Francisco completely escaped him. "Besides," he reminded me, "you never really experienced the full summer of freedom we had planned together five months ago anyway." I wonder what it would have been like if I had.

5 It Isn't as Simple as it Looks

Making the transition from high school to college had all the appearances of a cakewalk as I was handed my diploma in Holy Rosary Church in May of 1960. Not that I had huge intellectual aspirations, but going to college was not optional in my family. Even my dad, with only an eighth grade education, was firm on that score, maybe because he only had an eighth grade education. I had managed to become a decent student after my sixth grade experience; that is, once I got past the reading hurdle and made a few attitude and priority adjustments. Thus, going to college was going to be a walk in the park. Besides, my new classroom at Montana State College was only two miles from my front door and I had connections there, especially through church members. One had arranged a scholarship for me in chemical engineering and another had gotten me a track scholarship which, coupled with living at home, was going to allow my personal bank account to increase rather than decrease. The fact that I had no interest in being a chemical engineer seemed to be no impediment. They were paying me and I could switch majors any time I wanted. Shortly after being awarded the athletic scholarship, I was informed by my new track coach that I either had to play freshman football or run cross country to retain the scholarship. This was only more good news, and the decision was a no-brainer. I loved football and had no desire to experience the pain associated with running distances of greater than one mile. My stars were nearly perfectly aligned.

There are probably a reasonable percentage of kids who make the leap from high school to college without drama or at least mental gymnastics, but I was not among them. The parting shot by one of my high school nuns when she was leaving town after my graduation was "make sure you leave home when you go to college." I was startled by the comment but had no intention of acting on her advice. Why would I want to leave home? Didn't she know that I was committed to play football at MSC? She was probably aware, but also recognized something that I had overlooked. I needed to get out from under the security blanket provided by our little Catholic community, and two months in Daly City living with my sister was not the solution. I needed to grow up and she knew it.

One week before class registration was to begin for the MSC student body, new freshmen were required to report to the campus for an adjustment period. Nearly all except those from Bozeman moved into their new homes, called dormitories. During this week of adjustment, they began to form new circles of friends with their roommates and dorm mates. I did not have the opportunity to make these connections. Instead, I remained rooted in my comfort zone, sticking with my old group of friends that were still in town. Thus, I made little attempt to make the social transition into my new environment.

In spite of myself, I did come in contact with my new classmates during that first critical week in two happenings, neither of which contributed to my social adjustment. One was aptitude testing, a three-day marathon of knowledge regurgitation through a series of standardized tests. It took place in the MSC field house, a vast sports arena in which 1,500 chairs were placed side-by-side, row-after-row. After our group of new freshmen was packed in, promptly by 8 AM that first morning, the Dean of Students began his incantation.

"Dear new freshman," he chanted, "welcome to your new home at Montana State College. We are all extremely pleased to have you here. Before you get too comfortable, however, I want you to first look at the person on your left. Now look at the person on your right. Take a good look. Now do it again, and remember that only one of you will be here to graduate."

That was one inspirational speech. Welcome to college! His statistics were accurate but useless, sort of like an instruction manual written in Latin. I guess the goal was either to put the fear of God into each of our hearts from the opening bell or to attempt to arouse our competitive spirits. Since we were already uncomfortable enough, however, we didn't need to hear that disheartening lecture to make us even more so.

The second happening in which I came in contact with new classmates that first week was on the football field. That should have been fun; I loved football. I thought I was even reasonably good at it too, maybe because I had been on an eight-man team in a high school of 40 boys. My first clue that this might not go as well as expected was when I was introduced to my new equipment. What I received had once been new, sometime in the 1940's. The varsity had, of course, been provided their equipment first. Then the freshmen were assigned times to report to get theirs. I didn't become aware that I was dead last on the list until I reported late in the afternoon at my specified time. By then, some items on the equipment list were completely depleted, such as shoulder pads. The equipment manager said he would have to borrow a set from a local high school but it would take a few days. One piece of equipment he did have was a helmet – exactly one. It was two sizes too large and had padding equivalent to the helmet I received as a Christmas gift when I was six years old. I knew what a good helmet was since I had one in high school. In retrospect, I should have refused the use of the helmet I was assigned. The outcome of that discussion would have been interesting, especially since, as I soon came to realize, I was viewed as useless baggage in a freshman class with 40 teammates who had received true football scholarships. My track scholarship earned me the rock bottom position on the pecking order.

It may have been my ever-present fear that the new helmet would lead to my demise; it may have been the general disdain I felt from the coaching staff regarding my football abilities; it may have been my lack of confidence in this much larger arena. Whatever it was, I mentally checked out of football by the end of freshman week. Where was that competitive spirit that had been instilled into my marrow during 17 years of living at home with a dad whose primary goal was to teach competitiveness? Where was the inner courage that had been fabricated during years of training in the school of familial and personal hard knocks? Both apparently abandoned me when I stepped outside of my protective religious and social microcosm. I kept coming to the football practices but only because I needed the track scholarship. During these sessions, I avoided making tackles and being tackled whenever possible, and when I couldn't, I made sure my head and neck were not involved in the action. There was no way I was going to test that piece-of-crap helmet. I should have chosen my sport more wisely and gutted it out on the cross-country team. At least in that sport there may have been some appreciation for my athletic prowess and, best of all, I wouldn't have needed the helmet.

After the week of freshman orientation, it was time to register for our first classes. This process took place in a massive gymnasium filled with a separate table assigned to each of the curricula. Everyone enrolling was given a specific half day to accomplish this task, but even with a staggered schedule, the place was a mad house. The entire student body had to endure this punishment during a three-day period each school quarter. If you were assigned an early day, things generally worked out, but those given the last day typically found that at least one of their required classes was already full. This sometimes resulted in extra quarters and even extra years in school to complete requirements for graduation. So a lot could go badly during those mayhem registration sessions.

The only registration instructions given new freshmen were, "be there on time, bring money, and when you arrive, locate the table for the curriculum that is to be your major." I got there on time, but it still took nearly 20 minutes to find a banner labeled "Chemical Engineering." I had no idea there were so many potential college majors. When I finally found my table, it took another 30 minutes to get to the front of the queue. There I was assigned an advisor who spent the next 30 minutes trying to explain what courses I had to take and how to get myself registered in them.

The instructions from my advisor were to locate and queue up at a separate table within the gymnasium for each class I was to register in that quarter, and then pray that each of my specified classes was still available. If the process was derailed because one class was full, I would have to start the whole process again. After finally getting all the appropriate signatures, I still had to queue up to receive final clearance from my advisor before again lining up to pay for it all. To accomplish all this as an incoming freshman during the allotted four hours was not possible, and the longer past the allotted time it required, the more annoyed and angry the persons manning the tables became. Where were the sweet nuns at Holy Rosary High School now that I really needed them?

During the 30 minutes of planning I had with my new advisor prior to signing up for my first quarter of classes, he strongly suggested that since I was majoring in chemical engineering and would be having a class in general chemistry for my entire first year, I should consider taking a newly designed experimental course called honors chemistry. It was to be taught by an experienced and highly-respected Full Professor. I followed his suggestion, an act that meant nothing to me until I attended my first class. Apparently an excess number of new freshmen were given the same suggestion, and the class, which was assigned to a relatively small room, had students lining the hall outside. As might be anticipated, the first words uttered by my new professor were "many of you do not have the credentials to survive in this class and should switch to the less taxing general chemistry course."

That was all I needed to hear and I was out of there; my competitive juices had abandoned me once again. Within minutes, I had resold my textbook to the College Bookstore and was arranging the paperwork for the transfer. The latter required the signature of my soon-to-be ex-professor. I assumed that would be painless to obtain since he seemed more than happy to dump as many students from his class as possible. Surprisingly, he didn't just sign the withdrawal form, but instead, took the time to check my scores obtained from the three days of testing during the previous week. I had not been privy to the results of these tests and had no idea that I had scored in the top five-percentile in all categories. With this information in hand, my professor attempted damage control.

His opening remark was "you are not one of the group that should be withdrawing from my class."

Since my only thought was "then why did you try to scare me to death," I refrained from responding. This gave him the opening he needed to spend the next ten minutes trying to convince me to reconsider my decision, explaining in glowing detail why taking his class would be an opportunity of a lifetime. He might as well have been speaking in Greek. I had unloaded my honors chemistry book and was not about to pay the extra costs to repurchase it. Besides, I was playing freshman football and that was going to deplete the extra study time that would be needed for his course. I was out of there, switching to the general chemistry course taught to the masses by an inexperienced Assistant Professor who had received his PhD only three months earlier. This decision was to have a lifetime effect that I could never have anticipated on that September day in 1960, an outcome that took many years to fully materialize.

Within days of the start of classes, I realized I was withdrawing into myself, but couldn't catch myself in the freefall. My classes were progressing normally after abandoning honors chemistry, but it was a toss-up as to whether my sports life or my social life was in the greater disarray. Probably it was the latter. I wanted to say that this was due solely to living at home with ancient parents who were centuries removed from understanding what I was experiencing. In retrospect, all I had to do to rectify many of my problems was to become part of some social organization on campus, like a fraternity. However, I didn't even grab that lifeline when it was tossed to me by several previous Rosary High grads. I accepted the invitations to attend their fraternity houses, but had no interest in joining. It was not a family tradition to join a fraternity and, at that moment, I was keeping it close to home, sticking only with the familiar. Besides joining a fraternity would cost money, and I was determined to make more that year than I spent.

Using the "living at home with old parents" excuse for my social withdrawal could be taken only so far since Tommy, my high school classmate and companion for the trip to San Francisco, had decided for some unfathomable reason to attend college and had pledged a fraternity during his first week. His parents were almost as old as mine and neither of them, or his two older siblings, had darkened the doors of a college. Thus, guidance from the home front, either social or otherwise, was even more limited in his case than mine, but still he made the effort to fit into college life. This heightened my self-perception as a misfit, and added to my generally demoralized state. Maybe, I reasoned, I should have spent a year working outside the home like my siblings before going to college; maybe I should have taken the advice of the good nun and left home for college. However, I hadn't done either, and now I had to live with the decision. At least there was enough respectability left in my tank to do that, no matter how much I wanted to break and run. A little sound counseling at that moment would have helped, but I neither had the reasoning power nor humility to seek it. Someone with any sense could have told me that "this too will pass; you just need to give it a few weeks to allow the dust to settle." This was not to be; I never asked that "someone."

The ultimate career for a Catholic educated in the 1950's was in the service of God as a nun or priest. The cultural revolution of the 60's opened the door to other presumed selfless career choices, but as a finished product of the Catholic school system of 1960, the pinnacle was clear. Certainly the nuns and priests that were my teachers dared not say they were special. It was just understood. They didn't overtly direct those of us they viewed as having that special calling to the religious life. They just let it gradually seep into our brains that any other choice of a career would be either selling one's self short or worse, selling God short. Maybe those who made the leap and actually stuck with it just needed to justify their own decisions, or maybe misery simply likes company.

Thus, in the mist of my unhappiness with college life, I concluded that I must be one of those with a "special calling." This decision took all of two weeks to materialize after I had started classes, a bit premature by anyone's standards.

Deciding to become a priest was only part of my newfound aspiration. Two of my high school classmates were already on that course, enrolled in the local diocesan college in Helena. I needed to do one better, and decided the best priests were missionaries. I would become one and, thereby, save not only my soul but also those of the pagan children of the world. I was on a roll.

All this zeal for holiness was just an illusion. What really pushed my button was very simple, and had nothing to do with religion. I had just come off setting records in the State Class C 880-yard run for two years in a row, I had been voted the "Most Valuable Player" in both football and basketball at Holy Rosary High School, I was president of this and that and had graduated second in my class. I was real special, and if anyone didn't understand why, I was more than willing to explain it. What I forgot was that I came from a high school with less than 80 kids and everyone there was special in something by the time they graduated.

With a head twice the size of a watermelon, I started college. As with freshman everywhere, my transition to college life was an emotional roller coaster, but mine was mostly heading downhill. I played freshman football to maintain a track scholarship, but knew I wouldn't make the team, and really didn't care. I had enrolled in honors chemistry, but dropped out when the professor suggested not everyone there should have signed up for his class. I chose not to pledge a fraternity even though doing so would have provided me with a needed social base. There were no crucifixes on the walls of the classrooms at MSC to reassure me that any of my decisions were correct. God was gone, I was on my own, and I didn't like it. Living at home was more a burden than a help because it offered only more isolation, the exact opposite of what I needed in order to fit in. My grades were holding, but I hated my classes. I was convinced I couldn't compete and didn't really care. I spelled relief in the only way I knew. It was S-E-M-I-N-A-R-Y.

Within a day after I reached my life-altering decision, I was explaining to my pastor that I felt God was calling me, and asked when he thought I should inform the girl I had been dating for the past several months. He said "immediately. You will be taking the vow of celibacy and need to begin now." Did I ever regret I asked that question! My girl friend was still in high school, and she represented the one remaining thread to my glory days at Holy Rosary High School. However, I did as I was ordered; one does not ignore a priest's directive when one is about to enter the service of God. But it was October, nearly a whole year before I would enter Maryknoll, the missionary group I was planning to join. I don't know what my girl friend felt on hearing the news. I should have discussed my college adjustment difficulties with her but that type of conversation was beyond the comfort level of our relationship. I at least should have provided her with some forewarning of what I was thinking. However, I didn't. She was a good Catholic girl and had been taught the value of sacrifice. Maybe our breakup was even a relief for her. All I know for sure is that she was out of the door and running within seconds after our little talk, leaving behind the last ashes of my association with Holy Rosary High School. Now I really was on my own.

The shock waves of what I had just done hit quickly. I was not adept at being alone and desperately needed companionship. I finally sought it where I should have in the first place, at MSC, and this time my happiness meter began to climb. A whole crop of new friends of both sexes came out of the woodwork. My attitude may not have soared with the eagles but it was no longer sucking bottom with the catfish. By the end of the first quarter, only two things blocked a reversal of my decision to join Maryknoll. The obvious one was that I had already informed half of the people in Montana of the tremendous life of sacrifice on which I was about to embark, and was too proud to tell them I had changed my mind. Of course, none but my old pastor really cared at the time, but I was still arrogant enough to think they all did. The world was still revolving around me. The second reason for not backing out was the lingering need to satisfy the question about my special calling. Was I chosen or not? By the end of the school year, I was almost sure that this was going to be another bad decision. Regardless, I sucked it up and boarded the train for Glen Ellyn, Illinois, in September of 1961 where I began my career as a Maryknoller.

During my freshman year at MSC, I was consistently one of the top students in general chemistry. As a result, I was regularly quizzed by my chemistry teacher about my scholastic aspirations. Being young and idealistic himself, he felt compelled to urge the better students in his class to consider careers in science. Actually it was more than just becoming scientists; he suggested we all should become chemists. Before he opened his mouth on the subject, I had already redirected my ship toward the priesthood. However, I didn't share this information with my chemistry teacher during any of his speeches. It could have been that I didn't want to blunt his enthusiasm, and it was just easier to listen and keep my mouth shut. However, I had truly enjoyed his class, and felt that if this seminary thing didn't work out, I might actually follow his advice. Regardless, I was not about to blow up any more bridges on my way out of town. His interest in me, and my interest in chemistry, provided me a logical lifeline for a possible return to MSC, and I was at least going to keep that lifeline intact. It was a good thing I did.

6 1 Year, 3 Weeks, 2 Days and 7 Hours, But Who's Counting?

Time flies when you're having fun is a euphemism for "I spent a lifetime one year in the seminary." Why did I voluntarily put myself through a year like that? Second question: why did I stay so long if it was that bad? I have already provided some vague answers to the first question, but unless you were educated by nuns and priests, the explanation was probably incomprehensible. My ability to answer question number two is probably even more limited. It's almost like you had to be there. After all, people get themselves into lousy situations all the time and often can't find a respectable way out. Abusive relationships, dissatisfying jobs, poor career choices are just a few. So a year in a seminary was like a walk in the park. Tell that to an 18-year old who was thinking he had died and gone to Hell.

There is a lot more drama in those words than the situation warranted, but when the focus of life is solely on one's self, almost everything is high drama. After multiple life experiences, I now recognize that things and situations can change and usually do, often for the better. However, when I was going down an unhappy path at 18 years of age, and seemingly had little control over my life choices, this path seemed infinite. Did I really feel I had no other life choices once I committed myself to attend the seminary? Probably not really, but I felt convinced that I had to give this decision every chance to succeed before I cut bait. Every chance to succeed can be translated as "I had to be completely miserable before I could justify leaving." I think I got there. At least that is how I remember it.

When my brother John decided to enter the seminary during his college days, my dad proclaimed, "You better see this one through to the finish if you are going to start. We already had one child that was going to be a priest and quit. We don't want another one." The one child in question was our oldest brother Joe who was one year from being ordained when he finally realized he didn't want to live a celibate life. For being as smart as he was, he was a slow learner in that department. However, he was not alone as evidenced by the copious number of married ex-priests.

Confronted with the threat of family damnation, John did finish and became a priest, but I always wondered whether my dad's words kept him on course. Fortunately for me, the burden of those words was laid on him and not me. Still, I was convinced that when I committed myself to the seminary, my dad's thoughts on the subject had not changed, even if he didn't express them to me. With the patriarchal control my dad exerted, even his perceived thoughts were enough to alter the decisions of every one of his nine children. I was no exception.

But the blame for remaining in the seminary until complete misery set in was due to more than fear of my dad. I had a whole list of people that I was convinced I would greatly disappoint if I left. Most of this list was manufactured in my head, but some of it may even have been real. The cool treatment I received from my pastor, the one that had explicitly ordered me to lay off women 11 full months before even departing for Maryknoll, qualified him as one who felt betrayed by my departure when it finally happened. Certain family members also showed me a bit of disdain, even if they didn't verbally condemn me. This probably occurred because they had proudly told their friends I was going to be a Maryknoll missionary, and now they had to explain that I wasn't.

The main reason I couldn't pull the plug earlier, however, was I felt I would be abandoning the ultimate choice in careers, and it would all be downhill from there. Therefore, even though I made the decision to go to the seminary by October of 1960, and knew long before I arrived at Maryknoll in September of the next year that this was probably a bad decision, I still had to confirm to myself that I was not one of God's chosen few. In later years, I came to realize if I had no other virtue, I was persistent, and sometimes this has even helped. On this occasion, persistence was more a burden than an asset.

The road from Bozeman to the Maryknoll College Seminary in Glen Ellyn, Illinois, 20 miles west of Chicago, was the Northern Pacific Railroad. I always thought that the sound of a passenger train's warning whistle, as it moved away from me down the tracks, was the saddest sound in the world. When I was five years old, my mother had taken a trip east to visit a dying relative, and went by train. I accompanied my dad when he saw her off at the station. I didn't cry much as a kid, but I sure did that day. I remember, as if it was yesterday, the sound of the train whistle as it moved with my mother on board, down the tracks, and away from me. I hated passenger trains, and their forlorn whistling sound, for years after that.

Since I was actually in the train, the sound of its whistle as it left Bozeman for Chicago on that September day in 1961 was higher pitched than the noise I had grown to hate, but it was just as melancholy. Some of the sensation was due to early homesickness, but mostly it was anticipated loathing of that to which I had just committed myself. Even the Vista Dome car, with its 360 degree view of the world, held no interest.

The temperature in Chicago when I alighted in an early September afternoon at Union Station was 95 degrees, and the relative humidity was even higher. I had lived with heat, even sometimes in Montana, but dripping humidity was a new experience. Even in this blast furnace, however, I wanted to show my loyalty to Montana, and the only way I knew how was to wear my double-lined Montana State College letter jacket, earned in track the previous spring. There I was, standing in the middle of Union Station with three large suitcases and a foot locker in tow, rivers of sweat rolling down my face, and attempting to map a route to Glen Ellyn. I guess I appeared completely lost, or at least sufficiently so to draw the attention of a random young lady. Rather than asking me if I needed help, she instead inquired, "Did you earn that letter jacket at Michigan? My brother goes there."

The colors of the jacket were right, but the moment was wrong. In my mind, Montana State was heads-and-shoulders above Michigan, and besides, Michigan is in the Midwest where I certainly did not want to be at that moment. After explaining the true significance of my letter jacket to the girl, I was more depressed than ever. The jacket was not having the expected effect, and my body temperature was approaching boiling.

I eventually figured out that trains regularly went from Chicago's Union Station to the suburbs including Glen Ellyn. After making that transit and then the final leg by cab, I arrived at the Maryknoll Seminary. My first impression should have been a positive one since the seminary was built on a nine-hole golf course and eight of the holes had been kept intact after the seminary's construction was completed several decades earlier. However, the massive six-story brick monstrosity to which I was delivered was a postcard image of a penitentiary or sanitarium. With the cab idling in its driveway, and innumerable guys in cassocks milling around, I sat frozen in place. This was decision time. Do I leave now and have the cab return me to the railroad station or do I get out? The sweat continued to pour down my face since I still wore the letter jacket. That didn't help my ability to reason. Finally, the confused cab driver asked me if there was a problem. There sure as hell was, but it would have been impossible to explain it to him in less than two hours. His question did jerk me back to the fact that I had come this far, so it was no time to quit now. Thus, I willed myself to stumble the final step out of the cab and into the life of a seminarian. Later I learned that my dilemma was not unique and other first arrivals had made the opposite decision.

After putting my feet on the ground, one of the guys in a cassock immediately approached to get my name. Everything was well-organized, and my identity was quickly matched, from the sweat-soaked list the fellow kept tucked under his robe, to my assigned initiatory guide. There he was, shielded from the scorching sun by a corner of the mausoleum, waiting to perform his designated corporal work of mercy for the day which, in this case, was to "bear wrongs patiently." I was definitely in the wrong place and it was his job to bear with it.

My guide, black suit and tie notwithstanding, appeared quite normal on first glance. He was a sophomore like myself and had not yet been promoted to wearing the cassock. He introduced himself politely, and enthusiastically proceeded to help me get my luggage parked before showing me the lay of the land. He seemed almost euphoric but, in spite of his attempts, the euphoria wasn't rubbing off. During the tour, I inquired several times "how long does it take to get used to this place?" My guide just ignored the question and stuck with the script. I felt no semblance of bonding with this guy, and assumed I was breaching some piece of seminary etiquette by my direct approach but, frankly, I didn't care. It appeared that the question was not one he had heard, and he certainly did not want to answer it without a dispensation from the Pope. To the relief of both of us, the tour did finally end, just as the bell was ringing its command for the afternoon recital of the rosary and pre-dinner prayers.

I never really had another conversation with my tour guide; I think we just successfully avoided one another. We had only one class together and his daily activities were otherwise never parallel with mine. I know some people just don't hit it off but, from the moment I met this well-controlled robot, I felt he had a personality quirk that held those he encountered well outside the realm of his emotions. Later I learned he was a "lifer" which, as I met more lifers, explained a lot. Lifers were the boys who entered seminaries, with their volumes of rules and restrictions, as freshmen in high school. They were essentially ripped from their mother's laps and placed in the sole care of Catholic priests, and typically returned home only on special holidays and summer vacations. This type of upbringing, in my feeble mind, could have some negative impacts on one's personality. In my guide's case, behind the euphoria, I felt there was nothing but a barren, no-man's land. Just obey the rules, stick with the program, don't rock the boat, and life will be as it should. I was never able to fully buy into this philosophy. I guess that was at least one reason why I eventually left the seminary.

As already noted, my first formal activity on arrival was reciting the rosary. This was a mandatory event that was held every day between 4:45 and 5:00 PM. On days when the weather was anywhere within reason, it was held outside. Our entire battalion of 500-plus seminarians would parade in black suits or cassocks, side-by-side in packs of between four and five, from the entrance of our asylum, down the tree-lined lane to the property line and back, a distance of nearly a mile. As we strolled, the sing-song rhythm of the standardized prayers of the rosary murmured gently in the trees. One person in the pack would lead each decade of one "Our Father" and ten "Hail Marys," reciting the first half of each prayer. The remainder of the group would then mumble the last half in unison. Reciting the rosary must be the most "Catholic" activity ever created.

For me, recitation of the rosary was like going home. Every night at exactly 9 PM in our house, my dad would shout "rosary" loud enough to be heard in distant playgrounds of the world. He was like the crier on the minaret tower that calls Muslims to prayer. People in the neighborhood set their clocks by him. As the rosary was recited, it was passed from person to person to lead each of the five decades. The beads of our family rosary were olive seeds, and it took 59 beads, with medal links and a crucifix, to complete this potentially lethal weapon. When the rosary was passed to another person in our house, they were often completely across the room. If this was the case, the rosary was not passed, but instead was thrown, sometimes with purposeful force. If you were not aware of its flight and caught it on the side of your head, it took several seconds to get your bearings. This was several seconds too long by my dad's standards. One of his life rules was to keep the rosary on schedule. The possibility of being hit by this holy missile and the reproach of our dad did help keep me from falling asleep, at least sometimes. Some people love the mystical calming effect that can be produced while reciting the rosary, but this was a sensation I never experienced, even in my holiest days. While in the seminary, however, the relief of being released from the tomb in which we spent almost all of our time, even to say the rosary, made it worth the drudgery.

Immediately following the rosary, the entire community filed into the chapel which, based on the lack of natural light, appeared to be located within the depths of the earth. In reality, it was on the first floor, strategically encased within the surrounding portions of this massive structure to cut down on worldly distractions. Much of every day was spent in that chapel, a place dedicated to meditation and prayer. The afternoon service usually lasted only about 30 minutes, occupied as one might guess, by meditation and prayer. However, Sundays were special. On Sundays we had evening Vespers, a full 90 minutes of active singing and chanting, with meditation and prayer thrown in to keep us in the habit.

After the evening service, we marched down the hall to the dinner facility which, fortunately, did have natural light. Complete silence was mandated. Seating in the dinner hall was at assigned eight-man tables, and my seven companions were rotated on a regular two-week schedule. Nothing was left to chance or my volition, including my meal companions. During the first 12 minutes of the evening meal, verses from the Bible or the latest word from the Catholic press or a new edit from Rome was read by a chosen senior seminarian. Then with a sudden bang that invariably shot my heart rate up several beats, the rector who headed the seminary would hit a bell, indicating we now had permission to speak. The issuing of this permit was followed by an explosion of sound as over 500 suppressed voices were released simultaneously.

The meals were generally quite good, and they soon became one of the three desirable events in my routine. When all else failed, food was still there to get me through.

The evening meal was followed by 90 minutes of mandatory study time. Again, silence was maintained, whether you were in a study hall or your own room. The older seminarians actually had rooms but our younger group shared open dormitory spaces and group bathrooms which, when combined, occupied large portions of several floors within our cavernous building. Those assigned to the open dormitories were also assigned desks in an assigned study room. After evening study, we again visited the chapel for another 20 minutes of meditation and prayer. We then silently filed to our respective dormitories where we had exactly 20 minutes before lights out. The only permitted exception to the rule of silence during these periods was the ear-piercing bell that dictated all changes in our activities throughout the day and night.

The morning bell exploded at 5:30, permitting us 20 minutes to get ourselves to chapel. There was frantic noise throughout the zones of silence as we scrambled over each other through group bathrooms and down the stairs half dressed, attempting to put the finishing touches on our uniforms of black suits and ties before having our early morning meeting with God in the chapel. The older seminarians got a break here; they only had to throw on their cassocks.

The mandate during the first 30 minutes of early morning chapel time was to silently read Bible verses and meditate. During this mediation period, I did master one useful skill. This was the ability to fall into a deep sleep without allowing my head to slump. It is really an art form, probably known only to seminarians. The only sounds emanating from the chapel during that 30 minute period was occasional snoring and the bangs from dropped Bibles as they hit the floor. The latter were almost invariably released from the hands of freshman who had not yet acquired the ability to sit straight in place, hold the Bible firmly, and sleep. Sophomores rarely dropped their Bibles and juniors and seniors never did.

The early morning meditation period was followed by 45 minutes of Mass. After this, we filed in silence down the hall to breakfast. With the exception of Sundays, this consisted of milk and cold cereal. Sundays, however, were special. On that day, the nuns who prepared our meals presented us with magnificent breakfast rolls, thus making Sunday a special day. It really didn't take much to bring me momentary joy. Half way through breakfast, after more Bible reading, the bell was bonged and the pent up suppression in our vocal chords, acquired during the previous 13 hours of absolute silence, was released once again.

The remainder of the day until rosary time had a bit more freedom in that we could generally talk quietly without being reprimanded. Of course, silence was maintained during the 20-minute chapel period of meditation and prayer before lunch, and our every activity during the day was still scheduled. Each weekday and until noon on Saturday, we diligently attended our college classes and study halls. All courses were taught by Maryknoll priests. God forbid that an outsider would be allowed in to corrupt the untrained minds of aspiring missionaries, especially if it had been a woman.

Maybe it would have been okay if it was the Pope, but he never volunteered.

The highlight of my day, and the second desirable event in my routine, was the 1 1/2 hour period after lunch set aside for exercise and work. We had no gymnasium, but the seminary grounds were replete with tennis/basketball courts and football/soccer fields. Because we were training for the harsh conditions of the missions, it was mandatory that exercise be performed outside, regardless of the weather. This was a major pain to some of the group who truly detested leaving their tomb when the weather was not perfect. On cloudy days, which during my time in Chicago were almost every day, members of the "indoor club" could be heard wagering about the likelihood that they would be released from this hardship duty. I had a difficult time understanding their aversion to the outside world, but eventually realized that I was a Montana boy who was now surrounded primarily by big city kids. Most were from the east coast which housed the major seminary in Upstate New York, the true home of Maryknoll. The geographical imbalance of my fellow seminarians was so profound that, when we held the annual East/West Maryknoll football game, kids from Pennsylvania played on the west squad.

Before going on work duty or out for exercise, we changed clothes in a large locker room and showered there after we finished. The locker room also had its rules, the most amazing of which was "always cover yourself with a towel when you pass between your locker and the shower." At first, I thought they were kidding. When I realized that they weren't, I knew this was one rule I was not going to follow. I had grown up in locker rooms, and donning towels was never mandatory. Sure, I was aware of the pubic hair development of the boys in several of the grades at Holy Rosary School and even knew whether or not they had been circumcised. However, now I was apparently in an environment where a significant number of my colleagues might be led into temptation with this type of knowledge. For some reason, it was one law that was not enforced, maybe because any discussion would lay open the possibility that a portion of our group might have impure thoughts in the absence of the towel.

Sexual urges were to be ignored and, therefore, did not exist in the seminary.

Each day spent in the seminary was a lot like the last. The only regular respites were on Saturday and Sunday afternoons between 1:15 and 4:45. The Sunday afternoons were so lax that we were even permitted to have guests, if there were any to be had. I was generally out of luck on that score. The only visitors I had all year were sent from Heaven on an otherwise bleak Sunday in March. They consisted of my brother-in-law Bruce's parents, who lived in Chicago, and a friend. At the time of their visit, I had not seen a female, with the exception of our resident nuns, in nearly a month. Perhaps Bruce's parents realized the gravity of the situation and that was the reason for the "friend," an attractive girl about my own age. At that moment in time, any female not garbed in nun's attire could, in my discerning eye, have passed for Marilyn Monroe.

For the first 15 minutes of their visit, I tried in every way I could to convince my guests that they had not wasted a fully respectable Sunday afternoon. At the end of this warm up period, the girl, who was not a Catholic, suddenly became aware that the place was not a normal college. I guess the black suits and cassocks finally tipped her off. Bruce's parents had apparently spared her the details, probably assuming she would rather have spent the afternoon pulling cactus needles from her rear end than accompany them on this goodwill mission if she were given a choice. When I revealed our identities, she thought it was hilarious and exclaimed, "Are you really planning to be a priest? You'll never make it." I didn't know whether to consider her statement to be an insult or a compliment. I chose the latter, thinking maybe I hadn't really become one of "them" yet. You would think I had been abducted by aliens. Sometimes I wished I had been.

There were two potentially pleasant off-campus opportunities during that year, one in the fall and one in late winter. On those two days, we were transported in buses and released into downtown Chicago. As always, we were decked out in our black uniforms, thus simulating bus loads of Mormon missionaries prepared to preach the message of salvation, as we fanned out from our drop-off point on a street corner in the city. The first release date was in mid-October, by which time I knew I needed some type of relief, but had no idea of how to go about finding it. I had never been in Chicago, except the train station, and had no notion of what to do when I got there. Since I was with a group of classmates, one of which knew something about the city, the trip was not a total bust. We at least found our way to a couple of museums before the 3:45 PM curfew time.

The next trip was in March. By then I was so enmeshed in holiness that I volunteered to spend the day with three fellow seminarians cleaning an inner city Catholic school. I must have been really stupid, or at least had no imagination. The nuns who ran the place assigned us minimal duties that could have been performed by a blind third grader. The day was a complete waste and blown opportunity, something I fully realized when it was about half over. Thus, the volunteering did nothing but heighten my level of misery.

During my time at Maryknoll, I became the most prolific letter-writer in history. I wrote to every relative I could remember, every classmate for whom I could get an address, every girlfriend I had ever dated even one time, and anyone else in Montana that I could remember. Perhaps I was a bit homesick. I figured that if I got a return letter from 20% of them, it would keep me afloat. Most of my addressees did send at least a note in return. Every afternoon, just after the compulsory outdoor period, I would rush from the shower to my mailbox, always dreading the prospect that I might not receive a letter that day. I almost always did, thus constituting the third desirable event in my routine while at Maryknoll.

Another pleasurable pastime during my days at Maryknoll was participating in the whispered stairway conversations concerning departures. There were daily discussions about who was thinking about leaving and, more importantly, whose bed had actually turned up empty that morning. Leaving seemed infectious. I became close friends with some classmates and probably would have remained so had I met them under different circumstances. The ones with which I developed the closest ties had the highest percentage of departures. Perhaps the most disgruntled attracted one another. Our sophomore class had 172 members when we started in the fall and less than 120 remained when we checked out for home in the spring. If that defection rate had continued, none would have been left to be ordained seven years later. To stem the tide, our Director of Discipline sequestered us into the chapel on a Sunday evening in mid-February, this time to distribute advice, not to lead us in prayer. The message from the Director went something like this.

"You would not be here today if you had not received a personal invitation from God. Therefore, consider that if you choose to leave, you will be directly disregarding that invitation. For the good of your immortal souls, heed my advice."

I don't know how the others reacted to this threat, but his message made me want to flee more than ever. Years later, when I checked the ordination role for my class, I found there were a total of 21, but less than half were my identifiable classmates. The warning issued that cold day in February may have temporarily plugged the dike, but the emphasis is on "temporarily." One I recognized in the class of '69 was my initial tour guide, the "lifer." Maybe lifers had an advantage. They didn't know any other way. However, most of my ordination class had joined Maryknoll after they had graduated from college and did know "other ways." This seems like the more logical route into the priesthood.

One of my more depressing days at Maryknoll was my birthday. We didn't have major birthday celebrations in my family; there were far too many of us. However, my mother had a tradition of baking an angel food cake for each child on their birthday, and the birthday child got the first piece. My mother, God love her, attempted to keep the tradition alive for me, and mailed an angel food cake for my 19th birthday. She apparently didn't realize that a hat box was not sufficiently reinforced to withstand the pounding delivered by the US Postal Service. The cake arrived one-half inch high with the consistency of rubber. It looked like I felt. Even so, I still tucked it under my arm and surreptitiously wandered off into a corner of the building where I consumed its entire smashed remains in one sitting, hating my surroundings more with every bite. The rule was that goodies delivered from home were to be shared with your table mates. It somehow didn't seem necessary that the rule be followed with this smashed cake. Besides, I hadn't told anyone it was my birthday anyway. I guess I didn't want to share the cake.

Although my teachers were Maryknoll priests, all untrained as educators, they still did respectable jobs. In fact, they were probably above the average of my college teachers. I think the one from whom I learned the most that year was also the most austere. This awkward stick of a man taught theology which, during the year I was there, concerned the intertwined relationship between the Holy Spirit and the Bible. The Old Testament name for Holy Spirit was "Ruauch," so this name was adopted for our teacher. During my third day of theology class, Ruauch noted that the story of Adam and Eve was written to provide the "symbolism" of a loving relationship between man and God. I was horrified, but knew enough not to raise my hand and question his use of symbolism. Instead, I grabbed the ear of the fellow next to me and mumbled something about the six days of creation and the roles of Adam and Eve in the initiation of the human race.

In high school religion class, when asked whether we were "allowed" to believe in evolution, the priest who taught the class made it explicitly clear that only portions of evolutionary theory were considered acceptable in the eyes of Rome. He had dogmatically stated that "you must not accept that the human soul evolved and you must accept that we had one set of first parents." Now, after I had that bit of knowledge fully ingrained in my cranium, I had arrived at this seminary and was being taught heresy. Next, Ruauch would be telling me that Noah's ark and Samson's slaying of 5,000 or so Philistines with the jawbone of an ass were also written for their symbolic qualities. He might even suggest that I should begin to question some religious truths without his help. Unfortunately, he never took it that far. Ruauch did, however, open a chink in the armor of my memorized beliefs, but it was years before that armor was fully penetrated.

When I was in the first grade, I thought I was a tough guy and would take on any comer in a wrestling match. This phase passed quickly, and by the third grade I was a pacifist. Maybe this decision had something to do with the pounding one of my classmates gave me when I challenged his pugilistic superiority. Anyway, my only anger-related tussle came in the seventh grade when another student and I threw two punches each without landing one. Thus, it came as a complete shock when, during a heated basketball scrimmage a few weeks after joining Maryknoll, a classmate popped me with his fist, solidly in the jaw. I developed the appropriate amount of responsive anger, but retaliation in that setting was not in my vocabulary. Within seconds of being whacked, I exclaimed that the game was over for me. My attacker followed my announcement with the accusation of "you are a coward if you quit." More discussion might have helped since nothing was settled. I merely walked away and we avoided each other in the future. The moral of this story is that the only place I could find a fight was on the blessed grounds of a seminary.

Returning to Bozeman for Christmas during that year was a real vacation. I just did "whatever" with my old buddies, many of whom had also been away at college. One night we went tobogganing and, as always happened when we tobogganed, someone got hurt. This time it was me and the injury was to my wrist. It hurt so bad that I even chose to not play in the Holy Rosary High School reunion basketball game the next day.

By the time I took the return train to Chicago after New Year's Day, the pain had yet to subside. I didn't notice, however, since the hurt in my heart was many times more severe. On re-arrival in Glen Ellyn, the place never looked bleaker, especially since it was now set in a totally sunless Chicago winter. It took more than a week for my level of depression to readjust to its normal plateau. In the meantime, the wrist continued to ache, but to stop sports in that setting would mean that I would die entirely. By mid-February, however, the chronic pain was sufficient for me to request a visit with a doctor.

The seminary had an arrangement with a group of physicians located in a nearby suburb, and I was given an appointment with one their members. This guy moved my wrist around a bit and inquired about my level of pain. He then proclaimed it was a sprain. "All the wrist will need is physical therapy and it will recover fine." I lived with this explanation for the remainder of the school year, never really feeling I could use my wrist completely, but also feeling I was a wimp if I complained further. When finally released to return home in late May, the nagging pain in my wrist was still just that.

After about a week back on the family farm, where the wrist was being regularly used to pound rocks with a large steel bar around fence posts, I finally realized that this injury was more than a sprain, and was not going away. The doctor in Chicago had never seen fit to x-ray the injury, but the doctor in Bozeman did. There displayed on the x-ray film was a total vertical break through one of my wrist bones. Since scar tissue had filled into the break during the six months since the injury occurred, surgery was required to both scrape out the scar tissue and insert pieces of bone extracted from my hip to graft the broken bone back together. When the cast I wore for the next five months was finally removed, I promptly broke the same bone while tobogganing on the same hill where I broke it the first time during Christmas break the year before. This story has a moral but I'm not sure what it is. Regardless, the pain associated with my broken arm during much of that year in the seminary also contributed to my generally depressed state.

During the course of my first year at Maryknoll, no seminarian was asked to leave due to disciplinary reasons or otherwise. How could anyone be booted out after that motivational mid-February message delivered by our Director of Discipline? On the week before my departure for the summer, this all changed. I was amazed to hear that at least five of my remaining classmates were asked not to return. They apparently lacked the "right stuff." One was what I assumed was a close friend who replayed his exit interview to me. The reasons given for his dismissal had something to do with his inability to understand the subtleties of life. I guess they could have just said he was a simpleton. His response to the priest that delivered this assessment was that he actually was quite aware of the workings of the world. In fact, at least three nights each week throughout the year, he had removed himself from the seminary grounds to reinforce his understanding through the night life of Glen Ellyn. I had no idea there was night life in Glen Ellyn, but this guy surely did. The reaction of the priest who delivered the edict was complete and total surprise. I had the same reaction myself as I realized that I wasn't such a close friend after all. Then I was just ticked off because he had not invited me to accompany him. Of course, that would have been wasted effort because I would never have had the courage to break the rules to that extent. However, I always wondered how he got out of, and then back into our mausoleum without being spotted.

The road home to Bozeman that summer was not the railroad; this time three fellow seminarians and I made arrangements to deliver a car in Seattle. It has always seemed that there must be more reliable methods to move cars, especially if the assigned drivers have just been released from a seminary, and have not even been in a car for several months. The automobile in question was a nearly new Oldsmobile convertible whose speedometer went up to 160 mph. So, on a bright morning in late May, the four of us flew off the grounds of Maryknoll, gravel scattering in all directions, the convertible top down on our fine automobile, and the long-awaited sun beating down on our heads.

Our first stop was a local drive-in where a busty, half-clothed carhop waited on us. None of us had seen breasts for some time, and certainly had not seen them coming at us like this. To suppress our urge to grab something, we all began to laugh hysterically, thus providing another clear demonstration of why boys should not be kept in isolation for extended times. The carhop had apparently experienced this reaction before. She just sneered a bit, but otherwise ignored us.

Once we were free of the Chicago environs, we felt it our duty to test the full range of the car's speedometer. We drove at speeds that were unsafe in the daytime, but as we sped across the plains of the Dakotas at night, sometimes through blinding rainstorms, traveling at speeds of over 100 mph was truly insane. I think we relied on our recent close association with God to keep us on the road.

My stop in Bozeman was first, and we covered the 1,400 miles there in less than 18 hours, arriving just as the sun was peering over the mountains in our rear-view mirror. Having survived to that point, the others in the group decided to spend a day in my hometown before speeding on to their separate destinations. Thus, I had the opportunity to display some local highlights which included a new library that had been built at MSC since my departure. There, with the gushing and bubbling of the in-library fountain providing background music, they all had the honor of being introduced to my old high school girlfriend. I was really pathetic. My first reaction when I saw her was to run. However, she also saw me and responded like a normal person, coming over for a reunion and introductions. I stammered several times when trying to explain who she was, turning every shade within the color red. The discomfort in my reaction was blatantly obvious to my fellow seminarians. One of them concluded that, based on his learned observation, he had a sure bet if he wagered that I would not return to the seminary in the fall. I couldn't turn down the challenge, but it was a big bet; $50 to be exact.

That summer I decided several times not to return to Glen Ellyn. How much misery was enough? However, my competitive juices were running and the $50 bet was a contest I did not intend to lose. Finally, on a sad day in late August, I purchased train tickets for another ride east. On my return trip to Glen Ellyn, the same old misery set in, but I was determined to collect my $50. As luck would have it, the classmate that made the bet didn't return himself, so the debt was never paid. Instead, I just got plugged into the program once again, this time with three courses in philosophy, one course in theology, and a history class on my horizon. Would the thrills never end?

During my first year at Maryknoll, I had expounded upon the state of my unhappiness to almost every priest in the institution. All they had to do was sit with me for a few minutes and out it came. I even arranged a session with the resident psychologist who was also a Maryknoller. That was an experience. After he met me at his door, I quickly found myself on a sofa in his office where he asked me, in as formal a tone as he could muster, to relate my problems to him. During my recitation of woes, he nodded occasionally, but never uttered more than "and what do you think that means?" After this robotic one hour session, I just wandered back into my study room. I don't know what the psychologist thought, but my reaction was that I had just wasted another hour. He may have been more tuned into what I said if I had told him I was planning to assassinate the rector.

This strange experience, however, did not dissuade me from my quest to relate my miseries to nearly every member of the faculty, none of whom gave me the slightest inkling that my reaction was abnormal for one chosen to serve as a priest of God. On my return the second year, this pathetic behavior started all over again. After several tries in the first three weeks, I at last got the longed-for response from the Director of Athletics. He listened attentively to my tale of woe and logically concluded, "You have been here long enough to get past these feelings. I think you have given it a full shot. I'll take you to the train." I was packed in an hour and we were gone.

I got no comments when I returned home except from my mother who quietly said "I'm really glad you're home." The only inquiry from my dad was, "why did you waste the money going back and forth this year?" I told him it was because of the $50 bet I never collected. After all, he was the one that taught me to be competitive.

After leaving the seminary, I searched for something positive that the experience added to my life on which I could build. One positive was the attitude change I had on returning to Montana State College, something akin to pure euphoria that carried me through the next few months. Another was the development of the life motto, "Don't look for misery. Let it find you if it must." The most significant positive to come out of this experience, however, was the fact that I left the seminary and was able to get started on a meaningful career track. As it turned out, it would be a difficult track to keep under my feet.

7 School is Lovelier the Second Time Around

After taking permanent leave from the seminary, I returned to Montana State College a new person. I couldn't believe I had ever considered MSC to be anything but heavenly. It's amazing how wonderful normal becomes when you have been living in an apartment next to Hell. The old cliche about how good it feels when you stop banging your head on the wall is really true. I was fired up to do everything and be everything, at least until the seminary drugs wore off.

My first order of business was to change my major field of study. I had received a scholarship in chemical engineering as a freshman, so of course, I enrolled with this as my major. You couldn't turn down money. I actually had thought I wanted to be an engineer because I liked math, but the "chemical" part had never made my radar screen. When I entered college and encountered calculus for the first time, my opinion of a career with serious math involvement took a turn to the south. In contrast, the chemical part of chemical engineering had gained in appeal, driven at least in part by the urgings of my freshman chemistry professor.

When I was in high school, nothing by way of a career struck me as something I couldn't do without. Like almost every kid who had a desire to commune with nature, the standardized exam I took as a senior to determine my interests pegged me for a career as a forest ranger. Second on the interest list, however, was science. It may have been the resurgent national interest to get kids into any field of science after the USSR launched Sputnik that pushed my answers to test questions in that direction. But that wasn't the whole story. When plowing through our chemistry textbook during my junior year in high school, we eventually arrived at Chapter Eight. At this point there was a sudden change in direction from boring chapters about the general nature of matter to this chapter which concerned the basic nature of matter, i.e., the structure of the atom. Reading this was like a lightning bolt hitting my imagination button. The excitement elicited by this discovery had a short half life, but the flame of interest didn't completely burn out, even if it was too dim to be discernible when it came time for me to enroll in college. What my college chemistry teacher had done was to rekindle that flame. Thus, on my return to MSC, I switched my major to chemistry and entered the honors program under his tutelage.

My second order of business on re-arrival at MSC was to get my social life in order. I had no intention of making the same mistake I had as an entering freshman. I was going to fit into the social network or die trying. Since I was still living at home, this meant I had to join some social group on campus. Within days, I was again being invited to multiple fraternity houses. This time I was going to join one of them, family tradition and cost be damned. After a couple of weeks, I found the group of guys I related to the best, and joined their little group. Now I had a campus site from which to operate, other than a chemistry lab.

It should be noted that I did not mention a need to restart my athletic career. Football was done, but track would still have been a possibility. I had done well as a freshman, but was not offered a renewal of my scholarship when I returned. I could have joined the track team without a scholarship just to have the chance to again be a sports star. The "star" bit had lost most of its luster during my year in the seminary. More importantly, I knew it was time to study, and I didn't need more distractions than I had already arranged.

"Behind a successful man is a good woman" is not true for everyone, but if my experience in the seminary didn't do anything else for me, it alerted me to the fact that this little slogan would probably be applicable to me. In 1962, before the day of "partnerships without the benefit of marriage" was accepted into the general American vocabulary, having a good woman meant having a good wife. In those pre-modern days, it was even acceptable in most social circles for a 20-year old boy to suggest that he was actually interested in getting married. Thus, chasing girls when I took my leave from the seminary was for me more than just a social event; I really was on the lookout for a life partner.

During this early post-seminary period, I had several blind dates. These were always set up by friends who, by the end of the evening, I wondered if they really were. However, I did not let the bad times derail me. As a freshman at MSC, I had been on the debate team, a remnant of my training by Coach Doohan. Since the experience seemed worthwhile, I signed up again on my return. One of the members of the team was the Head Resident in a freshman girl's dorm. When I became aware of her job, it was obvious that she was a person of stature, one who could set me up with someone real special. After much arm-twisting, she grudgingly agreed and eventually managed to coerce one of her charges, a girl I already knew, into having one date with me. How hard could that have been? It was arranged for a Saturday night a couple of weeks in advance. On the Tuesday of the week we were to have our scheduled date, the chosen one phoned me to explain she couldn't make it on Saturday but had found a substitute. Being the resourceful fellow I was, I dialed the sub and suggested we meet for a short time on Thursday. That way she could decide whether a whole evening on Saturday would be worth her time, and I could make the same decision.

So on that Thursday evening, Shirley and I, along with my high school buddy Ike and his date, met for a little two-on-two basketball in the old Holy Rosary gym. Basketball went well. Shirley was a hell of a shot and we routed our opponents. That evening, I also learned that her life was like an open book, and several chapters got read while my car was idling in the -30 degree Montana weather in front of her dorm following our game. During that brief period, a fire was ignited, at least in this boy's heart. We agreed to meet again on Friday for several rounds of bowling, so when Saturday finally arrived, it wasn't a "blind" date after all.

The coming weeks and months became preoccupied with thoughts of Shirley. That winter quarter I received the worst grades I ever got in college. They weren't bad. They were just the worst. I accounted it to the difficulty of my courses, but my dad came to a different conclusion. After years of careful study, he had concluded that girls went to college only to get a husband. His studies were largely based on his own daughters. This fact, coupled with the knowledge that the new girl was not a Catholic, spelled bad news. He had never before shown interest in my grades, but suddenly his interest knew no bounds. It was expressed as, "you need to see a lot less of this girl if you are going to keep up your grades. Otherwise your future options are going to be real limited." This was coming from the man who had wanted me to be a farmer because in that profession I would have to "do real work for a living." At least his motive was obvious. My grades were up again the next quarter, so he had to come up with something else.

I have always been lousy at keeping things to myself, so I somehow felt compelled to repeat these and other mutterings of my dad to Shirley. Her grandparents and their friends were about my dad's age, so relating to this generation had, up to this time, been both natural and pleasurable for her. That would change. During the next months before summer break, Shirley and I saw each other multiple times each week, but I never suggested that she darken the doorstep of my home. In contrast, I met her parents within weeks of our first date and they lived 250 miles away. Shirley had nothing to hide; I guess I felt I did.

In the following summer, Shirley made one trip to Bozeman to attend a conference, and came early for a visit. I was working on my brother's farm, so I had what I considered a safe place for her to stay for a couple of days. What I didn't realize was that Shirley had a highly nervous stomach, and she had no more than alighted at our farm before she started vomiting -- steadily. It was so constant that I took her to my physician where the obvious query was asked as to the potential cause. The answer: she was scared to death of my dad. Amazingly, she only saw him briefly during her entire stay, and he was quite cordial. I guess I had successfully transferred my fears to her, not even realizing I had them to transfer. Perhaps I should have introduced her to him earlier; then again, perhaps not.

Religious discussions were top on the agenda from the opening bell in our relationship. Shirley quickly realized that what she had encountered here was a child born in the right wing of the Catholic Church. He had every answer to every religious question, and could even tell her on what page in the "Book of Answers" to find it. Is Christ really bodily present in the Eucharist or is it just symbolic? The answer: "You don't have to believe it but of course He is present. You know, 'This is my body, this is my blood.' What is your next question?" Why do Catholics believe in Purgatory? The answer: "You don't have to believe it but it is simple. If you die without having some minor sins officially forgiven through the Sacrament of Penance, you will need to work them off before you are allowed into Heaven. You do that in Purgatory. If the sins are big ones and the same situation applies, the next stop is Hell. What is your next question?" You notice the disclaimer about "not having to believe it" was always there; that was my only redemption. Even that bit of redemption was lost when, within weeks into our courtship, I stated, "I will only marry a Catholic. You are not a Catholic. Therefore, if we are to get married, guess what you need to do?" The apple hadn't as yet fallen far from the tree. Of course, the apple was still living at home getting daily tutelage from the tree. In retrospect, it was astonishing that Shirley did not call an immediate halt to our budding relationship. She must have felt there was a possibility that she could find a way to live with my decree.

As our courtship moved from months into years, my decree gradually melted away to the point that I no longer cared whether she became a Catholic or not. But that was not the case with a portion of my family, especially my parents. When my brother Bob was married in 1950, both of my parents would have had strokes if his wife had not converted to Catholicism before their wedding. This need was less poignant when it was my turn 16 years later, but it was still there. Thus, just two months before our planned marriage date, Shirley received an unexpected visit from my brother John, the priest, inquiring as to why she had deceived me into thinking that she would become a Catholic before we were married. Because she did not instantly acquiesce to his persuasive request that she reconsider and become a Catholic, he coerced my mother to join the battle.

When she could not reach Shirley by phone after several attempts, apparently to inquire about her religious status, I received a desperate call from her 1,000 miles away at school in California. This was the first time I was aware that my family had actually resorted to taking action. Fortunately, I was able to stem the tide during that brief talk with my mother.

In spite of the animosity engendered by this whole affair, Shirley and I were still married in June as planned with my whole family in attendance. Even though he did not approve, my brother John performed the ceremony. So, in the end, I had my life partner, someone who had earned her degree in determination and resilience well before we tied the knot, attributes that would help sustain both of us, and our marriage, in the future.

ॐ   ॐ   ॐ

Someone once pointed out to me that the most important decisions in life are those for which you have the wherewithal to acquire the least amount of information. This someone also supplied examples as backup.

"How can you know you will be able to spend the rest of your life with a person, no matter how well you think you know that person or yourself, when you recite your wedding vows?" Based on present divorce rates, you obviously can't.

Another example cited by my wise philosopher concerned career choice. "How does one make a career choice rationally? Mostly you just run out of time at some point, and have to make a decision based mostly on what you don't want to do."

After three years in chemistry, I concluded that I did not want to spend my life as a chemist. I had been in the chemistry honors program for all three of those years and had conducted experiments with three mentors on three totally different projects. The first was in organic chemistry where my knowledge was so limited that my only success was to destroy the glassware. When this happened, my mentor, who had also been my freshman chemistry teacher, decided I needed lessons in both manual dexterity and frugality. After demonstrating for me the intricacies of holding a test tube without dropping it, he informed me that I was going to pay for the glassware I had smashed. That took care of my stipend for the year. I felt like I was back with Sister Iona in the second grade after I ate my reading book and had to pay for it by pounding erasers after school.

My second honors project, one that loosely qualified as analytical chemistry, would have merited the Golden Fleece Award if it had been funded by a federal grant. I have filed the results obtained in that project into my memory bank as the ultimate example of useless information. My mentor, however, felt I had accomplished so much that he had me present my discoveries at a conference in Spokane, Washington, 400 miles from Bozeman. Even though I appreciated the opportunity, I felt sorry for the six people in my audience who had to suffer through a lecture on the "Identification of the hydrocarbons in the cuticular wax of a cricket." They had to have wandered into the room by mistake.

Things picked up during my third year. MSC had just hired a legitimate biochemist, and when he described his research interests, another light switch was turned on in my head. This was the time when astonishing discoveries on deciphering the genetic code were being published weekly, and our new biochemist had just finished his post-doctoral research in a lab where some of these discoveries were being made. He offered to mentor me during that year, but since he was just setting up his own lab on top of a full teaching load, my main accomplishment with him was to make a career decision, i.e., to go to graduate school in biochemistry.

Montana State College wasn't known as the "Harvard of the West." However, it still had sufficient reputation that a chemistry graduate with decent grades who scored near the top in the Graduate Record Exam could be accepted into most graduate programs in the country. At least it worked for me. I applied for admittance in what my mentor described as the "four best biochemistry departments in the country," and was accepted by three. Since I had already spent an extra year getting my undergraduate degree due to the seminary diversion, and was graduating with more credit hours than I could count, I picked the only graduate school of the three that would not require me to obtain a Master's degree before being enrolled in their PhD program. Getting an MS degree would have elongated my stay in graduate school by two years, something that would have been useful, but in my astute view at the time, not necessary. Besides, the weather is better in Berkeley, California, than almost anywhere in the country. So I scheduled another trip to the Bay Area, this time for a longer stay.

One of the prerequisites for me to enroll in a PhD program at the University of California was that I have a certified undergraduate degree. When I applied, I was under the illusion that I was about to get one. However, there was one hitch. When I had returned from the seminary and switched my major from chemical engineering to chemistry, I assumed all I had to do to graduate in chemistry was to have the proper credits in my new major. As it turned out, I had never officially switched majors; I just thought I had. Switching majors was a process that could only take place during registration periods at the beginning of each quarter, an event associated with specific formal requests and multiple signatures. I never did that. I was never told I had to. This oversight was not pointed out until half way through what I perceived as my last quarter at MSC when I received a letter from the MSC registrar saying I did not have the proper credits to graduate in June. I knew there had to be some mistake. In fact, there was. I was still registered in chemical engineering, and the registrar was right, I had not taken half of the courses required to graduate with that as my major.

For the registrar there was a simple solution. I merely had to pay my fees and register for the summer quarter, changing my major in the process. Then I could officially graduate at the end of the winter quarter. This plan was easy for her to say, but it would mean a lost year for me. If I didn't graduate in June, I would not be allowed into graduate school at Berkeley in September and would have to reapply to be admitted the next year. Besides, I was starting a summer job at the Lawrence Radiation Laboratory in Livermore, California, one week before the time of summer registration. I would be 1,000 miles away on registration day. It seemed logical that these extenuating circumstances, combined with my sterling record and such, would make it obvious that an exception needed to be made here.

This was my first official encounter with a registrar and I prayed it would be my last. A registrar invariably has right on their side, and if you don't believe it, you can read it in the "Book of Rules and Regulations." After a half hour of pleading, presenting every good argument I could drum up along with several bad ones as well, the answers from the registrar were a dumb look combined with "who do you think you are anyway?"

That battle was lost, but the outcome of the war was still in doubt. Within minutes of leaving the registrar's office, I was writing my sob story to the President of the College and the Chair of the Department of Chemistry. Neither formally acknowledged receiving my letter, but within two days my sentence had been revoked. There was a God after all, and He had seen fit that I should graduate in chemistry in June. I would be on my way to Berkeley after all.

8 I Went to School in Berkeley

It has always astounded me that all I have been required to tell most new acquaintances to convince them I have right wing tendencies is to say I grew up in Montana. However, if I want them to think I am a left wing radical, I merely mention that I went to school in Berkeley in the late 60's. The reaction following the latter explanation is typically an audible intake of air, a visible gulp, and the standard "isn't that interesting." This reaction has faded somewhat with time, especially in the younger set since many have never heard of Berkeley and certainly don't know anything about the late 60's. What I don't bother to mention, since those horrified by my revelation have generally fled by this point in the conversation, is that the Biochemistry Department in Berkeley was not only ranked first in the country when I arrived, but also had the reputation for being one of the most conservative. These facts don't fit the image, so they would detract from the desired effect anyway.

Before one arrives at a new school with suitcases in tow, one needs to have found a place to put them. Since I worked as a chemist in the Lawrence Radiation Laboratory in Livermore during the summer after graduating from MSC, it required only a short drive and a Saturday afternoon to find a place to live in Berkeley. My selection was an airy new apartment building about a mile from campus. The building was built for students because every set of apartments was composed of four miniature bedrooms and a shared miniature kitchen, eating area, and bathroom. Even though I was in Berkeley, the building manager still chose roommates to occupy the four bedrooms that were the same sex. Mine were an Indian majoring in anthropology, an American majoring in math, and a Japanese majoring in electrical engineering, all of whom were graduate students.

The one in the group that I gravitated to as a friend was Toshi, the fellow from Japan. About halfway through the school year, he suggested that rather than both of us wasting our time cooking each night, we alternate and cook for two. That was the best deal I ever made, but it was a lousy bargain for Toshi. I got acquainted with rather elaborate Japanese cuisine and Toshi experienced the joys of hot dogs and hamburgers, not a fair trade by anyone's standards.

My knowledge of Japanese people up to that time was that they carried out a sneak attack at Pearl Harbor, the price for which was two atom bombs delivered several years later. Not a lot of Japanese history was taught at Holy Rosary High School, and my curriculum at MSC was deficient in it as well. Thus, Toshi's opinions on life were like a course in international relations. I assumed, based on my extensive knowledge on the topic, that our involvement in Vietnam was fully justified. After all, we had to stop the commies somewhere, and Vietnam seemed to be as good a place as any. I was still thinking like I was in Montana. Toshi's first statement on the topic was, "No war is justified. It is just wrong to kill people."

How unrealistic was that? I came to realize that his was the prevailing attitude in Japan at the time, at least among the younger generation. Certainly the abrupt ending of the Second World War contributed to this philosophy. I was not a proponent of war, but always assumed it was a necessary evil. Toshi thought otherwise, and spent hours explaining why. I provided my traditional rebuttals but, in the end, had to admit he may have the better argument.

Toshi had not learned to drive a car, but his goal was to experience everything American, and this was to be part of it. His first step in that direction was to purchase a used Corvair, a car considered by some to be a death trap. After buying the car, Toshi needed to learn to drive it, so he recruited me as his instructor. My father had taught me to drive, so I applied the same learning techniques, i.e., yell loudly and often before your student has a chance to make a bad move. In spite of being regularly abused,

Toshi learned to drive, so well in fact that he drove his Corvair to Montana for my wedding in June, and lived to tell about it.

Toshi dodged that bullet, but he wasn't able to dodge them all. During the last several months we shared the apartment, he began complaining about an impending visit by his mother. This initially struck me as odd since I assumed he would love his mother as he seemed to love almost everyone. As the story unfolded, he revealed an even odder chain of events that explained his attitude. The "mother" in question was not his biological mother but a woman who, with her husband, had adopted Toshi. Apparently, Toshi's parents were not financially well off, and when Toshi attended college, he had rented a small room in his "to be" parent's house. This couple was childless, and wanted to have a son to care for them in their old age. Toshi was planning to come to America for graduate school, and felt this would cost more than his own parents could reasonably afford. Thus, when the adoption offer was made, Toshi accepted on the condition that his new parents would pay his way to America. The ink on the agreement hadn't yet dried when his new father passed away. When it came time to leave Japan, Toshi's new mother refused to pay the airfare, saying instead that Toshi was now her son and he should respect her wishes, which were that he remain in Japan and care for her. The only recourse for Toshi was to fall back on the generosity of his real parents. They scolded him for his earlier rash decision, but agreed to somehow get him to America. As Toshi left Japan, the pleas and threats of his adopted mother were ringing in his ears.

The ringing became augmented after his arrival in Berkeley. When Toshi showed no signs of acquiescing, his "mother's" next move was to come to Berkeley herself and retrieve him. She didn't word it that way; her plan was not fully revealed until after her arrival in July. However, based on Toshi's mood during our last months of rooming together, he was well aware of what she intended.

Soon after his unwanted visitor arrived, Toshi and his mother rented an apartment, and there they commenced their battle of wills. Who would win? Toshi was clearly not going back to Japan and his mother was not returning without him. It all got settled on an early morning in September, less than three months after Toshi's mother first set foot on American soil.

The story later related by the couple living in the apartment below Toshi and his mother was that they were startled awake at about 5 AM by a major commotion above them. There were repeated shouts from both male and female voices, all uttered in Japanese, accompanied by what sounded like a physical struggle. Not knowing what else to do, they went upstairs, knocked on the door, and inquired whether everything was all right. The response was a feeble "go away" uttered by what they described as a very dejected male voice. They returned to their apartment, and assured by the silence above them that the worst had passed, they returned to bed. Within an hour, they were again awakened, this time by a police siren and, subsequently, by a determined banging on the door above. The police had been called by a frantic woman speaking in Japanese, saying "we have committed suicide."

After the police smashed the door, they rushed into a blood-blotched apartment containing a dead Toshi in a bed and an elderly Japanese woman on the floor beside him with a small, self-inflicted knife wound. She had concluded Toshi would never return with her to Japan, and based on her view of ancient Japanese tradition, felt he had scorned her sufficiently to warrant death. To answer his insolent behavior, she planned to stab him to death with her ritualistic knife while he slept. She was quite serious about it; Toshi's dead body contained more than 40 stab wounds, mostly in the abdomen with only a few on the hands and arms. He apparently had fought back, but too late to save himself. After accomplishing her work, his mother put a small puncture into her own abdomen so that she could claim it was a planned collaborative suicide. Only then did she call the police.

After the incident, the Berkeley police decided that it was a domestic dispute and no blame could be placed. The woman had a few newly-acquired, traditional Japanese friends that supported her story. They reported that Toshi was an unappreciative child who would not honor his mother's justifiable request to return to Japan. This was all that the police investigator needed. He didn't understand the situation, and besides, the woman was both foreign and old. The solution was to merely deport her to Japan, knowing that she would not repeat this performance, at least not in America.

The fabricated story reported in the San Francisco Chronicle portrayed Toshi as an evil child, deserving of what he got. When I subsequently called the newspaper to report the facts as I saw them, the reporter responsible had no interest in printing a sequel. Thus was ended a wonderful and promising life. I never really understood what happened and never will. My only contribution to Toshi's memory was to acquire the address of his biological parents during his memorial service, and write to them of our friendship. It wasn't much, but it was something. They responded with a thank you letter that I had translated, accompanied by a small gift that I have kept as my memory of Toshi. He taught me a great deal in the short time I knew him; the rest of what I could have learned from him was not to be.

∾   ∾   ∾

I arrived at Berkeley in the heyday of the American science renewal following the Sputnik surprise. The challenge issued by the Soviets concerning space exploration was answered by a new infusion of grant monies for all the sciences, including biochemistry. Because of the optimistic prospects for the future of science that this infusion of monies provided, there was a major influx of America's brightest students into the sciences. Since the Biochemistry Department in Berkeley was ranked first in the country when I arrived, my classmates had been selected with the expectation that this ranking would be maintained. In addition, they all had undergraduate training in prestigious universities, and all had been biochemistry majors. The "all" parts here are probably not totally accurate, but that was my perception when I entered the ring with them. There really wasn't serious competition; you just had to do well and keep plugging regardless of what those around you were doing. It was intimidating, however, to realize they were light years ahead of me in their knowledge of biochemistry.

My deficiency of knowledge became most evident when we shared our first biochemistry laboratory course. This was high intensity training that incorporated only me, my 23 classmates, and our instructor. Within days it became obvious that my library of biochemical information ranked lowest of the group. The lectures that accompanied the course were delivered on the assumption that our knowledge of biological equilibrium and catalytic mechanisms of enzymes were all second nature. I had never heard of either nor was I aware of much else that was being discussed, an understanding of which was needed before stepping into the laboratory. Panic set in quickly, and I once again began looking for the door. The spirit of competition instilled by my dad just kept sliding away each time I needed it most. When I explained my situation to the professor teaching the course, he assured me that I would catch on – to just hang in there. It eventually worked out and I survived. It's a good thing I at least had sense enough this time to alert my teacher rather than to just cut and run as I had five years earlier.

During my last year at Montana State College, I had the privilege of panicking during a test. It is something you have to experience in order to appreciate the sensation. For me, it was a test in Advanced Organic Chemistry which, as it was taught, required heavy-duty memorization of synthetic pathways. I normally was one who studied for tests so far in advance that by the time the test was given, I was already studying for the next. I was the type that most people love to hate. This behavior also has disadvantages, mostly centered on the fear that if I wasn't totally prepared long in advance, my mind would explode as I crammed for an exam in the last few minutes. So, of course, that is exactly what happened.

I was still trying to jam synthetic pathways into my brain minutes before I was handed the exam. When a short time into the test I realized that I was having difficulty regurgitating one of the pathways, a cold chill shot down my spine followed in rapid succession by a drenching sweat. My mind went totally blank; I'm not sure I could have held a thought long enough to even remember my name. My first reaction was to dash for the door, but I knew that would have earned me a failure in the class. In lieu of that, I merely squirmed from side-to-side in my seat, praying that I could get a grip. Within several minutes, the fog began to clear a bit. Since it was a two-hour exam, I could afford to lose a little time. Some of what I had memorized eventually began to come into focus, and I was able to complete a portion of the exam. However, I received a 62% which was the lowest grade on a test I ever received in college.

This panic experience followed me to Berkeley. Most of my initial courses there entailed the acquisition of mountains of information that had to be regurgitated in detail during 50-minute exam periods. The worst exams were probably those given in basic biochemistry. Throughout the time between hesitantly walking into the room for those exams and staggering out, my internal panic button was screaming. Even though I never freaked out completely, the marks I got were consistently below 70%. I initially discussed this with my classmates, somehow assuming my experiences were not unique, but their responses were invariably, "I aced it." They were at least sensitive enough to not add, "What was your problem?" I ceased those discussions before I was totally disheartened.

When the final grades for the biochemistry course came out in late January, I was fully convinced they would spell the beginning of the end of my stay in Berkeley. Perhaps it was because grades were strictly determined by the class curve, or maybe that graduate students were given special favors, but I received an A- in biochemistry. Up to that moment, I had lived and died by my grades. This course in biochemistry may have reduced my life expectancy by ten years, but at least it rid me of that overpowering concern. I never obsessed about grades again.

One bit of extra knowledge gained during my first months at Berkeley was that biochemistry per se was no more exciting to me as a career choice than chemistry had become before I left MSC. However, I also took a course in molecular biology during my first semester which, at the time, was a study of the life cycles of viruses that reproduce in bacteria. These are called bacteriophages. Bacteriophages were chosen as models for understanding sub-cellular events because viruses are relatively non-complex and very little was known about animal or human viruses whose molecular behaviors might more closely resemble events in a normal human cell. As with other model systems, it was hoped that some of what was learned with the bacteriophages would later be applicable to higher order systems that were more difficult to study. This molecular biology course provided me with a glimmer of hope that science could still be interesting.

As the year wore on and my knowledge of biochemistry increased in spite of myself, it came time to select, or be selected by, our PhD advisors. When this selection process was completed, my advisor's work would become my life until my degree was in hand, so this was an important decision. Long before selection day rolled around, I felt certain that I had only one choice of advisor. This was because only one of the myriad of professors in the Biochemistry Department conducted studies that were remotely molecular biological, a field of study where, after my course on bacteriophages, I was convinced I belonged. As my classmates and I jockeyed for position in our choice of advisors, three others listed the same first choice as me. Since he would be allowed to take on only two new students at the most, I began greasing the skids to switch from the Biochemistry to Molecular Biology Department. My inquiries stimulated no positive responses, but when selection time came, I got the choice I requested, a result that set the tone for the rest of my career.

By the time I joined the lab of my advisor, he had been an assistant professor at Berkeley for two years during which time he had not only gained a reputation as an excellent teacher, but already had developed three disparate research projects, only one of which involved molecular biology. The purpose of that project was to decipher how the smallest bacteria viruses, called RNA bacteriophages, produce many thousands of new viruses after they infect their natural host, an *E. coli* bacterium. I attached myself to this project and thus began my life with viruses.

Most of the faculty members in our Biochemistry Department were veterans in training graduate students. They generally knew when to lay heat on their charges and when to ease off. Being young and inexperienced, my advisor hadn't yet mastered this art form. He himself worked around the clock and expected his graduate students to do the same. He was forever fired up about his most recent results and would hang over my shoulder to see what I had discovered. Ideas and suggestions flew out of his head like bullets from a machine gun. He would have been a great colleague for an established investigator, but was a source of serious confusion for a neophyte like myself. After each of our discussions, I would leave in a manic state, prepared to perform several years of experiments within the next 24 hours. However, I had no concrete knowledge of which experiments were of possible value, in what order they should be performed, or what I had really learned when they had been completed. It was an intellectual and emotional roller coaster ride with endless horizons but few check points.

Within days of my arrival in the lab, it was determined that I should establish a test tube system to monitor protein synthesis by bacteria viruses. My advisor had no personal knowledge of the system, but like almost everything in his life, he knew where to find it. I was mentored by an expert in the Department of Molecular Biology, and in several days, had the system running in our lab. With this system and a few weeks time, I made the most important discovery of my graduate years, i.e., one of the viral proteins needed in abundance to produce new viruses was able to block the production of another viral protein, needed in lesser amounts, by binding directly to the gene responsible for the latter protein. It was a nifty regulatory mechanism that saved the virus a lot of effort. At the time, this was cutting edge science.

So what happened with this earthshaking finding? By the time the discovery was made, my summer, free of all obligations except lab work, was replaced by a fall semester stacked with course work and teaching obligations. Of course, if I had the will and stamina to work nights in the lab with my advisor, the project could have been completed within weeks. One observation I made then and confirmed thereafter is that the most successful scientists often have no life. This seems to be a trait that helps separate them from less successful varieties. I was never willing to make that full sacrifice, even in graduate school when the living example was standing only inches away.

During the research hiatus that followed my initial discovery and before the essential experiments could be verified and the results published, I had my first experience of being scooped. It wouldn't be my last. Two papers appeared almost simultaneously that documented the same phenomenon I had uncovered. Both were published in high-profile, peer-reviewed journals. The significance

of this was recognized more by my advisor than me, and he wasn't
going to take it sitting down. Thus, within days, he fired off a report
on my discovery. It was old news by then, however, so the only place
our story could get published was in a journal that required no peer
review.

This method of publishing laboratory findings had by then
become a pattern for my advisor, a pattern that would soon have an
unpleasant effect on his career. He had been warned on several
occasions by the Chair of our Department and, by default, other
senior faculty, that publishing nearly every paper without peer review
was not acceptable for an assistant professor at Berkeley. My advisor
ignored their suggestions; he was "his own man," as he often
proclaimed, and was on a mission to get his results published
quickly. Respectable journals required far too much time and effort.

By the time my third year in the lab rolled around, it was evident
that this behavior was going to cost my advisor his job at Berkeley. In
spite of his brilliance and numerous major discoveries in basic
biochemistry, he was asked to vacate his position by the end of the
year. Berkeley may have been a wild and crazy place in the late 60's,
but none of this craziness penetrated the walls of the Biochemistry
Building. It stood like a rock of scientific conformity in an otherwise
disjointed world.

The edict issued to my advisor fired up my own after-burners. If I
had any chance of obtaining a PhD within the next few years, I had
better have it done in the next few months. I loved Berkeley, but not
that much. This was no time to be changing advisors.

My thesis was not memorable but it was completed by early May
and I graduated with a PhD in biochemistry in June of 1969, less
than four years after my arrival in Berkeley. I even beat my advisor
out of town, but not by much. I later suffered from the lack of
experience that a couple more years could have provided, like maybe
slowing down to get an MS degree as would have been required in
the other biochemistry programs in which I had been accepted, but
that was the price I had to pay. In the end, I left Berkeley well before
any of my classmates, in spite of their superior backgrounds. They
didn't have my advisor.

❧ ❧ ❧

Although three years had transpired since my days in the seminary by the time I arrived in Berkeley, my religious beliefs and practices had changed very little. Based on my need to be the living image of a perfect Catholic, my first act in Berkeley, even before checking in with the biochemistry staff, was to locate a Catholic church. As with most college campuses, UC Berkeley had a Newman Center that served this role. In Bozeman, I had attended daily Mass; I still lived at home while attending college, and daily Mass attendance was expected by the Head Resident. I had neglected this practice during my summer in Livermore, but only because it was impossible to coordinate daily Mass with my job and the 30-mile commute from the apartment building that had been rented to summer employees in Hayward. Now I was relieved that I could re-institute the practice. So I did, at least for awhile.

After attending Mass on my first day in Berkeley, I introduced myself to the priest and offered my services for anything he felt appropriate. He proposed that I could teach Sunday school, possibly the sixth grade class. I had never taught anything, but how hard could it be to teach sixth graders about God? I learned.

I lasted the year, but not without incident. I taught religion as the nuns had taught me, each class filled with dogma for memorization. My arsenal for controlling student behavior was more limited than those of the nuns who taught me. They always held the trump card of eternal damnation safely stowed in their habits for any child who did not conform to their wishes. Without this weapon at my disposal, some of my group of 12 students felt free to object to my teaching techniques. The objections were not to what I was teaching. They weren't that sophisticated. They were just disturbed by the memorization expected of them in a Sunday school class. I was a hard-liner, however, and stuck with my program, even when one student got under my skin enough that I sent him home. I don't know where he went when he left the class, and frankly didn't care. He did return without further flack, so I'm guessing he never told his parents. However, the priests that served the Newman Center did not request my return the next year.

My self-engendered obligation to be a religious zealot did not stop at the church door. One demonstration of this was that upon taking up residency in my first Berkeley apartment, I issued a standing offer to anyone in the building to deliver them to-and-from Mass on Sundays. One young lady living in an apartment upstairs randomly took up my offer. By "random" I mean she would randomly go to church depending on her Saturday night activities. I didn't condone this laxness with the rules of the Church, and attempted to keep her in the state of grace by urging her to attend Mass every Sunday. This entailed that I visit her apartment on Saturday evenings for my weekly lecture. On one such occasion, her boyfriend was present. On learning of my mission, he began a verbal assault on Catholics and particularly the clergy, saying they clearly either were women or wanted to be women based on what they wore. My anger level immediately peaked as I'm sure my tormentor had planned it would, and I let him have it with both barrels, calling him every unflattering name I knew. Whoever preached "turning the other cheek?" It sure wasn't me. My random rider disappeared after that.

I not only knew the Catholic Church provided the only way to salvation, but wanted others to be aware that I knew the path as well. I didn't preach on street corners, but did have a magnetically-attached, plastic statue of Jesus prominently displayed on my dashboard. When I was driving to church one Sunday morning, a group of pagans were playing ball in the street, and as I passed by, began to chant "I don't care if it rains or freezes; all I need is my plastic Jesus." I was infuriated and immediately hit the brakes, jumped out of the car, and provided them a verbal history of their ancestry. It's a wonder my religiosity didn't get me killed.

Making the adjustment from Montana to the Berkeley of the 60's has the appearance of a difficult transition. I was certainly naïve, but most kids were, even some of those who grew up in Berkeley. Besides, freedom of expression in Berkeley was generally tolerated unless it was harming someone other than you. A person could sit on street corners in rags smoking pot and reciting poetry or one could display a Jesus statue on your dashboard. Neither action typically elicited comment. I was even allowed to retain my Montana hair style. With that said, however, there were a few social behaviors I needed to learn, even if I wasn't obliged to assimilate them into my own lifestyle.

Shortly after Shirley arrived in Berkeley with me after our marriage, we were invited to celebrate the birthday of one of our new acquaintances. This was to be our introduction to the Berkeley counter culture. The party was held in the residence of our friend, a multi-room wreck of a house near campus that was about to be condemned. Apparently, every resident in this firetrap had invited numerous guests, so by the time of our arrival, there was standing room only. Many residents had pitched in with the food which did include some nutritious dishes. One had been a massive bowl of salad. When we arrived, however, the salad bowl was nearly empty and was situated squarely in the lap of a spaced-out guest squatted cross-legged against a hallway wall, his bare filthy feet pointed upward and both face and hands rummaging through the remaining contents of the bowl.

In the next room, a forlorn-looking lady with long, very greasy hair was rolling what I perceived as tobacco into a paper wrapping to be smoked. In Montana, many of our hired hands constructed their own cigarettes in that fashion so, to make conversation, I inquired as to whether she "rolled her own." It is unclear what she took my question to mean. Surely, I wasn't so stupid that I thought she was rolling tobacco. She mostly ignored my naïve introduction, but being a friendly type, offered me a drag. I still thought it was a cigarette, but knowing something about infectious diseases, I turned down the offer.

Soon after this encounter, I became aware that everyone present except us was quite elated and no alcohol was visible. Neither Shirley nor I were yet ready to celebrate with this group, so after excusing ourselves, we escaped to the comfort of more familiar social settings. We never really became acclimated to this branch of the "Berkeley Social Club."

The student protest movements of the 60's, as I recall, had their origin in Berkeley in 1964 during a Sproul Hall sit-in, the so-called

Free Speech Movement. After that, it was "power to the people" for almost any cause. This original sit-in was ancient history by the time of my arrival a few months later, and had been displaced by a protest movement over the war in Vietnam. This student-directed activity ignited a national movement that may even have had some effect on our eventual withdrawal from Vietnam. The folks at Berkeley had short attention spans, and the war protest movement was soon replaced by protests over a series of more relevant local issues for which student disruption was a necessity. How many protesters were actually Cal students during any of these clashes will probably never be known, but a whole lot of us were at least witnesses.

The order of happenings during these disturbances followed pretty much the same script. A potential infraction by what the group perceived as a complacent society would be identified, the protests would be organized, various police units would be mobilized, and finally, the National Guard would arrive to occupy the town and campus. The identity of the occupation force present on campus at any point in time could be used as a barometer to trace the progress of the protest. The campus police were the first responders, followed soon thereafter by the Berkeley police. When things began to heat up, the California Highway Patrol would be summoned, and when they began losing the battle, in would ride the Alameda County Sheriff's Posse.

The latter group was most easily identified, and also most hated. Every member appeared to be over six feet tall, weighed at least 250 pounds, and wore ugly blue coveralls. As the protesters were getting fired up in the plaza outside the Student Union Building on the edge of campus, the "blue meanies" would form a double-rowed phalanx, the face guards on their blue helmets would be lowered, and the 3-foot clubs they toted would be rotated to the ready position. These actions invariably inflamed the gathered crowd which would commence to chuck bottles and other available trash toward the blue lines. A "charge" order would then be shouted by the head meanie and the blue lines would rush forward smashing anything in sight. Immediately thereafter, the meanies would reform the lines to their original positions.

The arrival of the blue meanies invariably escalated the violence rather than curtailing it, and signaled the inevitable appearance of the National Guard who would arrive in force within days. The National Guard didn't consist entirely of foot soldiers; it also had an associated Air Force of helicopters that patrolled the entire city 24 hours a day. Their accompanying roar, day and night, could tip you into insanity if you weren't already tipped. Sometimes the tear gas used to disperse crowds was also dispensed from these helicopters. The patrol zone for the Guard and its helicopters was primarily near campus, but students attempting to return home from their classes would often be rerouted by the multiple soldiers that patrolled the streets. Curfews were issued during the height of most protests which played hell with lab experiments that needed late night attention.

For a student like me with little emotional attachment to these happenings, the protests were like circus acts. During a break time, however, I would be drawn to them like a magnet. After witnessing the maneuvers used by the various "law forces" prior to closing in to make arrests, I knew enough to watch from sufficient distance to not get enclosed when the kill was made. There were only so many troops available, so the circles they formed around their prey had a limited diameter. Fortunately, I was otherwise occupied when the entire National Guard occupation force decided to enclose a several block area that encompassed a large section of a Berkeley business district near campus during one protest, and arrested over 1,000 protesters and shoppers. Some of my classmates were not so lucky, and spent a frigid night in an outside, wire-mesh holding zone many miles from Berkeley.

The protest movement associated with the Vietnam War spread from the streets of Berkeley across the nation and created a divided populace. Initially only left-wingers were identified as protesters. The cry against them became "America, love it or leave it." This protest movement had a rapid metamorphosis, and by early 1968 included serious presidential candidates like Eugene McCarthy and Bobby Kennedy. The country was on a collision course with history which had begun to play out that same year with the assassinations of Martin Luther King, Jr. and Bobby Kennedy, and the mishmash of demonstrations and arrests associated with the Democratic National Convention in Chicago. Who of my generation will ever forget Mayor Daly as he screamed his anger into the TV cameras for a nation to witness while his troops were clubbing the heads of protestors a few feet from the floor of the Convention Hall? It was a turbulent period. As we drove out of Berkeley in June, 1969, my PhD degree in hand, we passed trucks loaded with National Guard troops that were just coming into town for another occupation. I don't remember why they were coming; I doubt anyone does.

9 Drinking Beer in Munich

A myth pounded into my head when I was in graduate school is that "meaningful" scientific research can only be carried out in a limited number of select institutions. Natural companions to this myth were that further in-depth training after receiving a PhD was required to perform this meaningful research and this training could only be acquired at the same select institutions. Since my life's ambition was to perform meaningful research, it seemed imperative that I continue my training in one or more of these respected institutions.

My need to identify an establishment in which to conduct meaningful post-doctoral training materialized well ahead of my Berkeley classmates due to the early release of my PhD advisor. There are potential penalties to be paid if a graduate student chooses a non-tenured faculty member as an advisor, and I had uncovered one. By the time rumors of my advisor's dismissal became reality during my third year of graduate school, I had developed sufficient self-confidence to realize I could leave Montana and live to tell about it. With this knowledge under my belt, I was keen to expand my horizon beyond our national boundaries. In 1969, most of the Centers of Science outside of America were in Europe. Ergo – I would apply for post-doctoral training in Europe.

My confidence in being content in a foreign land did, however, have its limitations. Because of this, I planned to commit only one year to this overseas interlude. This can be interpreted as "I wanted to spend one year traveling in Europe." However, I also felt the need to expand my scientific expertise in order to someday conduct meaningful research in my own lab. Next, due to a lack of a family slush fund, it was imperative for me to come up with monies to support this year on the road. Lastly, because I intended to stay for only one year in Europe, I needed to line up a second post-doctoral position in America where I could bounce to on my return, and from whence I could truly launch my own research career. Taken together, these added up to a sizable number of goals to accomplish in the few months I had left in Berkeley.

Even in my naivety, I recognized that a single year in Europe allowed insufficient time to introduce an entirely new research endeavor if I planned to accomplish something of value. That can be translated as "I needed to continue my research studies with RNA bacteriophages and get the results published, this time in peer-reviewed journals." By then, it was evident even to me that the research scientist's mantra was "publish or perish," and I was already chanting it several times each day, sort of like reciting the rosary.

Based on these requirements, I began to search Europe for a laboratory where reasonably profound scientific findings on RNA bacteriophages had been uncovered and where sufficient funds would be provided to survive for one year. The first task was relatively simple; the latter wasn't. I applied to six European laboratories and was accepted by each, but only one potential mentor was willing to provide me with any stipend. After performing a quick translation of the amount offered in US dollars, it came to slightly less than half of my $2,400 graduate student stipend.

Knowing that monies for a year in Europe might be difficult to come by, I had enough foresight to identify American funding agencies that might pay for a fellowship in Europe. I found a total of three. Although all three did support fellowships abroad, they much preferred that their monies be used at home. Thus, I was facing an uphill battle. My ace-in-the hole was that Wendell Stanley, a Professor in the Department of Molecular Biology at Berkeley and a 1946 Nobel laureate, was a member of the Board of Directors of one of the three, the Jane Coffin Childs Memorial Fund for Medical Research. Based on the proximity of our respective locations, I was awarded an interview with him.

His first statement to me after I slid into his office and diverted his attention from the manuscript he was reading was "Ward, why do you want to go to Europe?" After catching my breath, I regurgitated my previously memorized answer.

"Because I think learning science in a different culture would be invaluable for a research career in an institution of higher learning, Dr. Stanley." Heaven forbid that I would suggest a career in industry or even government.

"Humph! What would you do if you are not awarded this fellowship?"

"I would take the position where they offered me some money, Dr. Stanley." I didn't tell him it was marginal whether I could survive on what was offered.

"Humph! Spending time in that lab would be a waste of your time. Where else have you been accepted?"

After I rattled off my list of five other labs, he retorted, "Any of them is better than the institution that offered to pay you. "

I wasn't going to argue. He certainly knew better than I did. His next response was the one I was waiting to hear.

"Humph! I will get you the money so you don't waste your time."

That was it. I figured with the Nobel Prize, his word was golden, and it was. My salary for the year was to be $6,500 and, in addition, they would cover the travel costs for both Shirley and me. They even provided $2,000 to my laboratory of choice which was, by a flip of the coin, at the Max Planck Institute for Biochemistry in Munich. Things were working out.

While these events were transpiring, I also determined that on my return to America, I would embark on studies with a virus that actually caused a human disease, and one of the more obvious groups was the RNA tumor viruses which would later be renamed retroviruses. I knew that at some point in my lifetime, I wanted to conduct research that had the possibility of having a direct beneficial effect on human health. At that moment in time, RNA tumor viruses were believed to be the most likely infectious agents to be responsible for a multitude of human and animal cancers. Although this association has lessened with time, viruses within this family were eventually recognized as the cause of another somewhat important

human condition called AIDS. After spending less time than I should
have locating an American lab that was conducting cutting edge
research on RNA tumor viruses, I selected what I perceived to be one
of the best in the country. The director of that lab seemed to be
doing interesting things and appeared to have all the right
connections. At least he sold himself well. He also offered to pay me;
not much, but a little. I accepted the position well over a year in
advance of my planned arrival date, and left for Munich secure in the
knowledge that I had employment on my return.

If Shirley and I were going to have independence when traveling
in Europe, we would need our own car. By this time, the '55 Chevy I
purchased after returning from the seminary had amassed over
150,000 miles and was slurping more oil than Ike's red bomb when
we headed for San Francisco nine years earlier. The most popular
automobile in Berkeley was a Volkswagen. There were more of them
than hippies, and like hippies, most were decorated with peace
symbols. Since we were going to Germany, this seemed like the car
to buy if we could pay for it and still have enough funds with which to
survive until I received my first post-doctoral payment. Therein was
a potential problem.

At the time of our marriage, I had $950 in the bank and Shirley
was nearly $3,000 in the red due to college loans. My parents'
contribution to our marriage was a check for $200. It seemed logical
that there must be more where that came from, so I asked to borrow
another $200. Fortunately, I got it. The plan was that with Shirley's
new college degree in hand, she would be successfully employed
within weeks; the extra $200 was added just in case she wasn't. As it
turned out, it took her six months to find a teaching position in
California. During that period, we spent twice as much each month
than was covered by my $200 graduate student stipend just to live,
and not in a high style. Thus, by Christmas, we were down to the
$200 I had borrowed from my parents. Shirley's first check was due
to arrive in late January so we figured if we each spent $5 on
Christmas presents, we could just make it. Credit cards were almost
non-existent and we wouldn't have qualified for one if we had tried,

so charging was not an option. At least we avoided being swallowed up by that black hole.

That Christmas we lived mostly on love. I bought Shirley a cheap tennis racquet and she got me a World Atlas in the hope that someday we would personally be able to see some of what was displayed in it. Shirley's parents knew we were destitute and probably needed a taste of home, so they mailed us a Montana Christmas tree. We spent $2.25 on silver tinsel and blue balls to make it look like a Christmas tree, and $1.25 for a stand to hold it up. With that and a roasted chicken, we celebrated our first Christmas as a married couple.

With Shirley's checks from the California Department of Education coming in regularly during the next two and one-half years, and our combined frugality, she was able to pay off her college debt, I paid back the $200 my parents had loaned, and we saved enough to purchase a new $2,200 automobile. This purchase left us little financial wiggle room before I received my first check in Munich, which would not be until early in August. Thus, any traveling we did before that date would have to be done on a shoestring budget. We were about to become poster children for the book "Europe On $5 A Day."

After dropping off our '55 Chevy in Montana on leaving Berkeley, Shirley and I flew to Oakland on an early June morning with two suitcases each, the contents of which were intended to tide us over for a year abroad. Our charter flight was scheduled to leave from Oakland to London at 4 PM that same day. On arrival in Oakland, we had two pieces of bad news. The first was that one of my suitcases had not made the trip; the second was that our charter flight to London was delayed until 10 PM. Actually, the first bad news converted the second bad news into good news. At least I had a chance of retrieving the lost suitcase before it was untraceable. I viewed this as critical since we certainly did not have the cash to replace its contents. After multiple phone calls to the baggage department, I was finally informed that my suitcase was scheduled for a 10:35 PM arrival. This would be much too late for our 10 PM departure. The panic attack that ensued lasted until 8 PM when we were informed that the 10 PM departure had been moved to 2 AM, and would take place at the San Francisco Airport, an hour by car across the bay. As one problem abated, the other multiplied. The suitcase did arrive as promised and we were able to catch a ride with friends to the other airport, just in time to learn our flight was now scheduled for a 5 AM departure. This was developing into one long day.

Our plane eventually rose over the San Francisco Bay sometime after daybreak, but at least it did rise. I have ridden on many airplanes since that time, but never one like this. Its design mimicked that of the old slave ships. The cabin was built to accommodate two seats on each side of the aisle but they had packed in three. Likewise, the number of rows was double the comfort level. We were fully loaded, stem-to-stern, with 270 passengers in a plane built to handle about half that many.

Shirley and I stacked ourselves in, thankful that the extra inches in height that we both would have bargained with the devil for ten years earlier, had not materialized. Although we were exhausted, sleeping in the fetal position was impossible. Five hours into the flight, we refueled in Bangor, Maine, where no reprieve for our cramped muscles was offered. It was probably just as well since most muscles were asleep, and the pain associated with waking them would have exceeded the potential value of the brief respite. Some of our braver flight mates were making the trip with small children who could be pacified for only brief periods throughout the flight. These wee ones had no assigned seats, so had to somehow be assimilated on their parents' laps, if they had laps in their scrunched positions. We heard the pain of the children and felt the pain of their parents.

Six hours after leaving Bangor, we disembarked at London's Gatwick Airport. Getting through customs at that time of day was a breeze; we were nearly the only people in that part of the earth still awake. From there, the entire planeload was squeezed into buses that dumped us at a downtown London station. By then it was 2 AM, so late in fact that no one could be aroused to answer the phone at the hotel where we had booked a room. You couldn't even exchange money. Prior to leaving Berkeley, my advisor had gifted me a pound note which I was able to resurrect. With this in hand, we stowed our suitcases and headed out on foot for a night in the sleeping city.

It was a truly surreal experience. We were exhausted, and both of us were running only on adrenaline with those tanks approaching empty. Even so, during the next six hours we scouted the trails described by Charles Dickens through the streets and alleys of London, passing the Old London Bridge, The Tower of London, back and forth across the Thames, and through Piccadilly Square. The streets were essentially abandoned until delivery carts began moving at about 5 AM. There was no moon and few stars glimmered through the fog, but the sky never seemed to fully darken. I had never realized London was so far north since the weather was so mild; we appeared to be only a stone's throw from the midnight sun.

By eight o'clock, when the Bed and Breakfast establishments began opening their doors, our pound currency was spent and so were we, so much so that my muscles were beginning to lock-up. We had been awake for nearly two days and the intervening pressures made it equivalent to twice that long. Somehow we managed to exchange money, locate a room, and hail a cab before we both collapsed, which we did for a straight 24 hours. I didn't know anyone could sleep that long, but I also didn't know anyone could be that tired.

During the following days, we wandered around England in jet lag, spending only enough money to get by, and eventually headed for my ancestral home of Ireland. After traveling most of the day in second class compartments of several trains, we boarded the night ferry for the trip across the Irish Sea, arriving in Dublin with the sun. The hours on the boat's open-to-the-elements upper deck were spent in straight-backed wooden seats where the temperature hovered just above freezing. The combination of back pain and fear of hypothermia disallowed even dozing off for a few minutes, so we arrived in Dublin in the same rested condition as we had several days earlier in London. I guess we were not traveling first class.

Our initial order of business was to catch a cab to the automobile rental agency before the car we had reserved was given to someone else. The rental agency provided a map which showed where we were and the general location of the bed-and-breakfast where we had reserved a room. However, only about every fourth street was listed on the map, and the street names in Dublin changed so often that traveling nearly comatose from point A to point B on the wrong side of the road soon became a nightmare. I would pull over almost every block and yell expletives at Shirley, remarking on her inability to properly navigate. Twice on pulling out from the curb, I headed down the wrong side of the road, facing the oncoming traffic with blaring horns. It was an adventure. When we finally arrived at point B and fell into bed, it was for another 24-hour stint.

After a few days of driving on the wrong side of the road through the rustic Emerald Isle, it was time for another endurance contest. We again took the night ferry to England under the same frigid conditions experienced on our trip over, spent the morning traveling by train across England in our usual second class compartments, caught the afternoon ferry across the English Channel to The Netherlands, and were transported by bus to Amsterdam, arriving there late in the evening. It was a difficult method of travel to get from Ireland to the Mainland of Europe but it was the one that required the least amount of cash. That was the critical factor. Neither of us had slept on the journey so we were again barely able to walk on arrival in Amsterdam. They say you can survive almost anything when you are young; we were testing the theory. If our year in Europe were to have continued at this pace, we would have been transported home in the baggage compartment.

No sooner had we alighted from the bus in Amsterdam when I was firmly grabbed by a local entrepreneur who ordered us to follow him if we wanted a place to stay for the night. Times were apparently tough for our new host since the "place to stay" was to be in this guy's living room where a bed had been erected to accommodate tourists.

It was all very bizarre, and once shown our quarters, we never saw the man again until morning when he, his wife and four children all materialized to wake us for breakfast. We never knew where they hung out overnight because the only sounds came from cars passing in the street outside, and we were too tired to even hear them. They were a friendly group and all six spoke excellent English, one of the four languages they were expected to master in The Netherlands.

After a day in Amsterdam learning about Rembrandt and his companion artists, we boarded another train and pushed on into Germany, the country that was to be our home for the year. At the time of our arrival, I spoke only a few German words, and Shirley spoke even less. She at least had an excuse in that she had never studied any foreign language. I had taken a year of regular German in college and a second year translating scientific German. Even so, I failed the prerequisite German exam when tested after my arrival in Berkeley, even with the assistance of a dictionary. After studying the language on my own for several months, I finally got over that hurdle, but three years later I was again nearly speechless. In fact, I had always been nearly speechless; my only capability was to translate written German, and that was marginal. Our contacts at the VW Plant in Wolfsburg where we picked up our new car were quite proficient in English, so I had not yet uttered a word in German until we stopped the first night on the road to Munich. It was now time to take the leap.

After identifying a roadside Gasthaus (I at least could translate that), I timidly approached the clerk manning the front desk, planning the words in my head as I went. Out they came. "Haben sie ein zimmer frei?"

Fortunately, there was a room that was available, so my next utterance was "Wie viel costet das?" I was not about to pay $20 a night just because I didn't understand the language. In the end, however, I had no idea what the answer was to my question; I was just impressed with myself that I got one.

So began our year, attempting to survive in a foreign land. You would think we had been dropped off in the Upper Amazon. By the time we left Germany ten months later, however, we had grown to welcome signs in windows of hotels in other countries saying "Man sprecht Deutsch." It would have been preferable if they had said "English spoken here", but German would, by then, suffice. We did make some progress that year.

My first stop in Munich was the Max Planck Institute located on Goethestrasse, two blocks from the main railroad station in the center of the town and near everything. I became most aware of the latter during the two weeks of Oktoberfest when the crowds on the sidewalk in front of the Institute were so thick with people that you had to walk sideways to pass. But that was yet to come. On arrival day in July, there was an abundance of space since many locals were already on their summer holiday in the mountains or at the beach.

The Institute itself was a four-story structure that housed the laboratories of several of the most renowned biochemical investigators in Germany. My new mentor was only in his early 40's, so had not yet had time to reach the upper rungs on the pecking order. Thus, his quarters were located in the basement as I learned after searching the other three floors for his name.

My mentor offered his hand as soon as we were within shaking distance. It was a handshake I will never forget. He extended his arm with hand drooping off the end. I gripped it firmly as I had learned was expected when you shook hands. That was a mistake. My reaction was that I had just latched onto soft, wet rubber. I immediately jerked free, feeling like I had entered into forbidden territory, and was about to get slapped. My mentor never missed a beat; he just acted like my reaction was expected. I later learned that his handshake was infamous and was even the subject of spoofs played out by his lab staff.

The first significant character trait I learned about my mentor was that he took the time to care for the physical needs of his investigators. Both Shirley and I benefited from this behavior in that, on arrival, we were assigned a spacious room in the Institute guest house until we located a place to stay – which my mentor took care of as well. The guest house was like a small resort. Breakfast was served in the room, and you put in your daily request regarding its contents to Frau Schmidt, the octogenarian that ran the establishment.

Frau Schmidt spoke no English, so she offered us another chance to practice German. It was like communicating with an alien. Almost all was done in sign language accompanied by verbiage that helped emphasize points about which neither side had the least notion of what the other was saying. I never knew whether we were ordering breakfast or discussing Frau Schmidt's family life. Later I learned that Frau Schmidt didn't really speak German. As with other natives of Bavaria, she spoke Bayerisch, a dialect that even Germans living in other parts of the country had difficulty understanding.

Within a day of our arrival, my mentor accompanied us to the Max Planck Institute housing complex to check out a flat owned by a Professor of Theoretical Physics. There are many Max Planck Institutes in Germany and six were in Munich, so Institute housing could be owned by a variety of science types. The professor and his family were traveling to America where he was to spend a sabbatical leave. When we arrived, the whole group had their bags packed, so the professor did flip-flops to accommodate us. The place was heavenly. It had five very large rooms, plus two bathrooms and a central hallway linking them all. It was also fully furnished with a washer and dryer, television and even a dishwasher, and they were asking only $280 per month. One of the rooms was the study where the professor developed his theories, apparently with the door and windows closed. Cigarette smoke had seeped out between the door and frame, and had crept up the walls of the hall outside as brownish flames of stain. The study itself was fully caked with the same ooze. We inquired whether we could paint the room to alter the color and hopefully kill some of the smell. He graciously agreed, and even exclaimed that we could deduct the paint costs from the rent. He was truly desperate to get the place rented and we had a fabulous place to stay that we could afford.

The Germans were very intense about any activity in which they were involved, be it work or play. Official workdays were ten hours, but the expectation for post-docs was that this was only warm-up time. In Berkeley, I attempted to work normal hours, but in Munich I was expected to almost live in the lab, at least until it became time to play. Playtime was any religious or government holiday, usually accompanied by several days before and after. At Christmastime, the Institute was locked for nearly three weeks, time enough to explore a large section of Italy.

We drove out of Munich a week before Christmas accompanied by my sister Rose Marie, an ex-nun, and brother-in-law Jim, an ex-priest who was spending the year in Mainz on a Fulbright Fellowship. Italy had more than one tourist attraction, but being in the company of an ex-nun and an ex-priest who was getting his PhD in theology, the primary attraction was the churches. Italy has several churches and we didn't miss many.

The most dramatic "church experience" was visiting a newly-excavated catacomb under an ancient church in Rome. Jim learned of its existence before leaving America, and insisted that we pay a visit while collecting indulgences traveling from church to church on Christmas day. On arrival, Jim negotiated with a local guide to take us on a tour. This guy was more than happy to comply, but spoke no English. He supplied each of us with small candles, and after we thumped down two flights of centuries-old wooden steps, we made our entry into the catacomb. With candles lit, we passed through the narrow passages of ancient death. On each side, small indentations had been dug in the dirt walls, many housing the remains of early Christians or lost Roman soldiers. Our only light was provided by the candles, and the shadows of our little group of warriors flickered weakly off these same walls as we wandered by. I was bringing up the rear and just getting the feel of the place when I became aware of a distraught conversation taking place several persons ahead. Shirley was just behind the guide leading our pack, and her reaction to the place was less than pleasant. She later related that she had suppressed her first urge to run, but when the second wave came, she was out of there. She uttered a suppressed scream to the guide with sufficient forcefulness that language was no barrier. He grabbed her hand just as she began her sprint down the rear channels, and held tight. They passed me in a blur and were heading out. The only thing I saw was Shirley's panicked eyes which were six times their normal size. I don't know if I would have had the wherewithal to have stopped her had she not been linked with the guide. Since we had already passed several tributaries in our passage, God knows where she would have ended up before she could be located. Since that time, she hasn't done well in closets or elevators.

Although I attempted to forget the fact, my identity in Europe was that of a post-doctoral research fellow, not a tourist. This meant I was required to conduct research. Within days after arriving in

Munich, I was told I would be sequestered at a Max Planck Institute near the North Sea for three weeks to become familiarized with the latest lab methods in molecular biology. Having just left Berkeley where I had learned much of the same, I wasn't impressed. However, there were no options since my mentor was one of the teachers, and his lab would be locked for the duration. Shirley came along. Our home during this period was a non-refurbished Renaissance hotel where the one bathtub on each floor was usable for only two hours a night, and only on weekdays. The floor in our room was tilted such that it was an uphill climb from bed to closet when we retrieved our clothing in the morning. The building did have one modern appliance, a black and white TV located near the lobby around which our entire group of summer students gathered one evening in August to witness Neil Armstrong placing his feet on the surface of the moon, uttering "one small step for mankind." It was a fine time to be an American.

Even though I made a pretense of working during those three weeks, Shirley had no such distraction and spent most of her time lounging on a private beach located on the campus we occupied. The grounds were surrounded by an insurmountable barrier, beyond which the beach became public. Shirley's side of the fence never had more than a handful of bathers, but the other side was generally packed. However, the other side also had the only concession stand within walking distance, so after a week of eyeing this oasis, Shirley found a way to circumvent the barrier to procure a coke. At least she got around the barrier; she never got the coke.

When Shirley arrived at the stand, there were five customers in front of her. She lined up, assuming she would be the sixth. She soon learned, however, that forming a line was not part of the German vocabulary, and you were waited on only if you pushed your way to the front. After about 30 minutes, when there were now seven people ahead of her, Shirley realized that she was never going to make it to the front. That day, a coke wasn't worth the fight. She retreated to the other side of the fence to check her body parts for damage. Realizing that only her pride was wounded, it was time to plan the next battle. She was in a different country and here they had their own rules. She would have to suck it up and adjust. She did.

The next day she marched to the concession stand and arrived as the sixth patron, but this time she was the second to be served.

This lack of queuing wasn't restricted to concession booths. Even getting stamps in a post office required sharp elbows. However, the grocery store was a different matter. Our rented flat was located in an area near housing projects that lodged "gast arbeiters," the guest workers who almost all hailed from some Mediterranean country. Most had dark complexions that contrasted with Shirley's blond hair and blonder body. We never fully understood the politics, but the gast arbeiters were apparently unwelcome, at least in this neighborhood. Thus, when Shirley shopped, the clerks cleared traffic to wait on her first at the expense of those ahead of her with darker hair. She would object, but usually just acquiesced to keep the traffic flowing.

The aggressive behaviors encountered while we were on foot didn't hold a candle to those we met when driving. The rule in local car traffic was merely "to push on quickly or be pushed," but on the Autobahn it was more "kill or be killed." Driving cars on this roadway was serious business, and those with the faster, more powerful autos were required to demonstrate the same. Thus, as they streaked down the passing lanes of these racetracks, only one hand was used to steer; the other was used to flash their lights, demanding the right of way.

When I expressed my dismay about this behavior to one of my German co-workers at the Institute, pointing out that a momentary error in judgment by one of the slower vehicles would be invariably fatal to all parties, he proudly proclaimed that he would rather have it written on his tombstone that "he was right" than to have yielded and lived. Others who overheard the discussion agreed. With that warning, I generally drove only in the far right lane on the Autobahn. VW's did not qualify for the passing lane.

After returning from the North Sea, Shirley fully tanned and me still as pale as a sheet, work at the Institute began in earnest. My studies on the molecular biology of RNA bacteriophages continued with only a change in brand. My new mentor was credited with the discovery of one of these phages called M12, so his brand became the object of my experimentation. Prior to my arrival in Munich, one of the post-docs in my mentor's lab had begun a project to determine the gene order of this bacteria virus. I had already learned from my work in Berkeley that when one of the proteins of these viruses, called the capsid protein, was produced in sufficient quantities during the virus growth cycle in the bacterium, it would suppress its competition by binding to the three-gene viral RNA and thereby prevent the use of another gene that encoded the enzyme responsible for production of new molecules of viral RNA, i.e., the viral polymerase. Thus, large quantities of capsid protein and little polymerase protein were produced during the latter part of the viral life cycle.

With this information and the knowledge that the three genes were linked to one another in a continuous strand of RNA, it was assumed that the gene encoding the capsid protein was located nearest the end of the RNA used first. However, the third protein, called the "A" protein, was produced in very small amounts throughout the life cycle of the virus, thereby implying that production of the A protein was not controlled by the capsid protein. The location of the gene for the A protein was, therefore, a mystery. Wherever it was located, the mechanism of its regulation or lack thereof, was a potential biological goldmine yet to be discovered, and a major step toward this discovery would be to determine the gene order for this tiny virus.

The investigator who initiated the project had left Munich before I arrived, but the stock of biological materials he had produced was being retained in my mentor's freezer. This consisted of pieces of M12 RNA molecules, the genes for this tiny virus, captured at various stages during their production in its *E. coli* host. He had separated and stored these RNA fragments on the basis of their sizes, beginning with the smallest that would contain only a portion of the first gene, and ending with the largest that would contain all three genes. The assumption was that if these fragments were used in a test tube system that could decode the information they contained into proteins, the smaller pieces would produce only the first protein, the medium-sized pieces would produce both the first and second proteins, and only the largest RNA pieces would produce all three proteins. Thus, all that was needed was to decode these RNA pieces and see which proteins they produced. That was my new job.

I was not alone on this project. At the same time I arrived, a post-doctoral fellow from The Netherlands also joined the lab. Although our training partially overlapped, we both had our own unique knowledge to contribute to the project. It was a great collaboration. Ruud Konings and I not only became collaborators, but we also became lifelong friends. Within weeks, we had the system prepared and were ready to test the precious pieces of stored RNA. What we learned was that the gene for the A protein was actually first in line, followed by that of the capsid protein, and finally the polymerase gene. The bacterial protein production machinery used to decode the phage RNA would typically by-pass its entry site on the A protein gene and skip down to the entry site on the capsid gene. Thus, many times more capsid than A protein was produced during viral replication, but the capsid protein did not control production of the A protein.

This discovery flew in the face of doctrine taught a few years earlier by Jacob and Monod who received a Nobel Prize for their studies on the production of bacterial proteins from a set of linked bacterial genes. They reported that this process always begins at the first gene, and the protein production machinery moves onto subsequent genes only after it has passed over previous genes and produced the encoded proteins. Thus, the quantities of proteins encoded by the bacterial genes further down the RNA strand could not be more than the quantities of proteins produced from genes further up the strand. This became known as the doctrine of "polarity." Our finding flew in the face if this doctrine and was of sufficient importance that it was worthy of publication in a top journal. The one that appeared most suitable was called "Nature New Biology."

As we were preparing to report our discovery in the weeks after Christmas, another article appeared in this same journal that was a partial scoop. "Partial" in this case meant that the purpose of the published article was not to define the gene order of viruses, but rather to establish how it could be done. At the very end of the article, without any associated data, the authors claimed to have used their technique to determine the gene order of RNA bacteriophages, and it was "A protein-capsid-polymerase." They had it right.

Even with this information already in print, we still submitted our findings to Nature New Biology. However, to be respectful of the investigators of the published article, we sent a copy of our manuscript to the lead author. The outcome was that our paper was returned months later with minor comments, arriving two days after our competitor's actual report on the gene order of RNA bacteriophages was published in the same journal, accompanied with much fanfare in the journal's editorial section. Our paper was later accepted and published, but without comment.

One can interpret this chain of events in any number of ways. Ruud and I were new to the game, but still knew we had been screwed. However, what doesn't kill you makes you stronger, and we would both need the extra strength in the years to come.

Life in the lab in Munich was a daily adventure. One German post-doctoral fellow, who later became a world-renowned scientist, poked a glass pipette completely through his hand when he became impatient while collecting samples during an experiment; the one English fellow in the lab was asked to leave when he refused to share his results with our mentor; I was almost shipped off with him when I made the mistake of giving our leader a right-handed fist salute with clicking heels after he had issued an order. Germans were a bit sensitive about that. Probably the greatest adventures, however, were the pranks, and my mentor was either the instigator or recipient of them all.

The most awesome occurred just after we had celebrated a Christmas luncheon in our laboratory in the Institute, an unlikely place to drink and eat that would never be allowed today. Alcoholic beverages were also consumed in major quantities, as one might guess. After we had become sufficiently uninhibited, the suggestion was made that we have a snowball fight with the group located one floor up. This was to be an indoor event, lab equipment and glassware notwithstanding. Several of us, including me, visited the ice machine and loaded our Styrofoam ice buckets with its crushed contents, ideal for producing killer snowballs. I wheeled my collection to the elevator on a lab cart, and arrived in the hallway upstairs in unison with the rest of the gang who had traveled by stairway. We all grabbed ice and commenced chucking at anyone in sight.

My mentor took it one step further. He crashed into the office of the leader of the group and plowed an ice ball against the side of the guy's head. His target was engrossed in discussions with one of his fellows and had failed to hear the commotion outside his door. Thus, the event was a successful surprise attack. The thrown ice ball bounced off its target's head onto the data sheets laid out on the desk, causing the ink to immediately smear across the pages. The object of the attack reacted instantly. He roared, grabbed a full container of ice, and rammed it over my mentor's head. Then he punched him full in the mouth. Now it was my mentor's turn to be stunned. He picked himself off the floor, blood dripping from forehead and mouth, and retreated down the stairway without further ado. The other wounded party also did an about face and returned to his office to retrieve his data before it was totally destroyed. The whole scenario took less than one minute. I grabbed the cart and the overturned ice containers and headed for the elevator. Nothing further was said. I guess it was a draw.

This was a year of dichotomies. I loved the fun, but never felt fully at ease with it. The work was personally rewarding, but little credit for our accomplishments was given to either Ruud or me. Individual Germans were great friends, but I was put off by the aggressive behavior of the group as a whole. Space was at a premium in much of Europe including Germany, and I grew up in a part of America where this was not the case. I think access to space helps shape our personalities, but maybe this is mere conjecture. Regardless, I probably needed to stay more than one year to become comfortable with the customs of this country and the behaviors of its citizens.

Our best friends during the year in Munich were Ruud and his wife with whom Shirley and I interacted at least twice a week. We played a lot of bridge, so much so that I learned to bid in Dutch. When we left Munich, they took over our flat in the Max Planck housing until they returned to The Netherlands two years later. In 1997, Ruud and his wife returned to Munich for an invited lecture. When they were leaving town, their car was struck by a truck and Ruud was killed instantly. His wife survived, but had many broken bones. I lost another great friend in the accident, and ironically, he died in Munich where our friendship had begun.

10 A Bounce Through New Jersey

When we lifted off for a year in Europe in June 1969, I had carefully prepared a landing spot for my return. Well, maybe not carefully enough. We were still being served breakfast by Frau Schmidt in the Max Planck guest quarters, two days after our arrival in Munich, when this plan was nuked. A respected professor from Albert Einstein University, who was making a European tour, had dropped by my mentor's lab to discuss science. Since our visitor was a friend and colleague of my PhD advisor, I was allowed a personal audience. After introductions, the conversation was immediately focused on my projected career path, and our guest's first question was the obvious one.

"Where are you planning to go after your time in Munich?" The question was simple and I provided what I assumed was an equally simple but awesome answer.

"I plan to make a career identifying viruses that cause cancer, and have determined that RNA tumor viruses are presently the most likely candidates. Therefore, after carefully honing in on the best lab to get the needed training, I chose that of a world-renowned scientist" whom I specified. I knew that had to impress him.

Our visitor sort of gasped, and then uttered "I think that would be a horrible mistake." He was painfully direct.

How could this be? I had planned it so well. I was down but still not out. My confused comeback was "why would you say this?"

"Because your choice of a mentor is a lousy scientist and treats his post-docs like slaves."

"Is that all?" was my weak retort.

"Isn't that enough?" was his final argument.

I never really confirmed whether what he said had an inkling of validity, but it completely freaked me out. That same day, following our visitor's opulent advice on a list of acceptable labs in which to get the training I wanted, I was penning out letters rapid fire. The letters were all on their way within 24 hours, but it took several weeks to get all the responses, and this time they were all negative. Based on the consistency of their verbiage, it appeared I had started a year too late. The problem couldn't possibly have been due to flaws in my resume'. Since I was still not willing to spend a second year outside the homeland, the search went on with another flurry of letters. Again, there were no takers. I was becoming convinced that I would have to revert to my original next destination. At least I had not burnt that bridge.

Never despair, your rescuer is only inches away. Mine came in late February in the person of another visitor. Aaron Shatkin, who was on his own whirlwind tour of Europe, had only recently resigned from a respectable position at the National Institutes of Health, and had joined the pharmaceutical company Hoffman-LaRoche in Nutley, New Jersey. His move stemmed from the promise that Roche would build an in-house Molecular Biology Institute that would be filled with the world's best scientists. More importantly, their research would be supported without company restrictions, so long as it was deemed "cutting edge." This was to become a novelty within the pharmaceutical industry. Aaron had been at Roche for less than a year when he arrived in Munich, but reported that the promises were so far being kept. Although new investigators were presently scattered within older company buildings, the plans for the new Roche Institute, which would be sequestered atop a hill overlooking the other buildings, were already with the architect.

Another promise made by Roche was that all new investigators assigned to the Institute would have sufficient funding to hire several post-doctoral fellows. Aaron had already hired his first, and asked if I would like to be his second. Since Aaron was extremely personable and had all the earmarks of an outstanding scientist, and the stipend being offered was twice that of most post-doctoral fellowships, this should have been a no-brainer. Why wasn't it? Aaron's virus of choice was reovirus. Not only was reovirus not a RNA tumor virus, it was not even associated with a human disease. In fact, the "o" in reo stood for "orphan" which meant it had no known link to human diseases.

After putting some actual thought into this decision, I finally concluded that since I didn't know any virology except that pertaining to bacteria viruses, I at least could learn the fundamentals of animal and human virology with Aaron. This experience could then jump start a career with RNA tumor viruses at my next stop. What I had not considered was that becoming an expert in another new area of virus research would likely require that I conduct a third post-doctoral fellowship at this mythical "next stop." In fact, the primary reason PhDs conduct post-doctoral research is to provide the training they need to perform their own research. I had also not considered that after having been a post-doctoral fellow in two institutions, I would feel the need to have a real job on my next stop. In addition, I would probably be considered a weak or indecisive scientist if it required three post-doctoral fellowships before I felt competent to conduct my own research. So all in all, a stop in New Jersey did not have the makings of a great career decision if I truly intended to make a career conducting RNA tumor virus research in my own lab. However, I made the decision to go there anyway.

Shirley and I left Munich in mid-May to continue our European tour before my stipend expired in July. After spending a day traveling through southern Germany and Switzerland, we arrived after dark at the base of the Matterhorn on a still very wintry night. The elevation at our port of call was above 10,000 feet, and the temperature hovered at just above 10 degrees. We had a couple of blankets, so I figured that to save money, we could just spend the night sleeping in our VW. After an abbreviated discussion with the other party involved that went something like, "you can stay in the car and freeze your butt. I'm checking into a hotel," my position was adjusted and we checked into a hotel. By morning, the temperature had dropped another 20 degrees. I may have learned something about bacterial viruses up to that point, but my general reasoning powers still needed work.

After the Matterhorn, we dropped back to sea level into the gorgeous town of Nice on the French Riviera where I had another chance to demonstrate my superior education. The jug of water provided at dinner in a quaint French restaurant looked harmless enough, but my personal advisor suggested we should stick with the wine. I was thirsty and ignored the advice; after all, we had already survived nearly a year in Europe drinking local waters. After continual and extended toilet visits during the days that followed, most of which were hole-in-the-floor, hit-it-if-you-can varieties, I conceded it was a mistake.

My ego was resurrected a few days later in Paris. We arrived in the midst of a typical student/police standoff with the usual shouting, stone throwing, and head hitting that I became familiar with during my days in Berkeley. After locating a hotel and a place to park our car, we strolled into the night, ending up at a movie being shown in a small theatre housed on a narrow, boxed-in side-street. When we stepped outside after the showing, we were greeted with a whistling, bang-bang sound that shot up the cobblestone street past our feet like a rocket.

My experience in Berkeley was worth something, and the sound of teargas canisters being projected toward demonstrators was instantly recognizable. It took only a glance to comprehend that the troops were on one end of the street, their tormentors were on the other end of the street, and we were in the middle of the street. I grabbed Shirley before either of us was decapitated, and retreated into the theatre, attempting to explain to the French attendant why we were back. By the time of our next attempt at a safe egress, the warring parties had moved to other quarters. This fun continued throughout our visit, sometimes on the street just outside our hotel where we had parked our almost new VW. Several cars were torched, but ours was not among the chosen. In spite of the local uprising that occurred during our time in Paris, it became our city of choice for a revisit. Furthermore, as we were leaving town, Shirley acknowledged my graduate school experience was worth something. I humbly conceded that our survival during the teargas attack may have been due to skill, but the fact that our car was still intact when we left was pure luck.

❧   ❧   ❧

A couple of days after leaving Paris, we dropped off our VW at a port in Northern Germany. Since delivery at the port in Newark, New Jersey, was not scheduled for another two weeks, we headed by train for Scandinavia to fill in the time. Our first stop was Copenhagen where we had booked a room. We picked up a map at the train station and noted that our hotel was on the same street. Before grabbing a cab, I checked the street numbers of where we were and that of our destination. We were at 9510 and we were only going to 9820. It couldn't be more than three blocks, so we could surely manage the 70+ pounds each of us was packing in our suitcases for that distance. We were quick studies, and after a few minutes on the trail realized that we were only at 9540. My attempt at being both macho and frugal won out this time, so we trudged on, resting our rapidly deteriorating arms about every 30 yards. After two miles, I understood the meaning of "my kingdom for a horse." At the three-mile mark, we sighted our destination and in another 15 minutes we were there. The entire journey took over two hours.

About a week later, we departed from Norway for New York's Kennedy Airport. Europe had been an educational experience, but we were ready for home. Because of angst about missing the plane, we arrived at the Oslo Airport at nine AM, about three hours before our scheduled departure time. On arrival, we were informed that our plane had not yet left New York. This wasn't a charter flight, but it appeared to be setting up like one. At five PM, it was finally rumored that our plane was in the air. It arrived around midnight and by two AM we were on our way. We arrived at Kennedy Airport in the dead of night as had become our pattern. Without a place to sleep, we hung out in the airport until the docks opened in Newark before attempting to retrieve our car. This scenario was like a rerun of our arrival in London a year earlier.

We eventually caught a cab from the airport that delivered us to the Newark docks where we were provided an early demonstration of things to come in our next home. We were told that if your car contained anything transportable, it would be lifted on the docks. However, we didn't think our car radio fell under that definition. Apparently, it did. It took the dock caretaker over 15 minutes to locate our vehicle in his stack of papers; there was a lot of page turning and hem-hawing going on the entire period, but we assumed this was the natural course of events. Only after we had lived in New Jersey for several months did we realize he was waiting for a bribe. I guess he finally assumed we were brain dead and led us to our car. As I said, everything movable, including the radio, was gone. No one had lifted the engine, however, so it was apparently our lucky day. We drove west into the setting sun, just thankful we had something to drive. Besides, I had nearly two months to burn before reporting for duty at Roche, and we were going to spend it on the road, this time seeing our native land.

It was a great summer of fun. We had no responsibilities and lots of time. It was an adventure that everyone needs to experience at least once before they are too old and decrepit to enjoy it. During the course of the summer, we eventually revisited Berkeley where all our worldly possessions, other than what we carried in our suitcases, had been stored in a friend's basement prior to leaving for Europe. It seemed like a simple enough matter to merely have them shipped to an address in New Jersey where we would retrieve them in a couple of weeks. The moving company arrived as planned, and off they went with 24 boxes containing almost all we owned, much of which we would never see again.

From Berkeley, we wound our way to Denver where we stayed with my high school friend Frank and his wife who were in the midst of the baby years, completely inundated with diapers and other paraphernalia. Frank was still a year from receiving his PhD in psychology at the University of Colorado, so they lived where most married students with children live, known universally as Married Student Housing. It is a period in life one just gets through if you can, especially when you are doing it as a student. At the time, Shirley and I had just decided it was our turn to have a child; the

Denver experience made us reevaluate. Having children, however, is something people just did in 1970. You really didn't ask whether you wanted children or not. In my case, it may have been the Catholic training that dulled that part of my brain. I don't know what Shirley's excuse was. Regardless, we ignored what we witnessed in Denver and stayed on course.

We arrived in Nutley in mid-August, taking up temporary residency in a Howard Johnson's Motel. At least the plan was for it to be temporary. Early the next morning we began our quest for a more permanent residence, accompanied by my mentor Aaron who had by then become somewhat acquainted with the local landscape. We were grateful for his efforts but realized sometime later that we should have hired a local guide, one that truly understood the local customs. We worked through newspaper ads as well as just scouring neighborhoods for signs of "Apartment for Rent. Inquire with Building Manager."

After multiple stops, it began to appear that there really were no apartments to rent in this part of the country. When confronted with our simple inquiry about the rental signs posted in front of their buildings, the managers would invariably go through the same general routine as the caretaker when we had picked up our car on the dock. They would be courteous, always suggesting that something might be available soon, but never committing that they really had an apartment at the moment. During these encounters, we never saw the inside of one apartment, not even an example of what might become available. Clearly, we had a lot to learn about local protocol. All we would have had to do was slip any one of these dupes $20 and our search would have been over. After nearly two weeks of futility, the Roche Institute personnel manager got word that a new apartment building was about to be opened for tenants in Belleville, the town located just south of my work site in Nutley. Although we later learned this building was Mafia-owned, at least they had the decency to list the fee to rent an apartment upfront. We were able to comprehend this set of rules.

Within minutes of making our multiple payments (finder's fee, first and last month's rent), we were in a new, one-bedroom apartment where we continued our life out of four suitcases. The boxes we shipped from Berkeley several weeks earlier were already well overdue. Thus, the next day and nearly every day thereafter, I was on the phone with our moving company futilely attempting to locate our belongings. On every call, I was assured that the boxes would be scheduled for delivery any day.

This game dragged on for more than a month, by which time we had filled our apartment with secondhand furniture. The location of our original belongings, however, continued to remain a mystery. We surmised that they had "fallen off the delivery truck" as things did in New Jersey. Finally, around midnight on a Sunday night after we were dead asleep, we received a call from a guy saying he would be delivering our boxes within the hour. Some of what he said actually came true. He was there within the hour and he had some of our boxes. After a few back-and-forth trips from van to apartment, the driver anxiously pushed a piece of paper under our noses to sign, verifying that the delivery was complete. I was so elated that we had anything that I neglected to count the boxes, and almost signed the paper. Fortunately, Shirley was still alert at one AM, and immediately noted that we were short by about 50 percent. When asked where the other boxes were, the driver had a patent comeback.

"Yeah, I thought I was a bit short, but these were all that were in the warehouse in Pittsburgh when I picked them up." He feigned that he had never actually counted them.

So we didn't sign anything that night, and instead, continued our phone war with the moving company. After another four months, we finally conceded that our missing possessions would never surface, and filed our loss. There was, of course, no way for us to recall many of the items that were missing; that would only come later, piece by piece as they were needed. So this should have been the time for us to become creative. Instead, we were still under the illusion that honesty was the best policy, and merely reported the items we could remember, never realizing they would reimburse only about 10 percent of their worth. Things such as jewelry, even the inexpensive types, were not covered at all. So there went my MSC "M" jacket, Shirley's charm bracelet that I had regularly contributed to over the past six years, several pieces of jewelry passed on from Shirley's grandmother who had died in 1965, 45 silver dollars that Shirley's now dead grandfather had given us as a wedding gift, and a large fraction of our other wedding presents. Our only recourse in the end was to swear we would never allow that particular moving company to touch another piece of our belongings. As life would have it, we weren't even able to make that threat hold up.

Shirley loves to talk, and manages to learn the life story of nearly every person she encounters. Thus, within days of moving into our Belleville apartment, she knew almost everyone in the 36-unit apartment building. Most were locals, including the manager's wife, Sandy, who was a cousin of the building's owner. The manager's job was to keep the inhabitants happy. Within minutes into their first meeting, Sandy volunteered that her family had connections, and offered Shirley the possibility of purchasing anything from food to TV sets at much reduced prices. When in her naivety, Shirley asked if Sandy's family owned department and grocery stores, the answer was a simple, "No, they just pick up items that have fallen off trucks." She failed to mention that our car radio and undelivered possessions probably fell into that category. Another neighbor offered her services if we had any trouble with the law. For example, if we received any citation, such as a speeding or parking ticket, she had a cousin who would have it fixed. That is, if it was issued anywhere except in West Orange. That was the Jewish area, and his connections there were limited.

Our neighborhood was a zoning nightmare with apartments, houses and businesses all intermixed. Directly across the street was a nightclub that appeared to be rather exclusive, but also never seemed to have much by way of clientele. We seldom ate out due to our limited budget, especially at expensive places, but decided to treat ourselves to an evening at the club on my birthday. It was Saturday, but even though the place was elegantly decorated, it had almost no customers. During dinner, the person manning the bar, which was located within earshot of our table, became engaged with his one customer in a slowly heating discussion. As the volumes of their voices rose, it became evident that the primary topic had something to do with "territory" and who owned what. Threats were issued from each side, and the customer left with the parting shot of "my family knows your family, so I'll be back." Our appetites dissipated immediately, and dessert was the last thing on our minds. We were out of there before the sound of the other customer's footsteps had cleared the parking lot. The situation must have gotten resolved, or the war was relocated, because the building was still intact when we left town almost two years later.

Shirley became an adopted member of the local "families," and we were invited to all the serious happenings. One was the baptism of Sandy's first child, a momentous event in that part of the world. We weren't actually invited to the baptism itself, but we did get an invitation to the reception later that evening. This turned out to be a dinner for nearly 300 people held in a very expensive Italian restaurant. It was unclear how this affair was being financed because Sandy was not employed and her husband was a runner on the stock exchange, not exactly a lucrative profession. Toward the end of the evening, the mystery was solved when Sandy's cousin, the owner of our building and the child's godfather, made his appearance. He was about 60 years old and was dressed in a black shirt with a white tie and sports coat, and a black hat which he wore tipped slightly down and to the side. As he entered, it was like the Pope had arrived. Nearly half the room rose in unison and climbed over one another to shake the man's hand or kiss his cheek. The most ironic part of the evening came the following day when guests who ate the meatballs developed diarrhea. Sometimes it is difficult to control what goes on in the kitchen, even in the finest restaurants.

ॐ   ॐ   ॐ

The other part of my life in New Jersey was again supposed to be related to work. Roche did as they promised and, within a year of my arrival, had erected what was to become one of the most impressive research centers for molecular biology for the next two decades. It was also a post-doc factory as nearly 70 percent of the Institute's inhabitants fit that description. We all had the same mission: to gain sufficient credibility within the research community during our two-year tenures to be able to support research careers of our own when we left. "Support" means just what it says, i.e. get the money. In spite of the potential for secretiveness and jealousy in this type of setting, the atmosphere of the Institute was one of true congeniality. I made more good friends during my stay there than in all the years before or since. It also didn't hurt that Aaron was probably the best-liked and most trusted staff member in the Institute.

My project, as it evolved, was to determine how the gene segments for reovirus get assembled within the virus particle. The genes for most viruses, whether they attack a bacterium or human cell, are contained in a single molecule of DNA or RNA, but this is not true for viruses that belong to the Reoviridae family. The genes for reovirus itself, the original member of this family, are composed of ten segments of double-stranded RNA, and each gene segment encodes the information for at least one protein. The virus needs all of its encoded proteins to replicate after it infects a cell, so all ten RNA segments must be assembled into new virus particles during reovirus replication within the infected cell. Since the segments are not linked in any recognizable way, it was unclear how only the correct ten were assembled into the mature virus particles.

After spending two years trying to unravel this mystery, I walked away having contributed little lasting information on the topic. Perhaps it was a bit of a hard nut to crack because even today, it has not been determined how this happens. This lack of knowledge also applies to other members of the Reoviridae family including one called rotavirus that is responsible for over 500,000 deaths in young children each year. Although my research results with reovirus were not of great scientific worth, the experience did provide a fundamental understanding of this virus family which I capitalized on many years later when my attention became diverted into studies with rotavirus.

One of the most prestigious meetings within the virology community is held during each summer in one of several boarding schools in New England. Aaron, my mentor at Roche, was only in his mid-30s when I joined his group, but his reputation as a scientist was already established. This qualified him as a member of the club who would be invited to present their latest laboratory discoveries at this annual meeting. When meeting time rolled around during my second year at Roche, Aaron suggested that I present that year in his place. The significance of this honor only began to dawn on me when I arrived at the meeting site and was exposed to the remarkable accomplishments of its attendees, me being the exception. This significance has been enhanced with the passing years as many of those attending became members of the US National Academy of Sciences, and at least two became Nobel Laureates. Aaron had given me an opportunity to build on for a lifetime if I could have used it that way. Maybe I eventually did, but only after taking my career into several dead ends.

Although my discoveries while in Aaron's lab did not alter the course of science, I did come away with my name on three respectable manuscripts, and was the leading author on one. Armed with both experience in animal virology and my name on published papers on the topic, I set about trying to locate a more permanent home in a respectable university where I could learn about RNA tumor viruses, soon to be known as retroviruses, and be an independent faculty member at the same time. Little did I know that I had almost no chance of attaining both of these goals in the same institution, something that I was about to learn.

While still in Europe, I had written multiple self-invitation letters to universities scattered throughout Western America to alert them to the fact that I would be traveling through their vicinity during the following summer, and to offer a seminar presentation of my phage work. What I was really attempting to do was to interest someone in offering me a job after my time in New Jersey. As I said, my focus was strictly Western America. That was still my comfort zone. I received several invitations to present my story, but no place gave me even remote hope they were interested in having me join their faculty. In fact, only one university even sent me a response letter after my visit, saying "we are not interested in hiring a molecular geneticist at this time." I didn't even know I was one.

When the search for more permanent employment was renewed in earnest during my second year at Roche, I applied for jobs based mostly on announcements published in magazines, but sometimes followed up on the tips of friends or family members. One of the more unusual tips was from my sister Gen who lived near Austin, Minnesota, the home of Hormel, the maker of canned meats. I can't remember the exact description of the job that was planned for me at Hormel when I applied, but I do remember the salary suggested was well below poverty level. My mentor Aaron asked if they would also "throw in all the Spam you can eat."

Another response in my search came in the form of a phone call from a loud and boisterous individual who claimed he had been a Naval Officer, but had since started a university in Florida and was now its President. At the time of his call, he said "I am living on a boat which is part of the university campus, and have a multitude of gorgeous women on board." I assumed he really had been in the Navy because he kept repeating "you need to come aboard." I never understood whether I was being invited to board his boat with the women or to join the faculty.

Both of these job opportunities came early in my search, so I still had hope of landing the ideal job. My first interview was at the University of Kansas in Lawrence, and by the end of the interview, I knew I had blown it. The Chair of the Department of Microbiology was my tour director, but he didn't do the actual driving. He parked me in the front passenger seat and had some random student drive the car as he lounged across the rear seat, only rarely surfacing to observe where the student was even taking us. As he rested, he complained incessantly about the brain dead applicants he had already interviewed for the job. His under-the-seat chatter was a bit unnerving, especially since this was my first real job interview.

While visiting Lawrence, I interviewed with all microbiology faculty members and listened intently as each excitedly replayed their lab experiences. My own knowledge was still quite limited, so most of what I heard was novel to me. One project involved the use of bacteria that produced enzymes whose jobs were to destroy foreign DNA molecules by making chops at specific sites. These sites varied depending on the bacterium from which the enzymes were obtained, but they never chopped the DNA of their host bacterium. It appeared to be a method to gain an advantage over competitors, literally cutting them off at the pass. It was a neat mechanism, but neither the investigator nor I had any notion that these same enzymes would serve to revolutionize molecular biology within the next two years. The Kansas investigator was sitting on a scientific goldmine but didn't know how to dig. Several of those who did know how were awarded Nobel Prizes for their discoveries a few years later.

The quickest way to blow an interview is to be disgustingly honest. As I was leaving, the Chairperson, who was upright by this time, inquired about my degree of interest in the job. I was both naïve and stupid, so I answered, "This is my first interview. I need to have more in order to draw comparisons." Within a week, I received my rejection letter.

Two weeks after the Kansas experience, Shirley and I drove to Brown University in Rhode Island, where I had my only Ivy League experience. The interview started badly and got worse. Within an hour after Shirley had deposited me on the doorstep of the university, I was hunted down by the Chairperson's secretary who informed me that my wife had been in a car accident. After the dust settled, the story unfolded that she had missed seeing an oncoming vehicle when entering a main highway. Our VW was whacked by a car twice its size, apparently with little damage to the hitter, but a lot to our VW. However, no one was hurt, and our car was still drivable.

After receiving this bit of news, I began my interview process. This was the only place I interviewed where multiple appointments were ignored; I sat staring at the back of the head of the Chairperson's secretary for more time during those two days than I spent interviewing. Shirley and I were on our own for dinner both evenings, the excuse being that all Department faculty members had prior commitments. By the time my seminar presentation began at one PM on the second day, I was beyond mere anger. The final insult occurred when I was about half way through my presentation. I was in the midst of making some major point about my results when I called for the clincher slide. Nothing happened. I called for it again and still nothing happened. On the third call, which was more like a shout, I got my slide. The projectionist, who was one of the few faculty members I had actually talked with, had gone dead asleep. That is usually tough to do as a projectionist. Apparently my research was not his area of interest. After we left with our broken car, I never heard from Brown University again, nor did I want to.

My next stop was the University of Michigan in Ann Arbor. I arrived in early February, took one look around, and assumed I was back in Montana. The snow was several feet high where it hadn't been touched, so where it was plowed it had produced small mountains. School was open, however, and for the locals, it was life as usual. It really was like Montana. After my sham interview at Brown University, where it was apparent that they weren't really hiring new faculty, I thought I might as well determine if this was true at Michigan as well. It could take some of the heat off me during the interview process if they weren't, and I might as well know this from the beginning. I never made that mistake again. When I stated my question to the Department Chairperson soon after my arrival, he assured me there really was a position. However, he also explained that they had other applicants and one was a "very impressive Harvard graduate" who had been there the previous week. That was more than I wanted to know. Now I really was under pressure to perform.

In spite of this introduction, the interview process went normally and the various investigators all showed up at their appointed times. But one can easily guess who got the job. The final rejection came several weeks later via a phone call made only after I had left several messages inquiring about my status. The Chairperson merely said "no one had much interest in you." For my own self-respect, I rationalized that their disinterest was in reovirus and not in me.

Next I was off to Denver to interview at the Medical School for the University of Colorado. In my mind, this was the best of the job possibilities because it was in the Mountain West. But, once again, there was no job offer. The faculty members were all gracious, much like those in Michigan and Kansas, but the existence of a job mimicked the Brown University situation. They needed a spot to fill on their list of invited speakers and I happened to wander in on cue. After my departure, the Chairperson never felt the need to inform me of any decision; I guess he assumed I would eventually figure it out. This time I was truly disappointed, and after this fourth failure, my worry wagon was kicked into high gear. I only had two more interviews lined up, so something had to give soon.

The first of these last two interviews was in the Medical School at UCLA. My impression of Los Angeles, up to that time, was less than favorable even though I loved the Bay Area to the north. I had visited LA only once during my time at Berkeley, and came away feeling that the combination of smog and traffic were incompatible with human life.

I arrived at the Greater Los Angeles Airport quite late at night and was beginning to doze off during my trip from airport to hotel when my escort, a junior faculty member, began to describe the pastimes he enjoyed most. On the top of the list was fart-lighting. He swore his group of party animals would regularly challenge one another to determine who could shoot out the longest flame. Apparently, the contestants would strip to their briefs, then bend over and release their best farts while a colleague held a lighted match behind their anuses. The fireballs created by the top combatants were measured in feet and not inches. It had to be spectacular. My guide was certainly pumped about the whole affair. I inquired about the "burn factor" and he assured me the briefs they wore minimized it. My imagination soared when I envisioned what might have happened if the briefs had been removed. This was my introduction to science at UCLA.

My communications prior to this interview were not with the Department Chairperson, but instead, I was contacted by a faculty member who was seeking a junior investigator to work in his lab on projects concerning herpes viruses. My hand didn't fit that glove, but by then I was prepared to force it in anyway. At the end of the interview, I was not offered a true faculty position supported by university "hard" monies, but instead was offered a "soft" money position supported mainly by grants awarded to the person who had issued the invitation. At least I had an offer.

I left LA not really liking what I was being offered, but not really disliking it either. The job certainly had nothing to do with retroviruses and it wasn't an independent position. At this point, I wished I had been more pro-active with the folks in Kansas, saying something subtle like, "I'll take the job in a heartbeat if you offer it to me." But that was water over the dam.

I had one last stop on the interview circuit, and could approach this one with the confidence that I at least had an offer in hand. This last was in the Cell Biology Department of the University of Kentucky in Lexington. The Medical School there had several excellent departments but Cell Biology was not among them. There were eight faculty members besides the Chairperson and four had just been asked to leave. This was not a good sign. The unattractiveness of the situation was heightened by the less than impressive credentials among the remaining members of the Department.

The Department Chairperson behaved like I probably had in my previous interviews, i.e. desperate. He never let me out of his sight except to sleep. When I interviewed with the various faculty members, he was there to run interference. His presence insured that no one slipped in anything negative during our conversations, even though there was ample room for it. I could have handled negative comments more easily than knowing they were being suppressed. The Chairperson also had the nasty habit of lighting one cigarette off another, so much so that his smoke-screened body often seemed to be headless. The whole experience was like attending a second tier spook show. Two days of that were enough. As I was running out the door, the Chairperson's final bit of encouragement was, "I will bet you that I have all four departing faculty replaced within a month." I never took the bet, so am unaware of the outcome. I received a good offer, but was never tempted to look back. So, by process of elimination, my next stop would be Los Angeles.

New Jersey had a lot of positives, but the finest came two months before our departure. As already noted, even experiencing the full drama of the baby years when we visited my friend Frank and his wife in Denver did not dissuade us from trying to have a child ourselves. By the summer of 1971, when we were on our annual trek to Montana, we had been in this mode for well over a year without results. While there, a short article was published in the Bozeman paper that described four Northern Cheyenne Indian children, ages one-six, whose parents had just been killed in a head-on car accident. Fortunately, the kids were not in the car. Shirley's inability to get pregnant combined with our residual '60's idealism prompted us to investigate whether the kids could be adopted. The answer, which may have saved us years of turmoil, was a definite "No, the tribe will take care of its own." One wonders where life would have taken us had we received a different response.

One month later, Shirley began regular vomiting and it didn't let up. She wasn't deathly ill, but she was always just sick. After several weeks of this, she located a physician who pronounced her pregnant. We were a long distance from biological grandparents, but both our neighbors in Little Italy and my lab associates were superb surrogates. It was an unusual day when one of us did not receive advice on proper prenatal care. While at work during the month preceding the birth, at least one person besides me was posted within hearing distance of my phone. My co-workers even staggered their lunch schedules without me realizing it.

During a scheduled visit on the day before her due date, Shirley was assured by her physician that she would deliver that night. It was one very long night, associated with nothing that remotely resembled childbirth. One week later, Shirley again visited her physician and received the same pronouncement, but this time with some caveats. However, the caveats weren't necessary. At about nine PM that evening the contractions started.

Shirley comes from tough stock and had long since resolved that this baby would be delivered naturally without medication. She had also resolved that she was not in this alone and that I was going to be present at all times during the birth process. Presence of a father during birth was rare in 1972, and was generally discouraged by most parties involved. However, Shirley had hooked up with an obstetrician who not only allowed it, but encouraged it. Thus, we had enrolled in Lamaze classes, and I had diligently learned all the breathing techniques. I had also paid close attention to the advice of "don't go to the hospital too soon. You will likely just be hanging out there for at least a full day if you do." Thus, when the contractions began, I was still listening to our instructors, in spite of Shirley's suggestions that we start getting the car packed. Things progressed as we were told they would, and by two AM, Shirley was becoming quite uncomfortable, but the contractions were still about five minutes apart. We were told to stay home until they were less than two minutes apart. We hung in there for another couple of hours until Shirley had had enough. It's a good thing that we lived only five minutes from the hospital.

We arrived at five AM, and Shirley was in the labor room only long enough to determine she was dilated eight centimeters before being wheeled to the delivery room to begin pushing. I was one step ahead of her, following my Lamaze instructions to a tee. They had said to bring a boatload of items to sustain all parties during the labor process. Amongst these were pillows which they said to bring into the delivery room for the mother's comfort as well. At least that is what I heard. So I burst into the delivery room with three in tow, followed closely by Shirley on a gurney. After my first step inside the room, I was met by the largest woman I had seen before or since, and she was truly enraged. She ordered me to "leave instantly and take your damn pillows with you. This room was sterile, you idiot, and you just broke the barrier." There seemed to be no room for compromise, and I certainly was not in a bargaining position. As I was fleeing, the doctor grabbed my collar and stepped between me and the monolith. Her eyes were spitting fire, but he still ruled and I remained. He assured her I would behave, and might even be of some use. She muttered something about "that will be the day," but gave way, even though she towered over the doctor and tripled his weight.

The birth progressed rapidly and on June 23 at 6:02 AM we had a new baby boy. It was not the custom to have the mother hold their baby immediately after birth in those days, so Christopher Corey was toted off to another part of the room for various rituals. At one point, Shirley looked over at him and gasped, saying "he must be dying; his feet are black". That was when I made my one contribution. Before she stroked out, I assured her that they had just gotten his foot prints. I was at least paying some attention.

After that, Christopher was taken away, Shirley was wheeled into the hallway, and I was ordered to the waiting room until further notice. The big nurse was in charge again. This ended the saga of the birth of our first child. We had gotten to the hospital on time, I wasn't scalped by the delivery room nurse, and both mother and child were healthy.

ȣ ȣ ȣ

At this time in our lives, I was still adhering to the dictates of the Catholic Church, among which is the command to attend Mass every Sunday. I had been dutiful, and had found a church not far from our apartment where the priests provided some reasonable messages. Thus, shortly after Christopher's birth, I approached one of the clergy at the end of Mass with a simple inquiry about having him baptized. The answer received was anything but simple. The priest first asked whether I was a member of the parish. I assumed I was since I had been attending Mass there for nearly two years. However, that was not sufficient qualification. The priest then asked where I lived. Once he had my address, he informed me that I belonged to another parish and shouldn't have been attending his church at all. I had, up to that point, assumed that the Catholic Church was universal, as I had been taught by the nuns in grade school, and that Catholics at least were welcome in any Catholic church. At first I was just surprised; then I was angry.

I repeated this conversation to my brother-in-law Jim, the ex-priest, who suggested that these events provided a unique opportunity rarely pursued by today's Catholics. He explained that in the early days of Christianity, it was the duty and privilege of the baby's father to perform the baptism, a practice that was still permitted if not often carried out. I decided it was the time to become an early Christian. So I performed the baptism with Jim and my sister Rose Marie as witnesses. I think this event marked the beginning of my easing away from the Catholic Church.

ȣ ȣ ȣ

After our bitter battle with the company that moved our belongings and the belief that all moving companies are probably the same, at least in New Jersey, where items routinely fell off trucks, we decided to self-transport our household belongings to California. This was to be an arduous journey since Los Angeles was the most distant point from New Jersey in the contiguous 48 states. I rented a massive truck to transport our belongings and Shirley's mother came from Montana to accompany Shirley and Christopher in the car. On picking up the truck, I was aware that the steering was a bit tight and reported this to the rental agent. His comment was something about "it will warm up." This seemed a bit optimistic since the temperature outside was already over 90 degrees, but our bags were packed, our helpers were already at the apartment, and our lease period was over. It turns out that not only was the power steering not working, but the steering was much tighter than in a normal truck without power steering. Driving it 3,300 miles across the USA provided a unique opportunity to develop my upper body strength.

On a very hot and humid afternoon in August, we again headed west, this time fully loaded, me struggling with an infirm truck, and Shirley with her mother and Christopher in our non-air-conditioned VW. Two hours into the trip, just after making our first baby-feeding stop, we somehow got separated. I thought I was ahead, and slowed down to allow the others to catch up. They were nowhere in sight. I slowed more and, after another 20 minutes, finally stopped and waited beside the road. This was in the day before cell phones, and we had made no arrangements for this set of circumstances. I waited and waited, thinking that maybe we could both make contact through Shirley's father who was still in Montana, if we could ever track him down. After nearly a lifetime, they finally showed up, saying they had taken a wrong turn. After that, we developed a contingency plan.

When traveling across country with our first new baby, the obvious scenario was to show him off to everyone, whether they were located anywhere near our normal route or not. What is an extra 600 miles if you are already going 2,700? By the third night, we finally made it as far a Minnesota, the home of two of my sisters. This was not out of the way since we were going to Montana anyway. By then we realized we had caught a lucky break for the trip. At two months of age, Christopher was essentially a perfect baby. He slept multiple times during the day, and since no law required he be kept in a car seat, he did so in a prone position in a stroller carriage top. At other times he was merely held. At night he went to sleep when we did, and woke when we did. He only cried during the day when he got really hungry before Shirley could get off the road to breast feed him.

We eventually wound our way to my parent's home in Bozeman. By then, we had been on the road for five days and were 600 miles off course. This impressed my parents about as much as meeting their 41st grandchild. The only comment from either came from my mother who pronounced, "He doesn't look like a Ward." I was wondering why we had bothered to make the trip. When my father died nine months later, I was thankful he at least saw his youngest grandson. I think he appreciated it, but as with other personal things, was unable to express it.

Eight days after we left New Jersey, our little caravan crept into smog-laden LA. It was time to begin another chapter in our lives.

11 Staying Above Water in LA

After years of precise analyses, I finally deciphered how titles for PhDs, at least in the sciences, are determined in American universities. The simple answer is "money." If you have your own supply procured through grants or the like, or the university decides to pay you for your contribution as a teacher, you are sometimes honored with a tenure track position. Even that isn't always a certainty. What is certain is that if you don't have money from some source other than a mentor, you will not be on a tenure track. For a PhD who conducts laboratory research, this is usually designated as the research track. The biggest discrepancy between the two tracks is independence, something that is at the heart of every PhD's agenda when they step into a university lab. You either conduct your own research or that of someone else.

I had hoped to obtain a tenure track slot when I left Roche, but the only offer was from a Department in distress at the University of Kentucky. Thus, I had settled for the research track position offered at UCLA. This might explain why the satisfaction I felt with my job choice was below par even before I drove into LA. My new mentor was to be my primary source of support, and the funds would be siphoned from his research cache. I did have one-third of my salary paid by the university, probably to provide me with hope that I would eventually be bumped to the tenure track, but that was the limit of their responsibility. Thus, in reality, I worked for my new mentor and not the university.

Prior to my arrival in LA, my new mentor generously provided a house-hunting trip at his expense. Before making the trip, Shirley and I had decided not to buy a house – at least not until we lived in Los Angeles for sufficient time to get some feel for the area. There was also the legitimate concern that my already bad attitude about my new position would deteriorate further with time, and our stay in LA would be of short duration. Under most circumstances, it would have been a logical choice. However, this was the time of a booming housing market in LA, and had we purchased a house at the time of our arrival, it would have made a better salary than I did during our stay. Since this was something that could not have been foreseen, my mission was to rent an acceptable apartment near the UCLA campus.

Having lived in Little Italy for the past two years, I had forgotten that everyone did not love children. Thus, it was a shock to realize that in most apartment buildings within a two-mile radius of the UCLA campus, no children were allowed. Interestingly, there were generally no such restrictions on pets. So even though the area around UCLA had ample, affordable apartments, only a few permitted children. Thus, it required a full three-day search to locate something "acceptable near the university."

"Near" to me meant within biking distance; we had only one car and it would need to remain available to Shirley and her new companion. In the end, I visited with more building managers than I had in New Jersey but, for a totally different reason, the availability of apartments was just as scarce. At least this time, no under-the-table passing of money was expected; they just didn't allow children. I finally settled on a small but respectable upstairs apartment in a house occupied by its owners. I seemed to be doing a lot of settling before this venture even got off the ground.

One of the typical perks of university living is its community. It is generally accepted that university faculty members don't get paid much, but they have companionship to compensate for their low salaries. They often live near one another in communities situated within walking distance of their campuses and are, thereby, professionally as well as socially intertwined with their neighbors. Such universities are viewed by some, at least from a distance, as little utopias. This was not UCLA.

Few UCLA faculty members could afford to live anywhere near the campus in Westwood, nestled within the most expensive part of West LA between Brentwood and Beverly Hills. As a result, their homes were scattered over at least a 50-mile radius. This was not conducive to the development of close social relationships with others on the staff, especially for a junior faculty member who wasn't really even that. These were also the baby years for Shirley and me, and they were being played out in a locale that didn't take kindly to babies. I felt I had placed my family on an island in a huge archipelago without a boat.

The apartment I had rented was within biking distance of UCLA as I had planned, and the campus could be accessed during normal hours, mostly via side streets and a path through the Veteran's cemetery. However, the gates into the cemetery were locked early in the afternoon, blocking my route when I headed for home many hours later. Thus, on my daily return trip, I would metamorphose into a nearly invisible streak as I pedaled for my life in the dark down the outside lane of eight-lane Wilshire Avenue, attempting not to be converted into road kill by the commuters as they sped toward the freeway ramp. There were no bike lanes or sidewalks, so it was just me and the cars. I somehow survived. I remember it being predicted during my time at UCLA that the next major breakthrough in the biological sciences would be accomplished, not by one of the factories of science, but by a lone university investigator riding to work each day on his three-speed bicycle. Mine was a five-speed, so I wouldn't have qualified.

The weather in LA was fantastic and the lab in which I worked was built to capture the essence of this fact. It was located in the Reed Neurological Institute, a glass plated, six-story building attached to the west side of the massive medical school complex. Because of its location and wall of windows, I was provided a daily panoramic view of the setting sun. Physically it was an ideal place to work. Psychologically something was missing.

In order to work in this Institute, one was required to study a disease or disease agent associated with the nervous system. My mentor had chosen herpes viruses for his research, and since I worked for him, that would be my choice as well. Knowing in advance that this would be the arrangement, I had spent most of the last two months before my arrival in the library at Roche attempting to come up to speed on the topic. In addition, Roche had generously paid my way to the annual Herpes Virus Workshop, which that year was held a short distance away at Cold Spring Harbor on Long Island.

This introduction to the herpes virus community was an eye-opener. My observations were that socialization was not the overall strong suit of this group, and personal recognition at almost any cost was more the order of the day. The latter was often not accomplished as much through the presentation of sound data as by repetitive interruption of other speakers, shouting down anyone who dared disagree. I had previously witnessed only brief outbursts of this behavior, even though I had rubbed shoulders with many internationally known scientists and heard them present their experimental findings in high-visibility meetings. A steady four-day diet of these confrontations was rather discomforting, especially knowing I was about to become part of this action.

During my days in the Roche library, I had deciphered that little was known about the methods employed by herpes viruses to control their own reproduction in an infected cell. This was surprising since herpes viruses had been popular research targets for some time, and substantial information was available on this topic for other large DNA viruses. With this knowledge in hand, I entered my new lab with the rudiments of what was to become my primary research project.

A short time after beginning my job in Los Angeles, I was requested to participate in another project in addition to the herpes virus work. My new mentor had just embarked with a UCLA colleague on experiments to determine the nature of the agent responsible for scrapie, a disease of the nervous system found primarily in sheep. Once an animal was infected with the agent, scrapie was invariably fatal. The colleague was an expert in scrapie research but had little biochemical knowledge. Hence, he needed my mentor, and hence, my mentor needed me.

Scrapie agent belongs to a group classified as "slow viruses," primarily because their presence leads to the slow but steady neurological degeneration of their hosts. Human counterparts are Creutzfeldt-Jakob disease, kuru, and mad cow disease. Kuru is especially interesting. It was a disease endemic among the Fore tribe of Papua New Guinea who ate their dead relatives in order to return the life forces of the deceased to their hamlets. Women and children contracted the disease more frequently than men who consumed the choice cuts and left the residual to the others. This included the brains of the deceased where the disease agent was concentrated.

Based on certain of its properties, such as its resistance to heat and other physical stresses, it had been suggested that the scrapie agent might be composed solely of infectious nucleic acid (RNA) as had recently been determined for the agent responsible for potato spindle tuber disease. If scrapie agent was, in fact, a viroid as the potato pathogen was called, it would be expected to remain infectious when extracted by a process used to release nucleic acids intact from biological samples. My job was to perform the extractions. The extracted material was then inoculated into mouse brains, and the mice were monitored for development of neurological disease six months later. This study provided a full understanding of the name "slow viruses." The end result of our seemingly endless experiment was that the extracted material did not produce scrapie, indicating that scrapie is not a viroid, a conclusion that we subsequently published.

Shortly after our finding appeared in print, I received a phone call from an investigator at Stanford University who identified himself as Stan Prusiner. I had never heard of him, but he said he was interested in my work with scrapie and invited me to present my results at Stanford. I declined his offer with the explanation that "I have published everything I have learned, so I don't think I have anything to add. This was a one shot project and my efforts are now being concentrated on herpes viruses." Nineteen years after this phone conversation, Stanley Prusiner was awarded a Nobel Prize in Medicine for the discovery of prions, the infectious proteins responsible for incurable degenerative neurological illnesses such as mad cow disease and scrapie. Maybe I should have accepted his invitation and ditched the herpes virus project.

I blasted into herpes virus studies with the optimism that I would make a significant contribution to the field. Herpes viruses were not retroviruses, but there were reports suggesting they might cause some form of cancer, particularly cervical cancer. That suggestion never became a reality; in fact, another group called human papilloma viruses were later found to be the cause of cervical cancer. Regardless, in 1973, I had hope that I was working with viruses that caused cancer, a topic which I planned as the target of my research since graduate school. I also had the satisfaction of knowing that even if the cancer connection was never established, herpes viruses were at least established causes of multiple human diseases. That was an improvement over reovirus.

From the day I walked into the lab at UCLA, my time was mostly spent in scientific isolation. Maybe it was a personality defect on my part, but I always had the impression that others in the lab had little interest in what I was trying to accomplish. I rarely even talked with my mentor about an experiment. The laboratories and offices controlled by my mentor were occupied by a somewhat random group of investigators, from lab assistants to PhD students to visiting scientists. However, all were attached to my mentor and his research. No one had much understanding of, and little interest in molecular control mechanisms. I didn't even have a lab assistant with whom to discuss ideas and plan experiments. This was in contrast to previous positions I had occupied where experiments were typically discussed ad infinitum before a test tube was touched. Thus, even in a crowd, life can be lonely.

After about a year of day and night work, I discovered that herpes viruses behaved much like other large DNA viruses. That is, certain viral proteins are produced only minutes after the virus infects a cell while the production of others is delayed for hours. This regulatory mechanism was used by the virus to conserve its resources and those of the infected cell. I was about to prepare my discovery for publication when my mentor returned from a herpes meeting with less than encouraging news. He reported that I was about to get scooped again.

This news presented another opportunity to regroup and move on, drawing on the competitive spirit I felt many years before when being benched during basketball games. Thus, I set out to finish the experiments I had started and publish the results, even with the knowledge that a competitor was about to publish similar findings. If nothing else, I was still persistent.

By this time in my career, I had written several papers, but each was judiciously revised by my various prior mentors without overtly calling to my attention that I was a lousy writer. My new mentor was not so merciful. I was under the illusion that I had done a decent job of preparing a draft manuscript of my results, but that thought was scuttled with one swing of my mentor's ax.

"You have no beginning or ending to any of your sections. And there is no story here. I don't even know what points you are trying to make." He was right. Even though it was discouraging, his comments did stimulate an improvement in my science writing.

Before I submitted my manuscript, my competitor's paper was in print. There still could have been a place for my story if it had something extra to add. It really didn't. In fact, the methods used in the published work were so vastly superior to mine, and the conclusions were so much better defined, I felt I had been operating sometime in the last Ice Age. Perhaps I had been working alone too long. Eventually, I uncovered and published several features of herpes virus replication that had not already been reported, so all was not lost.

હ હ હ

In early May of our first year in LA, Shirley renewed her regular bouts with morning sickness. By this time, Christopher was a proficient walker and would doggedly follow Shirley to her designated position in front of the toilet. To put an end to this, Christopher would forcefully attempt to drop the toilet seat on Shirley's head as the process was being played out, day after day. None of us thought this would ever end. But it did. Stephanie Jill was finally delivered in St John's Hospital, Santa Monica, at 5:14 AM on February 3, 1974. Even though I was present throughout, this time I didn't tick off the delivery room staff.

In less than one hour after the delivery, I was heading home. My dad had died nine months earlier and my lonely mother, who was 75 years old and quite slow of foot, had come to "help" us. In spite of her lack of speed, she was the one left in charge of Christopher who was minutes from awakening when Stephanie emerged into the world. Once that happened, the only hope was that my mother could keep the doors locked and somehow not let Christopher escape. I knew he could open any lock in any door and would be gone in the blink of an eye. Once he was outside, my mother had no chance.

By this time, we had moved to a small rental house with an oversized back yard filled with great climbing trees. When left to his own devices for a short time, Christopher had shinnied up one of these trees and onto the roof of the adjacent garage. The roof on the end of the garage where he entered was only a few feet off the ground, but the other end, where Christopher was perched when Shirley located him, was two stories above the concrete driveway. She talked him into retracing his steps, but the lump in her throat that developed as a result of her suppressed scream took weeks to dissipate. Another time, Christopher escaped out the massive back gate of our yard into the adjoining alley. Somehow he had squeezed around the gate and was nearly a block away before he was captured. This explains why I so quickly deserted one part of my family in favor of another the morning of Stephanie's birth.

࿇   ࿇   ࿇

When I began seeking a "real job" at a university after two stints as a post-doctoral fellow, my assumption was that I would be able to land a respectable tenure track position in one of the better universities. This was unrealistic in light of the fact that I had been studying human viruses for less than two years, and the discoveries I had made with one of those viruses (reovirus) when I began the job interview process were not exactly earth-shaking. Still it was a disappointment when my only reasonable job offer again entailed working for someone else. Once at UCLA, however, I was allowed almost complete independence, but instead of using it to spread my wings, I relegated myself to a form of scientific isolation. My goal before beginning this little adventure had been to study retroviruses and one of faculty members in our Department was an established investigator in that field. If I had an ounce of foresight, I would have learned the system from him and utilized this experience to launch a research career with retroviruses. I ignored this opportunity and, instead, kept my eyes focused on the negatives, such as the fact that another junior investigator, whom I viewed to have similar credentials to my own when I came to UCLA, had been awarded a tenure track position in our Department just before my arrival. Somehow, I felt I had been rejected, and this feeling was continually fueled by my self-generated scientific isolation. However, the distaste I had for my job was due to more than this.

During my first year at UCLA, I gradually began to comprehend what was required of a junior faculty member at a prestigious university. It was assumed that you would be an outstanding teacher of at least two courses per year, conduct cutting edge research, obtain full funding for this research through grants, publish manuscripts on this research in the most prestigious journals, review submitted manuscripts and grant proposals of other investigators, hire, direct and support several laboratory assistants, graduate students and post-doctoral fellows, and be both a member of and leader in several university committees. All this was to occur while attempting to be a decent father and husband. I began to wonder why anyone in their right mind would willingly choose this lifestyle. It seemed like it would have been easier to breathe under water without an oxygen tank than accomplish all that was expected of an Assistant Professor on a tenure track in a major university.

In spite of escalating discontent with my choice of a career, I still began negotiating for a tenure track position at UCLA, hoping that my perceptions of the life of an Assistant Professor were not entirely accurate. This process had been going on for several months by the time Stephanie was born. On the day she was brought home from the hospital, I received an urgent message from my mentor saying he needed to see me immediately. From the tone of his voice, I knew it wasn't good news. So up I went to the laboratory, prepared for the worst on what should have been one of the happiest days of my life.

The topic of the meeting was a message my mentor had been delivered concerning a presentation I had made to the graduate students in our Department. By this time in my negotiations for a tenure track position, I had already presented my results as a formal seminar in the College of Medicine. Because my tenure-track position was to be potentially managed through the College of Dentistry rather than the College of Medicine, I had also presented a formal seminar in that College to a group housed in the same complex as the medical school. After these two dog-and-pony shows, I was told I also was required to meet with the graduate students to inform them of my research plans, but that it was to occur during their lunch break and would be strictly informal. Somehow "informal" to me meant informal, like I would casually discuss with them my past research and future plans while they gobbled their sandwiches. Apparently, I insulted them by not making a third formal presentation, and they voted unanimously that I not be hired for a tenure-track position in the College of Medicine. This was to have important implications.

Because of my concerns that I would not be offered a tenure track position at UCLA, I had already begun seeking employment elsewhere by the beginning of my second year in Los Angeles. My first stop was at Texas Tech University in Lubbock. The Chairperson of Microbiology met me at the airport, and during my first hours in town, provided the grand tour. Later that evening, we were joined for dinner by two junior faculty members. The evening was cruising along as we consumed several cocktails and worked our way into the main course. Then, out of nowhere, one of the junior faculty members turned to me with an expression of intense interest, just before introducing his version of the Inquisition.

"Do you realize how difficult it is to get grant money?" was his opening volley. This was followed closely by, "How do you plan to present your research to the grant reviewers to make it sellable?"

His remarks sufficiently jolted me out of my alcohol-induced trance to mutter, "I will be presenting my results tomorrow and assume you will understand my research plan after I present the complete package."

I don't know which of us had the more to drink, but my response only added more coal to his furnace as he knowingly pontificated, "You seem to be very naïve about the funding situation, and I don't see anything in what you have done that makes your work fundable. Perhaps you can enlighten me now." Those were fighting words.

My first inclination was to punch him; my second was to tell him to go screw himself. I can proudly say that I did not act on either of those options but instead merely told him, "I was not born yesterday, I know the situation, and I don't like your attitude. When the time comes, I will write fundable grant requests." That pretty much took care of the rest of the evening as well as the interview.

When I did make a formal presentation of my data the next afternoon, my buddy was not around to hear it. In fact, the only faculty member in attendance was the Chairperson, and I don't think it was of his choosing. Apparently, the word had gotten out that I was a hothead. Interestingly, three years after this debacle I received a phone call from the other junior faculty member in attendance that evening who said my buddy was no longer at Texas Tech, and that he himself was leading a search committee to find a replacement. This was followed by, "since you were the best recruit we have had for this position, would you be interested in reapplying?" He was going out on a limb and was a perfect diplomat. I still declined the offer.

My next job interview was at the University of Illinois, one of the country's top universities. However, after being in Urbana-Champaign for only two days, I was ready to run. The expectations for an Assistant Professor there appeared to be even greater than those at UCLA. The junior faculty member who was my guide during those two days told me he had a full-time teaching load and, coupled with his university committee obligations, was able to conduct his own research only after dinner in the evening. We visited his lab at about 10 PM, and the place was a madhouse of activity. Apparently his students were expected to follow the same schedule as him. This observation further reinforced my need to flee from the life of a university faculty member. When asked whether I would accept a position at the U of I if it were offered, I gave the same response I did two years earlier at the University of Kansas. "I need to see more places before I can make a decision." This time, however, I knew how they would respond and, within a week, they had made the decision for me.

The next stop in my job search was a break in my pattern. Until that time, I had interviewed solely for university positions. I was brought up in the school that taught no decent research ever materialized outside of a university or, possibly, government laboratory. Industry was strictly off-limits, and if you went there it was to sell your soul and not to conduct meaningful research. The Roche Institute was an exception since research conducted there was not controlled by the company. Freedom of choice was everything. However, I was now at a university and felt I was drowning. Thus, any option that could throw me a lifeline was appealing.

My next interview, therefore, was for a staff position at G.D. Searle & Co., located in a northern Chicago suburb. It was a whole new experience. I was picked up at the airport in a stretch limousine with darkened windows that blocked any view of me from lowly spectators, and was delivered to a five-star hotel. After I was well-situated, my prospective supervisor escorted me to one of Chicago's finest restaurants.

It was a bizarre interview. Knowing my background, my prospective supervisor emphasized the challenging research opportunities I would be given at Searle, and attempted to verify his claim by introducing some of the company's finest research programs. One was the development of a new sweetener that was going to be a block buster. He was eventually right; the sweetener was NutraSweet. However, I was a basic researcher and none of this impressed me at the time; I took a different view later in life, but that would require time and more attitude changes. I was even less enthusiastic about the job after my chaperon explained that the project he had in mind for me was to screen for potential antiviral compounds synthesized by the company's chemists.

The voices of my previous mentors drowned out any words of encouragement delivered during that interview. I was still a product of university thinking, and what I was hearing confirmed previous warnings. I left Chicago with the belief that there had to be something better out there somewhere.

By this time, my family members had learned of my frustrations at UCLA and some even offered their condolences, probably because they wouldn't be caught dead living in Los Angeles. One family member took it a step further. Perhaps she remembered me as the child who needed her care during the summer I spent with her in San Francisco after graduating from high school. Regardless of why she did it, my sister Clo suggested I investigate positions at Sandia National Laboratories in Albuquerque where her husband Bruce now worked. She had discussed this with him, and Bruce had taken the time to determine that Sandia was actually looking for biological scientists. Clo even gave me a name and number to call.

Bruce was right, Sandia was looking for a PhD in some area of biology, but it was unclear why. Other National Laboratories all had respectable programs in the biological sciences, but Sandia had been strictly a haven for physicists, chemists and engineers. The group with which I would be interviewing was dabbling in biological research but had no real biologists. This should have provided me with sufficient warning to cut bait before even visiting the place. However, Sandia Laboratories was located in Albuquerque which had mountains and, in contrast to LA, clean air; not much water or many trees, but certainly mountains and clean air. I accepted an interview which became my introduction to the American military/industrial complex.

Sandia Laboratories sits within the confines of Kirtland Air Force Base and most of its activities are weapons-based; nuclear weapons to be exact. This should have given me another foreign body reaction, but then I looked at the mountains and breathed the air. Besides, Sandia was neither a university nor the dreaded industry, even though it was managed by Western Electric, a branch of AT&T. In addition, I was offered a job with a starting salary of $23,000 which was $2,000 more than was offered by G.D. Searle & Co.

There were a lot of factors that went into my decision to leave LA, but most had some connection with my job. Due at least partially to the objections of the graduate students, I was never offered a tenure-track position in the Medical School. I was, however, offered a position in the Dental School. The rub was that my salary, which would have been $23,000 in the Medical School had I gotten the appointment, was to be $15,000 in the Dental School, a $1,500 decrease from what I was already being paid. We were on the brink of bankruptcy as it was, so a reduction in pay meant we would be near the poverty level for the LA area. When I shared this piece of information with my graduate school advisor, who by then was living nearby in San Diego, his only comment was "they certainly want you to stay." I got the message.

I discussed the Sandia possibility with several of my science friends, and each of them expressed disbelief that I would even consider making this move. The assumption was that a move to this type of job would cause me to lose the small amount of respectability that I had gained within our community of scientists. I reasoned, however, that they all had the same university indoctrination as me. They also didn't understand what I was experiencing at UCLA, and that I had little desire to join another university. In the end, I convinced myself that other National Laboratories had an abundance of PhDs in biological sciences, and it was just a matter of time before the contributions of biologists would be needed and appreciated at Sandia. Besides, I would be getting in on the ground floor and, thereby, could lead the charge that would inevitably blossom into major biological programs. So I suppressed any residual desire to launch a research career with retroviruses, ignored every piece of advice I received, and accepted the offer at Sandia.

Sandia had agreed to pay for our move to Albuquerque, and about one week before our departure from LA, the assigned mover arrived at our door. He was from the same company we had on our move to New Jersey. We vociferously objected to this being our only choice, but were assured that this was it or nothing. The moving agent who made the visit was to be the driver, and he promised us that this move would be perfect. He was right. I guess you just have to let some things go.

On a sunny day in early August of 1974, we loaded items not put on the moving truck, including two babies, in the back of our non-air-conditioned VW, then headed east across the Mojave Desert. We left California at the town of Needles where the thermometer registered 105 degrees. Later that evening we arrived in Flagstaff,

Arizona, where snow was in the forecast. This radical change in weather foreshadowed an even more radical change in my professional life.

12 The Prince of Sludge

Welcome to New Mexico, the land of enchantment! When we arrived in Albuquerque on a mid-August afternoon in 1974, we were warmly greeted by the ethereal desert air and nearly unending sunshine that were to be our daily companions. For me, it was like the prison break I had carried off several years earlier when I escaped from the seminary. At least I began this venture with optimism. But all good things have a price, and Sandia Laboratories would expect its pound of flesh; it would just be extracted from a different body part.

Although my starting salary at Sandia Laboratories was superb by my standards, they were unwilling to pay for a house-hunting trip. I could have made the trip at my own expense, even though our bank account was approaching empty. As it turned out, I should have done so. My sister Clo had lived in Albuquerque for several years, however, and should have been familiar with local housing. It may have been a lot to expect, but based on her expressed knowledge on the topic, I asked her to rent a house for us. The plan was to live in this rental only long enough to scout the town and determine if this move was going to be more permanent than its predecessors. Once those lines were checked off, the assumption was that we would then buy a house of our own – for the first time.

Clo agreed to do our house-hunting. After a few days, she reported back that she had located "a darling little place" that would be ideal for a small family. She had six children, so that was her point of reference. In order to close the deal, we were required to sign a one-year lease and provide rent payments for the first and last months. In addition, we would not be allowed to sublet the place unless the owner personally interviewed the prospective renters. He was moving to California and would not return to survey his property for a full year. Based on his requirements, it was clear that we would be stuck with the house for a year if we signed the lease.

The only concrete feature of the house described by Clo over the telephone was that it had six rooms. She also exasperatedly complained that she had been searching for days, and this was all that was available. I found both assertions difficult to believe, and was beginning to recognize the mistake I had made in asking her to perform this favor. However, the deed had been done, and there seemed little choice but to show our appreciation by signing the lease agreement. So we did.

Clo had been given the keys to our new abode, and was anxious to showcase what she had accomplished on our behalf. Thus, within minutes after our arrival in Albuquerque, she brought us to our first viewing. Since Clo was present, an open expression of shock was not permissible, but it was immediately obvious that she had severely underestimated our needs. The house did have six rooms as Clo had promised, but she had neglected to point out that if more than three people were standing in any one of them, there would be little space left for furniture. In fact, our new home was no bigger than most of our previous apartments, even the one-bedroom place in Belleville. The most spacious room was the kitchen, but it wasn't large enough to accommodate a table and four chairs, and still leave space to slide around the sink and stove. Thus, our dinner table and chairs would have to be placed in the family room. That would leave just enough additional space for our oversized sofa and a floor lamp. There were three bedrooms, but the largest would need to be relegated to the storage of our remaining furniture, including our washer and dryer, all of which was eventually jammed in from floor to ceiling.

Even before we began stacking our furniture into the new house, we were plotting how to break the rental agreement. The only solution that seemed plausible, without paying rent for an entire year whether we lived there or not, was to renegotiate our contract with the owner. By then, he was already living in California and wasn't scheduled for a return visit until the next summer. Fortunately, he could be reached by telephone, so after several exchanges, he exasperatingly conceded that we could sublet the place. However, this was accompanied with the threat that "the monkey will be on your back to repair any damages." It was like one step forward and two back, but at least there was a place to step.

The plan to wait until we knew the area and better understand my job stability before attempting to buy a house was rerouted. Instead, within days of our arrival, we were touring Albuquerque with an aggressive realtor. Simultaneously, we were showing our luxurious estate to prospective renters. The quantity of lookers was surprisingly high, but was inversely matched by their quality. I'm sure I would have been sent to prison if those who toured our establishment had compared notes on the contracts I required them to sign before they rented the house. Individuals who seemed anywhere within the realm of respectability were offered the same deal we received, but the fees went up from there based on my degree of apprehension. One well-manicured but otherwise shady-looking character arrived with four scantily-clad, fine-looking women as his escort. I did a rapid calculation and muttered that the owner expected an entire year of rent paid in advance. Since he didn't blink an eye after digesting that bit of information, I was wishing I had extended it to two years. As he wheeled off with his covey of ladies, I was convinced he would be our replacement. Fortunately, that never materialized.

Several days later, a mother of three teenage boys arrived at our door. This would normally portend the absolute destruction of the house within weeks if they became the renters, but this lady had the appearance of someone in charge, even of three teenage boys living in a matchbox. The thought of charging her and her boys more than we paid to cover potential damages didn't even enter my head. Sometimes one makes the correct judgment and this time it was my turn. It all worked like a well-oiled machine; the only report we had after handing over the keys was delivered a year later by the owner who proclaimed that our period of house servitude was successfully completed. In fact, the place was immaculate when he visited, all 630 square feet of it.

One of our requirements in house searching was that the place be available immediately. Thus, within days of starting the house search, we were moving into an almost new Southwestern style home, a flat-roofed, one-story, adobe-like structure sitting with a panoramic view of the city and accompanying Sandia Mountain peaks. The house was built on a concrete slab as is typical of Albuquerque, so everything was on one level. It wasn't huge, but was still three times larger than what we had just left. We thought we were moving into a section of paradise.

Based on the time and energy required to establish meaningful friendships during my stay in LA, nearly the first item on my agenda in Albuquerque was to jump-start a social life that didn't revolve around baby care. Thus, on my very first day at Sandia Laboratories, I inquired about the existence of a social group within the organization that a new employee might join to find new friends. The welcome response from one of my new colleagues was, "Sure there is. My wife and I belong to The Sandians, and the group is having an outing in the mountains next Sunday. Why don't you come?" I thought I had hit the jackpot on my first pull.

The outing was to be a hike and picnic in the Monsanto Mountains just south of town. The other participants would bring food and drinks, so all we had to do was show up. We knew the hike part would be hopeless with babies, so we arrived just as the others returned from their time on the trail. The picnic site was half-way up a mountainside, and the participants had randomly parked their cars where they would be retrievable without becoming high-centered or sacrificing their oil pan to a granite boulder. We picked the least hazardous of the remaining spots on the slope to deposit our VW before alighting to greet our hosts.

The mountainside was swarming with kids, so our two-year old son drifted off with the mob and introductions were commenced. We were only being introduced to a third couple when a warning scream echoed across the valley, followed by a resounding crash as one of the cars parked higher up the mountain collided with another several yards below. We all rushed to the scene to learn the cause and assess the damage. Even in the short distance the offending car had traveled, it had gained sufficient speed to produce major damage to both vehicles. The assumption was that an emergency brake had failed, and the free-falling car was fortunate to have contacted another vehicle before it plunged into the forest below and exploded. The latter supposition was correct but the former was not. The car that initiated the collision did have a driver. He was just unlicensed, and in fact, was only two-years old. When I opened the door to retrieve our renegade son, he was bubbling with laughter, clearly relishing the fantastic ride he had just experienced. As I was handing him to Shirley, the car's owner forcefully blurted out, "Aren't you at least going to whack him?"

Too much had occurred too quickly to give the appropriate response which should have been, "who is going to whack you for leaving your car unlocked without the emergency brake engaged on the side of a mountain?" We were just thankful our son was still alive. What had happened was the troop of kids had paraded through the front seat of the unlocked car, and Christopher, who was bringing up the rear, had lingered just long enough in the driver's seat to pull the gear lever out of park. In the absence of an engaged emergency brake, he sent the car pummeling down the mountain.

Somehow it was determined between the owners of the two damaged cars that we were responsible for our son, and since he caused the accident, we were responsible for the damage. We lingered only long enough to exchange insurance information. Our insurance company did pay for the damages, but they couldn't repair the animosity I felt toward some of our new acquaintances. Fortunately, they were not representative of the community.

❧   ❧   ❧

Sandia and other National Laboratories are high security government institutions managed on behalf of the Department of Energy. Before an official offer of employment is issued at these establishments, the new hire must be cleared through extensive inquiries designed to weed out potential security risks. I was informed of this eventuality early in the recruitment process which stimulated an instant flashback to my days in Berkeley. It was probably acceptable that I signed a petition to have Ronald Reagan impeached as Governor of California, but to have registered in the Peace and Freedom Party seemed likely to bite me. My party's presidential candidate was Eldridge Cleaver who had fled to Algeria to avoid imprisonment, and our most prominent party slogan was "Free Huey Newton," who had been imprisoned for killing Oakland cops. The "our" part here was a major stretch since my involvement was summed up in a sidewalk registration to make the P & F Party an entity. I wasn't convinced that the investigators, who eventually interviewed nearly everyone I had known since birth, would take the broad view of this situation. Apparently they did, and I received my security clearance.

This security thing was a serious matter at Sandia, and for good reason based on the nature of most activities being conducted within its boundaries. Every employee was issued a badge and was required to wear it in a fully visible fashion when inside the gates of the Laboratories. This is commonplace today, even in elementary schools. However, it was not commonplace in 1974 to require a security guard to physically hold your badge and compare your face to the image when both entering and leaving work. God forbid that you should lose your badge. It never happened to me, but I was told that one might survive the first incident. However, the powers of Hell would devour you if it happened twice. I still have nightmares in which I have lost my badge inside the gates and am not allowed to leave. Those who worked with classified documents were, of course, under constant scrutiny. These documents had a bold, red "classified" stamped on every page, and if you happened to leave one exposed when you were out of the room for a few seconds, and a security guard or fellow employee happened to witness this careless act, you were history.

I seldom saw a classified document, so the biggest security issues for me were associated with my visitors or new employees under my jurisdiction who had not yet received their security clearances. The paperwork associated with the entry of any visitor was monumental, and the process had to be initiated several weeks in advance. Even then, not every visitor was given a permit, and I might as well forget it if my visitor was not an American citizen. Once everything was in place for those who did make the cut, I would meet the visitors in an office outside the gates of the Laboratories to verify in writing that I would accompany them at all times while inside the gates. Surprisingly, I did not have to accompany visitors into the restroom. That was the only exception to the rule. I did, however, have to remain at the door while they were inside. If for some unexpected reason, I was not attached to my visitors for even a few seconds, I was required to turn the paperwork over to another employee who would sign the document and continue the surveillance.

A few months after I joined Sandia, I hired my first ever laboratory assistant. Because the clearance process was not complete by the time we needed his services, I had to escort him at all times. One morning during his probationary period, I received a frantic call from Shirley saying that Christopher had smashed Stephanie's thumb in a door jam, and it was hanging to her hand by a thread. We still had only one car and that day I had it, so it was either up to me or an ambulance. Without a seconds hesitation, I was out the door and gone with escort papers in hand. I arrived at home within minutes to witness that the thumb was not dangling, but was certainly smashed. After a police-escorted rush to the hospital, the situation became as controlled as it could be, and we returned home. We were greeted by a ringing telephone and a frantic fellow employee on the other end. His only statement, issued in a loud, high pitched voice, was "you abandoned your charge, and had better get your butt up here before you get fired." Once my terrified assistant saw me flee the lab and realized he was without paperwork or an escort, he went into hiding for several hours and only revealed himself to one of our group after he had given up all hope of my return. It wasn't a reported security breach, so I lived another day.

The security situation at Sandia was not unique, and has become a way of life in many jobs today, but it was an annoying novelty to me. It personified the military establishment to which I had attached myself, something for which I had no tradition or appreciation. In order to even access the gates of the Laboratories, I had to clear the check point at the entrance to Kirtland Air Force Base which encircled Sandia. This was relatively simple since it merely required a visible sticker on your vehicle to be signaled on by the military guards. When my vehicle became my bicycle, however, the sticker wrapped around the handle bar was nearly invisible and required a daily full inspection before I even got beyond this exterior gate. It doesn't sound like a big deal, but it was an annoyance that reminded me each day of my lack of independence, both inside and outside of the laboratory.

Sandia Laboratories is the largest and probably least known of the National Laboratories. Almost everyone born in America before 1950 has heard of Los Alamos National Laboratory located about 100 miles to the north. That was where the first atomic bomb was developed and assembled. However, within months after the end of World War II, Sandia Base, as it was called at the time, became the designated peacetime assembly site for atomic weapons. Because of the classified nature of its primary business, Sandia Laboratories remained anonymous until it seriously branched out into other activities many years later. However, nuclear weapons assembly and delivery was still its primary mission when I arrived in 1974.

Although Sandia was not strictly part of the military, it was similarly managed. Every project required a highly specific, attainable mission for approval, something with which I had previously been unfamiliar. Even side projects, like the one to which I was assigned, were managed toward attaining a carefully spelled out end product, and experimentation was directed solely toward that goal. Scientific innovation was not totally stifled, but it certainly was vigilantly controlled.

The project to which I was assigned had been initiated several years prior to my arrival, but progress had been slow. Nuclear reactor waste had already become a national burden, so it was determined that any acceptable use for even a small fraction of this waste would relieve a portion of the unpleasant notoriety of this material, even if it didn't solve the problem. One radioactive isotope contained in the waste that had potential use was cesium-137. This isotope emitted high energy gamma rays as it decayed, similar to those released by cobalt-60, a source of radiation traditionally used for medical applications such as cancer treatment. Although cesium-137 represented only a tiny fraction of the radioactive isotopes in nuclear reactor waste, the hierarchy that controlled the finances at Sandia were convinced that its retrieval from this waste could be cost-effective if the end use was of sufficient value, i.e., it was used to irradiate materials of high value. Human tumors may have qualified as high value targets, but it was unlikely that sewage sludge would make the cut. Regardless, it was chosen.

The justification for this decision was that mountains of sewage sludge, which is the solid material that settles out of sewage, were being created daily, and most was being disposed of using costly and environmentally unsound methods. The images portrayed were either mountains of human waste as high as Mt. Everest being constructed within smelling distance of major cities or boatloads of the same being dumped near our shorelines. Animal manures had been used as fertilizers for years, so it didn't take great imagination to envision similar possibilities for human waste. In fact, several cities had already joined forces with commercial enterprises to treat, bag and sell their sewage sludge as popular and expensive garden fertilizers. The folks at Sandia had concluded that if human disease agents in the sludge could be destroyed, the product could be applied directly on farmland. Cesium-137 extracted from nuclear waste was to be the destroyer, and my role was to insure that the planned treatment would inactivate human viruses present in the sludge.

It wasn't exactly flattering, but during the following years I became recognized as the "Prince of Sludge" in the environmental sciences community. My one lab assistant and I produced a publication on virus destruction in sludge in some refereed journal nearly every three months during my years at Sandia. The timing of these submissions coincided with obligatory quarterly reports; I just couldn't fathom wasting time on a report that had no positive outcome except to become filler for a filing cabinet. Therefore, my quarterly reports and journal articles were one and the same.

During these years, I learned that viruses were destroyed during aerobic and anaerobic digestion, drying, and certainly heating of sludge. The only treatment that was generally ineffective was gamma radiation unless you applied amounts sufficient to eradicate most of the world's human population. I not only learned what killed the viruses, but also why they were killed.

The methods used in these studies were to produce enteric viruses containing radioactively-labeled proteins or RNA and seed them into sludge prior to treatment. My assistant and I would then extract the radioactively-tagged viruses or virus pieces to determine what happened to them during the treatment processes. Enteric viruses are those that replicate in the intestine and are, therefore, released intact in feces and become components of sewage sludge. Polioviruses were the model enteric viruses used for most of our experiments. Even though polioviruses are the cause of devastating neurological diseases after they pass from the intestine into the bloodstream where they can access nerve tissue, they are also released in intestinal waste and thereafter spread from person-to-person after exposure to and consumption of fecal matter. The use of poliovirus vaccines developed by Salk and Sabin in the 1950's and 60's had already nearly eliminated polio in the Western Hemisphere. Furthermore, the polioviruses we used were similar to the weakened strains administered to infants in Sabin's orally-delivered, live virus vaccine. Thus, the cavalier use of these viruses by ourselves and multiple other laboratories as models in environmental studies was deemed safe.

During these studies on viruses in sludge, we learned polioviruses die during sludge digestion in the absence of oxygen (anaerobic digestion) due primarily to the toxic effects of the ammonia generated during the digestion process. They also die during the drying of sludge, probably because they are ripped apart during the process of evaporation. Besides poliovirus, we also seeded sludge with another model enteric virus that had been obtained from monkey feces called rotavirus, the human version of which had only been discovered a few years earlier. After the discovery of human rotavirus in 1973, it became recognized as the primary cause of severe diarrhea in young children throughout the world. Therefore, the certain presence of rotavirus in sludge had major significance if this waste product was to be used as a fertilizer. Rotaviruses are members of the Reoviridae family, so my experience at Roche was paying dividends. These studies with rotaviruses also foreshadowed what would eventually become my life's work, something I never envisioned while serving up sludge.

The monkey rotavirus we used for our experimentation was also killed after being seeded into sludge, but interestingly, the agents responsible were found to be common detergents rather than ammonia. Much of this had little practical value, but it provided a small breath of life for my personal credibility in the science community. Strangely enough, it was an enjoyable period for me in the lab even though I had little ability to affect the overall direction of the project, and the project itself was about as connected to my dream studies with retroviruses and cancer as turnips are to space travel.

It sounds like this all came easily, and relatively speaking, it probably did. However, it didn't seem that way when I was living it. Prior to accepting the job at Sandia, I had been promised any equipment items that would be needed to support virus studies, whatever those studies might entail. To accomplish what I perceived as required for the sludge project, I judiciously determined that I would need two moderately-priced items: an ultracentrifuge and a scintillation counter. The former was needed to purify viruses that I would seed into sludge to observe their fate; the latter would be used to trace the radioactively-labeled components of the viruses during their destruction. A formal request for these two equipment pieces was issued within days of my arrival at Sandia, but their delivery required nearly eight months of wrangling. Several months after my request was submitted, I was told that these items were sufficiently expensive to require formal submission in the annual budget. That meant their arrival would be delayed at least another year, and there was no assurance they would ever come. My typical, knee-jerk response was "I was looking for a job when I came here and I can continue to look now." I think this threat actually had an effect because the equipment was ordered shortly after my ultimatum was delivered.

The excruciatingly slow progress on the sludge irradiation project prior to my arrival was partially due to the lack of an experienced biologist on the project. I was the first such creature to be hired at Sandia and would be nearly the last. My arrival didn't exactly jumpstart the sludge project, but it did help, and within a couple of years, the group was actually irradiating sludge in a pilot project.

Part of the presumed novelty of this project was associated with the combined use of radiation and heat during sludge treatment. The logic behind this was based on an observation that this combination could be synergistic, i.e. the magnitude of microbial destruction by the simultaneous treatments was greater than the sum of the individual treatments. To demonstrate the effectiveness of this combined treatment process on a moderately large scale, a truckload of liquid digested sludge were hauled from the Albuquerque Sewage Treatment Plant to the Sandia irradiator, and just before the sludge was exposed to a high intensity source of gamma radiation, it was heated to several degrees above body temperature. After treatment, the sludge was pumped into a holding tank and several hours later, the bacterial levels remaining in the sludge were measured. Lo and behold, it was found that the bacterial concentrations actually increased as a result of the treatment. Someone, including me, had ignored the fact that bacteria multiply in warm growth medium, and our heated sludge was exactly that. Thus, the bacteria that survived the treatment found the conditions ideal for their multiplication, and multiply is what they did. I think Sandia needed a real microbiologist on the project, and that apparently wasn't me. So it was back to the drawing board.

This was when a project on drying of sludge was initiated. The logic was that if the moisture levels in the sludge were low, bacteria levels would expand slowly after irradiation if at all. So this time truckloads of raw liquid sludge were hauled to a site within the Sandia properties, out of range for public smelling, and deposited inches deep in an open-air containment area. Three times each day for the next several weeks, weekends included, the "product" was turned by hand (actually by shovel), and the intense desert sun was expected to accomplish the rest.

During the time required to drive off most of the moisture, it rained several inches. That was why it required the raw sludge several weeks to dry. We all had our assigned "turning" duty. Even the most potent farm smells I experienced as a child paled in comparison to those generated in the warm, raw sludge. We never determined the nature of the inhabitants that multiplied in the drying feces, but every shovelful uncovered an array of magnificent creatures. The drying process did, by definition, reduce the sludge volume, so it also reduced the quantity that would need to be passed through an irradiator, thus cutting down on costs.

Eventually a pilot irradiator was designed, constructed and supplied with a large source of gamma radiation. By this time, the love affair with sludge irradiation within our group was growing cold when it was finally realized that the end product had little value, and food irradiation was filling the gap. To my knowledge, the only material that was ever passed through this multi-million dollar irradiation facility was grapefruit. A few years after I left Sandia, the irradiator was disassembled and the entire project was moved into the history book. My most lasting memory of the project resulted from a contest that took place during a neighborhood social outing. The competition was to guess "who had the most unusual job." I chose myself saying "I irradiate poop." I had no viable competitor.

During my entire stay at Sandia, my comfort level with longevity remained in question. I had a difficult time envisioning a future for my immediate project, and saw little overall progress in the establishment of a biology-driven organization within the Laboratories. Attempts were made but with marginal success. Within weeks of my arrival, my supervisor and I were already trying to build a functional biology group, but interested candidates were scarcer than alligators in Siberia. Most respectable scientists were unwilling to take the chance I had. The applicants we did interview were a random lot. One guy from North Carolina had a project which required immediate access to large members of the feline kingdom. He indicated during his interview that the job would be of interest to him only if he could bring several panthers, lions and tigers with him. My supervisor was unrealistic enough to consider the possibility, but the actuality was not surprisingly nixed by upper management.

Another interviewee was from the National Institutes of Health in Maryland. His project involved a human genetic disease in which DNA damage resulting from UV radiation was not repairable, and affected persons would develop devastating skin cancers after exposure to even brief periods of sunlight. This project did have some potential association with a facility where radiation from various sources (such as nuclear bomb blasts) played a role. However, when offered a job, this candidate turned it down before he even left town.

After multiple attempts at recruitment, our group was finally joined by two PhD biologists. Both were New Mexico natives, and both would have accepted almost any job just to return home. One had developed a serious case of claustrophobia as a post-doc in New York City, and the other was being slowly destroyed by the heat and humidity while a faculty member at the University of Florida. Once they joined, the question was what could each do to enhance the Laboratories' mission. One began a project to identify potential detrimental effects of exposure to high voltage power lines, something quite removed from his past experiences as a cell biologist. However, he did use cells in tissue culture as his target, but his model system was a far reach from a real world situation. Needless to say, little practical information came from the project.

The second new member of the group joined the Waste Isolation Pilot Plant (WIPP) project to write environmental impact assessments. The purpose of WIPP was to determine if low level nuclear waste could be safely stored in an underground salt deposit located near Carlsbad in southern New Mexico. This pilot plant did begin accepting defense-related nuclear waste about 20 years later, and celebrated a successful ten years of operation in 2009. However, I would have a difficult time identifying a more boring project for a PhD in a biological science than assessing the environmental impact on a desert surface that might result from the construction of a nuclear waste burial site located 2,150 feet below the surface in a 250-million year old salt deposit. However, for our new biologist, the ticket to New Mexico was satisfaction enough. Neither of our new hires, however, did much to help establish a stable biology program at Sandia Laboratories.

About halfway through my time in Albuquerque, our group had a serious management shake-up. Reorganization is always a way of life in government and industry, and the more it happens, the less that seems to get done. Our reorganization involved, among other things, the acquisition of a new Department Head, a 33-year old engineer who had never opened a biology book since high school. However, that didn't deter him. Within days, he was grilling me about how I was conducting my experiments, following which he judiciously provided his personal critiques. After listening to several of his suggestions, my underlying sense of diplomacy evaporated.

I calmly inquired, "I am really curious about something, and maybe you can enlighten me. A week ago you knew nothing about biology and today you know nearly everything. Does the promotion to Department Head also entail the infusion of divine knowledge?"

To his credit, the new Department Head didn't miss a beat and merely responded "yes it does." He was only half joking.

After this shake-up, it became apparent that my dream of a serious biological organization within Sandia was evaporating. I finally began to realize that you don't build an organization of this type from the ground up. Big changes are strictly top-down, and Sandia had no senior leadership inclined to push for the establishment of a biological research program. They did not understand it and thereby saw no need for it. Besides, their careers were progressing well, so why fix something that isn't broke?

Even in this rather hostile atmosphere, I kept my eye on the ball as best I could. However, the constant uncertainty forced me to keep my resume' updated and remain on the interview circuit. One interview was with DuPont in Delaware where I was offered a respectable job with a respectable salary. However, I had been at Sandia only three years at that point, and wasn't yet ready to commit to leaving the Mountain West for a more permanent home on the East Coast. Things had to deteriorate further. They eventually did.

When Stephanie was two months old while we were living in LA, she contracted a respiratory syncytial virus (RSV) infection from her brother. Christopher was old enough to cough up the crud, but Stephanie was more vulnerable to the effects of the virus because of her age. We had been advised by our pediatrician to take her to the hospital as soon as warning signs developed. Early one morning a short time later, Stephanie's inability to get her breath during a coughing episode provided the warning. Since someone needed to be with Christopher, the trip to the hospital was a one-parent operation, and this one was mine. Stephanie had not been baptized, and my Catholic training was screaming at me that it needed to be done in case she didn't recover from her illness. Therefore, I found an unoccupied restroom near the emergency room waiting area and performed the act, just as I had done with Christopher in our home in New Jersey. Stephanie did recover without permanent damage after a traumatic week in the hospital, though I doubt her restroom baptismal ceremony had any effect on that outcome.

During our first week in Albuquerque, my sister Rose Marie and husband Jim paid a visit. Their presence reignited my concerns about a proper baptism for Stephanie and, whether I really felt the first one was valid or not, I thought she deserved the same official ceremony provided Christopher. Thus, while Rose Marie and Jim were in town, they stood as witnesses to another of our children's baptisms as I poured the water and recited the words once again. This act marked my continued effort to remain within the graces of the Catholic Church.

Albuquerque is a very Catholic town based on the fact that many of its inhabitants were descendants of religious benefactors associated with Spain's conquest of Mexico. As a result, the town has an abundance of Catholic churches from which to make a selection. My first attempt was with the Catholic parish located nearest our home. I attended Mass there several times before this choice imploded. On one particular Sunday, the sermon was delivered by the pompous pastor who exasperatingly chided his congregation for calling the rectory to inquire about the schedule for Sunday masses. He droned on with his chastisement for some minutes before summing up his concerns with an inspirational conclusion.

"You housewives do nothing except sit around watching soap operas and eating bonbons. At least you should have enough time to read the bulletin." Surprisingly, my colorful exit was not joined by the rest of the congregation.

After several more attempts at locating a Catholic church where I could leave Sunday Mass with new energy and optimism rather than anger, I began attending the Church of the Holy Spirit. It became my spiritual oasis within this desert town. For some reason, the messages of Vatican Council II that were issued ten years earlier were still in vogue among the priests that served this congregation. They preached that acceptance of others regardless of our differences was more important to God than protectionism of the rules created by several clergymen during the Dark Ages. This attitude was perhaps best demonstrated in a few quiet words delivered at the end of an Easter sermon in which the pastor invited "everyone to share in communion who believes in Christian values, regardless of their personal situation." My first reaction was to take cover before the lightening strike hit. Once this fear passed, I realized that the changes enacted during the brief tenure of Pope John XXIII had survived in some circles, and that his message of a loving and rule-disdaining Christ was at least present in one parish. This recognition provided me with the hope that I could still find a home within the Catholic Church.

Living in Albuquerque was a real pleasure. Once I gained an appreciation for the nearly endless days of sunshine, I began to disregard the scarcity of natural vegetation. I even began to appreciate the fact that, although we weren't exactly militants, a neighborhood filled with Air Force officers had advantages. They were all transplants like us, without extended families or established friends. Thus, they too were eager to reach out and develop new relationships. Unlike our experience in LA, making friends was easy in Albuquerque.

Even though things were going exceptionally well at home, satisfaction with my job continued to receive low marks, mostly due to its uncertainty. It was also a serious struggle to maintain an even rudimentary skill level as a virologist, something foretold by my colleagues when I left UCLA. The work I was doing was totally disconnected from the avalanche of biological discoveries being made in laboratories across the globe. My only local touchstone with real biological science was at the University of New Mexico which was a 40-minute commute from my work site. The library at the university also provided my only access to the scientific literature in this time before the Internet. Thus, I forced myself to make the trek to the university library at least twice monthly to retard the unrelenting progress of permanent scientific isolation. I knew something eventually had to give. Either I had to give up the dream of making significant scientific contributions in virology or we would have to abandon our first real home and move on again. After years of vacillating on the topic, I finally resolved that I could find a way to live with the former choice. Then, on a bright springtime afternoon, our Department Head called an emergency meeting for our Division, the outcome of which was that my resolution had a short lifetime.

Our Department Head was blunt. His proclamation started with "it has been decided that the expenditures of time and money required for the maintenance of a respectable experimental biology program is more than the Laboratories is willing to sacrifice. Therefore, the present program will be terminated within the next few months."

He ended his speech with these inspiring words. "Those of you who wish to remain at Sandia can attempt to find programs in which to become assimilated."

I sensed that the message gave its messenger more pleasure than regret. His promotion to Department Head two years earlier came with the condition that he would be required to manage an activity for which he had no understanding. Thus, complete amputation was the only means by which he could envision dealing with this unwanted appendage. His edict certainly forced a rethinking of my earlier decision to remain in Albuquerque.

This round of restructuring my career came at a time when jobs were few and far between. It was one of those times when the average education of cab drivers made a considerable advancement as unemployed PhDs took what they could find. On a personal level, I had also taken myself out of the mainstream of science, so even if there were research jobs, I would be an unlikely candidate to fill them. However, that didn't prevent me from attempting to move on once again. After several months of job searching, my only interview, and consequently my only offer for employment, came from the US Environmental Protection Agency in Cincinnati. My reputation as the "Prince of Sludge" did have one appreciative audience.

Both during the time it took to negotiate this position with the US Government and several months thereafter, I attempted to keep my options open at Sandia. The only job I could uncover within the Laboratories was as a chemist in a group investigating the feasibility of disposing nuclear waste in Nevada's Yucca Mountain. It was going to be a road show in that I would be commuting to Las Vegas every week en route to my new work site. I had no interest in being retreaded as a chemist; I had made the decision to leave that field years earlier and could muster no desire to alter the choice. Still Albuquerque had become a safe haven and a welcome home for both me and my family.

We had two months in which to make a decision before the EPA job would vanish. After seemingly endless and heart-wrenching discussions, I decided that our house would make the decision for us. If we sold it, we would move; otherwise, we would stay. After a month on the market, we received an offer for our house. I pitied the realtor who made the call, reporting what he expected to be joyous news. Shirley took the call and completely fell apart when she realized our decision had been made. We would be moving on again.

13 Fun Times in the Government

During our years in Albuquerque, I made several work related trips to Cincinnati. Although none were pleasure cruises, I became familiar with the landmarks between the Cincinnati Airport, located across the Ohio River in Northern Kentucky, and the US Environmental Protection Agency, which was my inevitable destination due to our shared love affair with sewage sludge. In my initial visit in 1974, the EPA was housed in a massive brick structure set on a hillside on the eastern edge of town. Within a few months, however, the Agency moved into new quarters near mid-town next to the University of Cincinnati, a large urban university bordered on most sides by what had been modern homes in the late 1800's but had gradually evolved into slum housing. But even this area held topological appeal in that it resided amongst hills. In fact, the entire city of Cincinnati is spread over a series of hills, and many areas have a designation of Mount something.

The new EPA building became my home away from home before it became my real home. I had already performed multiple studies with EPA staff members there before I began conducting my own experiments. Some of my work at Sandia was even funded through EPA grants. Thus, the move to Cincinnati was not a step into the unknown, at least not for me. However, it was for Shirley. She had never laid eyes on the city before a house-hunting trip was carried out a short time after our home in Albuquerque was officially purchased.

Even though I felt Cincinnati had charm and appeal, it was still in the Midwest which both Shirley and I had been taught to disdain. Her father had suffered through the heat of the dust bowl years on a farm near Paris, Missouri, and in 1936 at the age of 17, had moved with his parents to the pine-filled mountain air of the Bitterroot Valley in Western Montana. Paris was only about 100 miles south of Melrose, Iowa, where my father almost died from asthma before being rescued near death's door by his flight to Montana in 1938. Thus, both of our dads had a deep-rooted hatred for the Midwest which we were taught to appreciate. When one of my older Sandia colleagues and I were flying into the twinkling night lights of Albuquerque after spending several days in Cincinnati, he remarked that he felt he "was being delivered from Hell." I didn't exactly share his sentiments but certainly had been fortified with a tradition to understand them.

By the time we left Albuquerque, we had two cars, so there was one for each of us. Shirley's, however, would initially be heading north rather than east. Her parents were having their 40th wedding anniversary and she was due in Montana to help with the arrangements. She and our six and eight year old children would make that 1,200-mile trip while I headed east with our neurotic cat to meet the movers.

Although Christopher didn't display signs of anguish on leaving Albuquerque, the same cannot be said for his little sister. As Shirley was pulling out of our driveway for the last time with Stephanie at her side, she began to weep. Stephanie observed the tears and inquired about the cause. Shirley explained that she was just sad because she was leaving many friends that she never expected to see again. It is unclear what things register with a six year old, but even with all the moving plans and the empty house, Stephanie had apparently not gotten the message that we were actually leaving town. But at that moment, she began to get it.

"Aren't I going to be able to play with Jackie and Tracey again?" They were twin sisters, almost exactly Stephanie's age, and since they lived next door, had been her daily companions for several years.

"No Stephanie, we are moving to Cincinnati, don't you remember?" was her mother's response.

"But you never said I couldn't play with Jackie and Tracey anymore." And then the deluge began. She survived, but I think the move may initially have been hardest on her of anyone.

We stayed with friends our last night in Albuquerque, then headed in our separate directions at the break of dawn. I had the cat, a creature that disdained traveling in cars. My assumption was that he would eventually get the hang of it. I was wrong. On leaving, I had placed him in the back seat without restrictions. He immediately started to howl, pace, and sweat. When we were just leaving town, he decided he had already had enough, and jumped over the seat, sinking his claws deep into my neck as I attempted to stay on the road. I somehow got him dislodged and threw him against the passenger seat window. Fortunately it was still early, the day was cool, and the window was closed. Otherwise, it would have been "good by Tumble."

Tumble then headed underground. He burrowed under the passenger seat where he continued his persistent howling and panting for the rest of the day. When we stopped to sleep late that night, I was able to grab his neck, pull him out from under the seat, and force him into the cage I was carrying. His claws were whirling like a windmill during this operation, reaching for any possible resting point on my body. He made several contacts before my immediate mission was accomplished. The next day he stayed in the cage, howling, panting, and sweating as before.

In planning for our arrival in Cincinnati, we had contacted a first cousin of Shirley's mother who lived with his family in Northern Kentucky. When he and his wife learned I would be alighting first, alone, and with no immediate home, they offered to make me and Tumble their guests until we closed on our new house. I didn't know them, but soon did. They were true Godsends, providing me with some measure of sanity during the craziness that occurred during the next several days.

When I drove into town, there was no official word about the home loan we were waiting on, and my realtor was still debating about whether to alert the sellers of the fact. He was almost certain that the closing would be delayed. After another day of indecisiveness, when it was absolutely certain the closing would have to be rescheduled, he at last informed the other realtor. This person was seemingly understanding and even somewhat forgiving of the lack of a timely warning, but the sellers were not. They called their friend the lawyer immediately and he began issuing threats. The expectation was that I would pay for any charges the sellers would accrue due to their inability to have a timely closing on their new house in Tennessee It was clear that they felt deceived, and had no faith in my ability to acquire the loan monies within the foreseeable future. My realtor did have a comeback for all this. He said "we will agree to this if the sellers guarantee the basement of the house has no leaks." I didn't see the connection, but the ploy did cause the sellers and their lawyer friend to pause.

Being a peacemaker at heart, I decided to at least visit the sellers to provide my version of the story. As I walked up the steep front hill leading to the house, I nearly collided with movers as they were transporting a massive sofa from the premises. I had never met the owners and can't say I really did that day either. I rang the doorbell, and when it was answered by the man of the house, I attempted to explain who I was. My introduction was cut short by, "get the hell out of here." Welcome to Cincinnati!

By this time, our household belongings had arrived, and our driver was biting at the bit to unload them. Fortunately, he allowed me four days to finish my transactions before he would park everything in a warehouse. I made the deadline by a few hours.

The sellers were not present at the closing but were represented by their lawyer friend. He arrived loaded down with a very large list of demands and extra costs from his clients. My realtor looked over the list and again repeated that we would pay it if guaranteed a lack of water in the basement. If looks could kill, we would all be dead. After several minutes of mumbling, the lawyer signed the closing papers for his clients and disappeared.

Early the next morning, with Tumble in the hands of Shirley's cousin, I was on a plane to Montana to retrieve my family. Several days later, as we were leaving Montana and heading east, just at the point in the road when we normally would have turned south to

Albuquerque, we all participated in another moment of sadness. For some unknown reason, Christopher exclaimed "we are all going to die in Cincinnati." As it turns out, his words may have been prophetic. But life for that moment was moving on and so was our little family. We arrived in Cincinnati two days later, retrieved our cat, and began life in a new house and another new town.

After parking my family in our new home, I began the process of locating a Catholic parish to replace the one I had left in Albuquerque. While there, the priests that served the Church of the Holy Spirit had begun to convince me that the Second Vatican Council had accomplished lasting changes toward a vision that we are all children of God, a designation not reserved strictly for Catholics. That belief began to gradually seep away after my arrival in Cincinnati. I was confronted repeatedly with what I considered to be a lack of appreciation for any other religious beliefs as I made my passage from one Catholic Church to the next. There were certainly differences between parishes, but the theme of "the Catholic Church is right, and that makes all other beliefs wrong" seemed to be pervasive in all that I attended. Maybe I was hoping for too much.

My expectations had changed dramatically since leaving Holy Rosary High School and then the seminary. It was sometimes a frustrating spiritual journey, but it was a road I had to travel. Today I still hold out hope for lasting attitude changes within the Catholic Church, but my expectations for such changes have dwindled. Perhaps someday I will find another parish where true acceptance of persons of other faiths is more in vogue. I'm still looking.

So how were things going at the EPA after our arrival in Cincinnati? I had learned while at Sandia that large, government-related organizations all have defined missions, and the boundaries of those missions are dependent on the organization to which you belong. The USEPA was more than a government-related organization; it was the government. Thus, the range of permitted research activities was even more restrictive than it had been at

Sandia. These restrictions were further narrowed based on the "Laboratory" to which one belonged. Mine happened to be the "Health Effects Research Laboratory." Regardless of this seemingly broad title, the only way I would be allowed to attack any of the myriad of serious health problems in the world was if it could be done by inactivating viruses in sewage or drinking water. My mission was clear, but it also had all the earmarks of becoming very boring.

The niche I was hired to fill at the EPA was that of a junior manager defined as a Section Chief. This activity had been handled by the Microbiology Branch Chief, the next rung up the ladder, prior to my arrival. Since his administrative responsibilities were spread thin, this left little time to guide the four junior investigators in the Virology Section, one of the three Sections for which he was responsible. As Virology Section Chief, my job was to provide this guidance and conduct my own research without the benefit of a lab assistant. It wasn't clear whether this was a promotion from Sandia because there I at least had an assistant. The hooker in all this was that the free-for-all situation with the four investigators had been in effect for several years prior to my arrival. Thus, they had grown accustomed to doing or not doing about whatever they wanted within the limitations of "the mission." This would not have been all bad if they had the training and experience to conduct meaningful experiments. But none of them did. So my first task was to gingerly position myself between these freelance investigators and the Branch Chief whom they loved, possibly because he had given them almost total freedom.

Two of my new troops welcomed me with open arms. They recognized their limitations and were ready for some steady and, hopefully, constructive advice regarding their day-to-day research planning. One of the other two was a man with nearly 40 years of government service whose formal education ended with the delivery of his high school diploma. He had been free to do his own thing for so long that my arrival in his life was more mystifying than annoying. I approached my relationship with him with feathered gloves. He would listen to what I suggested, but would generally ignore my sage advice and revert back to what he felt was tried-and-true. This sparring match lasted several weeks before I was able to win his respect. My trump card turned out to be a manuscript that he had attempted to get published. It concerned a study to grow almost every known human enteric virus, 105 in all, in each of 17 different established mammalian cell lines. Since our mission was to detect and destroy these viruses, having the ability to monitor our success was a worthy cause. It was just mind-numbing work.

The old fellow had diligently and successfully performed the work over a three year period, but when it came time to get his results published, it became another matter. He had little ability to write and whoever helped him with this task either didn't understand the data or couldn't write either. Writing these types of papers had almost become second nature to me after my six years at Sandia, so I volunteered to rescue the manuscript. It really was rather simple, and the revision and resubmission required only a couple days of my time. The manuscript was reviewed and accepted within a month without further revision. For my newly found devotee, I had worked a miracle. From that point forward, he followed my advice like it came directly from God.

Gaining the confidence of the fourth member of our team was a bit more challenging. This fellow was a relatively recent college graduate who was confident he knew at least as much as I did about virology. His project was to use electron microscopy to examine diarrheal stool specimens from subjects collected during waterborne outbreaks in an attempt to identify possible viral causes of the outbreaks. It was another worthy goal, and the method was one that pioneers in the field had used several years earlier to identity Norwalk viruses and rotaviruses as major causes of severe intestinal illnesses in adults and young children, respectively. My new associate had been at this task since the time he had been hired after college graduation. Even though he was having little success, our Branch Chief was convinced that he was still "the man" and would eventually make a major breakthrough if I didn't interfere. When I asked whether I really was this young tiger's supervisor, our Branch Chief assured me with "sure you are. I just wouldn't interfere in his work if I were you." That certainly defined my role.

After I had been on the job for about a week, I risked annoying "the man" by inquiring about his work. He curtly provided me with a one minute review of his last two years of activities, and then promptly left, saying he needed to get back to work. That was pretty much how our relationship remained throughout my stay. His loyalty was to our Branch Chief, and only to him. Any attempt on my part to learn what he was doing was viewed as an intrusion that he would promptly report to his real Chief. Then I would get the same advice. "The man is doing really good work. He just needs to have his space." After a few attempts to see if I could provide some small measure of guidance, I gave up, hoping that the Branch Chief's assessment was correct. Nothing of note was accomplished on the project under my watch, and I never read reports of significant findings thereafter. I probably just haven't read the right journals.

During my short stay in the government, I continued to pump out a manuscript about every three months. Some were from projects I had completed while at Sandia, some were collaborative activities with three of my four group members, and some were my own new initiatives. The most fascinating was a project to determine if viruses could be taken from soil into plants. If they could, it was theoretically possible to acquire an enteric virus infection by merely consuming a vegetable irrigated with poorly treated sewage or fertilized with undertreated sewage sludge. To answer the question, I reverted back to my graduate school experiences and used a RNA bacteriophage as the model virus.

It was clearly impractical to attempt to observe possible virus passage into plants directly from soil spiked with even very large numbers of viruses. Therefore, the plants (beans and corn) were grown with their roots directly in well-aerated water (hydroponic conditions) under artificial lighting. The water was spiked with variable amounts of phage and the upper parts of the plants were harvested over the next days to detect live virus. These were not experimental conditions conducive to the use of even weakened human viruses, such as live poliovirus vaccine strains, since there was no containment. In fact, the aerosols created by the bubbling air probably saturated the room with the seeded viruses. What was learned was that the roots of both plants had to be severed in order for viruses to be transported to their upper parts. I'm sure this finding will eventually be recognized as a seminal discovery; its time has just not yet come.

The US economy was in lousy shape when I arrived at the EPA in 1980, so it became a goal of Jimmy Carter to reduce government spending as his group was leaving office. For whatever reason, the Health Effects Research Laboratory (HERL) of the EPA became one target for this cost savings. There are multiple methods to enact such savings, but a reduction in force (RIF) became the method of choice in this instance. I thought when I signed on with the government that, if nothing else, it would be a secure job, but that was another myth. Rumors of a RIF in HERL began about eight months after I joined, and spread like a wild fire. I was quickly made aware that government policy in these cases was that the "last one in was the first one out." Knowing I was the last one in, I began beating doors to learn the extent to which my job was in danger. The leader of Cincinnati HERL scoffed at my concerns, saying my position was probably the safest in the organization. He was correct; the position itself was secure. However, the occupant of my position was not necessarily secure if the job of a senior person with more longevity in the organization was eliminated. In that case, the person with the longer time-on-task could bump me.

Within days of the first rumors of a RIF, a second set of rumors began circulating with the message that several senior positions within HERL were to be eliminated. Amongst these was that of a Director, two tiers in the pecking order above me. Again, I was assured that my position was safe because the individual in jeopardy was incapable of doing my job. Besides, why would he want it since he was 65 years old, already a retired Public Health Officer and could take a second retirement from the EPA as a result of the RIF? Why indeed! But who can predict the ways of man and the workings of our government? Within a month of hearing the first rumors of the RIF, I was told I would be bumped. The good news was that they gave me a six month warning.

So it was back to job hunting again, and the job market had not improved from a year earlier. It was especially disconcerting to know I had left a job at Sandia and had ripped my family out of their security to walk into this. I responded to every vague job ad I came across during the next several months, over 250 in all. All my letters were addressed to a point person in some Human Resources Department which was comparable to sending them into a black hole, at least during the time of a serious recession. I received no positive responses, and only a few of my targets even had the decency to say they had received my application.

In the midst of all this, my Branch Chief, who was feeling a tinge of guilt about his lack of effort in preventing all this from happening to me, suggested I inquire about a position at a small research institute that was just down the street from the EPA. He had contracted a study to this institute, and had been told the Director was interested in hiring a new investigator. That suggestion ignited a four-month-long series of elusive negotiations.

The institute in question was called The Christ Hospital Institute of Medical Research, a title far removed from anything with which I had been associated in the seven years since I left UCLA. It was a tiny research institute attached to a major Cincinnati hospital. It had a total of six investigators, and one of these was the Director. He was the only MD on the staff; the other investigators were PhDs like me who conducted basic science studies in virology, largely from funds provided by The Christ Hospital Board of Directors. The Director of the Institute was the only investigator to be fully funded. His specialty was performing viral challenge studies in human volunteers, primarily to test new vaccines or antiviral drugs. He had fallen in with the EPA because he was one of only a handful of persons capable of and interested in determining how many live enteric viruses consumed in drinking water would be required to initiate an infection.

When I discussed my background and recent interests with the Institute Director, it appeared I had little to offer him. Other investigators in the Institute were all molecular biologists, and I had lost what little edge I had in that specialty during seven years of floundering in sludge. Even the viruses these investigators were studying, which included influenza, measles and RSV, had no connection to my previous experiences. I also was not a clinical virologist like the Director. All told, these deficiencies on my part might explain why the negotiations drug on for months.

So what were my fallback positions during this dreadful period? At Sandia, the old sludge project was still rambling along. Even though they had eliminated their in-house biological capacity, they still had a need for an experienced biologist to support the project. I reapplied for my old position and was interviewed by the same cast of characters as the first time. I was a known commodity, so was offered a rerun with little fanfare. The main problem was that I would be part of the same, seemingly useless project I had left, but this time without a laboratory. Another downside was that my salary was to be $6,000 less than when I left. They were offering me a job but also paying me back for leaving.

My other fallback positions might better be termed "fall off the earth" positions. One came from my brother Bob who owned an irrigation supply business near Bozeman and needed a salesman. He generously offered me a job for $20,000 a year, half of what I was receiving at the EPA. The other offer was for better pay but was not much more attractive. Several months before we left Albuquerque, I encountered my high school girlfriend who had recently moved there with her family. During our brief interaction, I told her about my remarkable job as a sludge artist. I guess she remembered what I said because, just as I was about to be pushed out the door at the EPA, her husband called to inquire about my availability to become his employee. The job I was being hired to fill didn't exist as yet, but he was making me an offer on the chance that it would. This job was to manage a contract with Sandia concerning irradiation of sludge and food. Apparently, the position I had been previously offered at Sandia really didn't exist since what I was being hired to do was being turned over to a contractor. I listened long enough to learn that my starting salary would be nearly $50,000 a year, $10,000 more than I was making at the EPA. However, I had had my fill of sludge and irradiation, and the lesson in humility of being employed by the husband of my old girl friend was too much to even imagine.

Eventually, I was offered a position as Associate Member at The Christ Hospital Institute of Medical Research. This, in theory, was equivalent to an Associate Professor at a university. Furthermore, my salary was to be comparable to what I was being paid at the EPA. Several stars had to be aligned to make this possible. One star was that I was in Cincinnati, so the Institute Director didn't have to leave town to recruit me. My second star was that I had a sterling recommendation from my EPA Branch Chief who was funding the "viruses in drinking water" study at the Institute. The third star, and the one my pride considers most important, was that I really did have something to offer to the Director's program due to my experiences with enteric viruses. So on Friday the 13th, I was issued my walking papers at the EPA and on November 16, 1981, my 39th birthday, I began a new career at The Christ Hospital Institute of Medical Research. At least my family didn't have to move again.

14 A Second Chance

When I left UCLA for Sandia National Laboratories in 1974, disenchantment with the life of a university faculty member derailed my plan to conduct research in cancer virology. It became apparent over the next seven years, even before being handed my walking papers at the EPA, that this desperation move was leading in only one direction, and it wasn't up. Thus, by joining the Christ Hospital Institute of Medical Research, I was offered a potential resurrection of my old dreams.

If I had learned nothing else during my sludge years, I did become familiar with the word "reality". The main reality that accompanied the new job was that I would now be responsible for obtaining funding for my own research, something that had not been required in my previous jobs, and I would be allowed limited time to make this happen before my next set of walking papers would be issued. This is the price paid for independence. And for what type of research was I realistically qualified to obtain money within my allotted time? It certainly wasn't to study retroviruses.

This was the time to take a panoramic view of the entire playing field, identifying both the positives and negatives of the hand I had dealt myself. The first positive was that in my new job I would be free to do almost anything in a biomedical science that I could get money to support, quite a change from the restrictive environments I had been in most recently. The negative was I had to have both the skills to conduct the work and the ability to get the funds to support it. Another positive was that there were still viral-related environmental monies floating around, and my most recent experiences should help me land some of it, especially if I worked the guilt angle with the EPA. They truly felt chagrined about what had happened, but these feelings would only have a limited lifetime. The negative was that those types of monies would merely be a stopgap solution until I identified a passion that actually led somewhere.

The minimum infectious dose study that my EPA Branch Chief had supported at my new Institute was essentially finished, but a follow-up study was being planned. This was also a positive. The next study, however, would need to be conducted with a different virus. The completed study had been performed by making a series of dilutions of an enteric virus, echovirus-12, into drinking water before known quantities were consumed by adult volunteers. The subjects in this study were then monitored for intestinal virus production through detection of echovirus-12 in their stools during the subsequent week. From this it was determined that consumption of nearly 1,000 live viruses was required to initiate an infection, thus suggesting that drinking water would need to have significant contamination to present a viral hazard. Echovirus-12, however, causes no known illness in humans, so its use as a model virus in this type of study had limited applicability.

Many other enteric viruses clearly do cause human diseases, and some produce severe disease, even death. One of these is rotavirus which is estimated to cause over 500,000 fatalities worldwide each year due to severe gastroenteritis. However, severe illness and death due to rotavirus occur primarily in infants and young children, while the healthy adults with which viral challenge studies are conducted, rarely experience severe rotavirus disease. On the other hand, adults can be infected with rotaviruses but usually experience few, if any, symptoms, thus making a minimum infectious dose study with adult volunteers administered this virus potentially more useful than the one conducted with echovirus-12.

The EPA bought off on this plan and my new Institute was awarded the monies to perform a new minimum infectious dose study with rotavirus as the challenge virus. In the end, they not only funded this project, but personally awarded me two additional, moderately-sized grants on sludge-related projects. At least I had monies to keep myself temporarily afloat.

The use of rotavirus in a minimum infectious dose study had appeal beyond this one project. I was looking for a virus that caused serious disease and rotavirus certainly did that. I also needed to utilize my experiences if I hoped to obtain serious funding for my own work within the foreseeable future, and I did have experiences that could pertain to human rotaviruses. Rotavirus is an enteric virus, and I had just spent seven years studying enteric viruses. I had even used one animal rotavirus strain to seed sludge while at Sandia, and had published two manuscripts on the topic. Finally, rotaviruses are members of the Reoviridae family of which reoviruses are the prototype, and I knew something about reoviruses because of the time I had spent at the Roche Institute. So, at that pivotal moment in my life, I switched my loyalty and hope for the future from retroviruses to rotaviruses.

How does one obtain the necessary tools to begin studies on a new virus without the assistance of a mentor? It was time to find out. Given the opportunity, I soon uncovered instructors of multiple shapes and sizes. Some were merely journal articles and reviews on the topic. Others were new colleagues who provided both advice and materials, such as the viruses themselves and the cells in which to grow them. It is remarkable what you can obtain from fellow investigators who will be competing for some of the same monies as yourself if you are willing to take hat in hand and ask for it. Thus, within weeks of committing myself to rotavirus, I was already conducting preliminary experiments with my new virus.

Although the sky was the limit on possible rotavirus projects, the most immediately pertinent was to conduct a successful minimum infectious dose study. Since this was to be done with a virulent human rotavirus (one that causes human illness), such a virus had to first be procured, and then prepared as challenge material. Rotavirus illness is a winter disease, and during the winter rotavirus season stool specimens from children hospitalized with severe diarrhea were routinely collected and stored for analysis at Cincinnati Children's Hospital, located about one mile from my new workplace. Thus, my first collaborative study was with investigators in that institution, and their stored stool specimens became the source of my challenge virus.

The next task was to make the stool material acceptable for purposeful consumption. Although this would have been a much more rigorous process in subsequent years, all that was required to make this happen in 1982 was to filter the suspensions made from stool materials to remove microbial agents and debris larger than viruses, then to test the filtrate for residual disease-producing agents other than rotaviruses. The latter was done by inoculation of the filtrate into rodents or cultured cells, and wait for the outcome. Human rotaviruses obtained directly from infected children were known to produce no visible effects on mice, guinea pigs or cultured cells, so if our filtrate elicited a measurable response in any of these, it would have been deemed unacceptable for human consumption. Using these methods, I identified only one stool specimen with a sufficient number of live rotaviruses to be useful after filtration. Fortunately, this filtrate produced no detrimental effects after inoculation of mice, guinea pigs or cultured cells. Thus, I had a potentially usable challenge virus.

As this work was being done, my two laboratory assistants and I also developed the techniques and reagents required to work with human rotaviruses. The techniques of most importance were a reasonably sensitive method to measure the quantities of rotaviruses in human stools after the virus reproduced in an infected subject's intestine, and a reliable method to quantify rotavirus antibodies in the blood of these subjects made in response to a rotavirus infection. Both methods were to be used to determine if our volunteers actually experienced a rotavirus infection after swallowing different amounts of the stool filtrate.

Prior to conducting viral challenge studies, volunteers are typically screened to identify those with the lowest amount of blood antibodies against the challenge virus because these subjects would theoretically be the most susceptible to a new infection with the virus in question. These blood antibodies are made by our immune systems in response to a virus infection. Normally one hopes to find subjects with no antibodies against the challenge virus, thus suggesting that the individual had never been infected with this virus and should be fully susceptible to becoming infected when challenged. With rotavirus, however, that is nearly impossible in adults. Essentially every child in the world experiences at least one rotavirus infection by the time they reach three years of age. Better sanitation can delay the first infection, but doesn't prevent it. The reasons are obvious. Rotaviruses are readily transmitted by the fecal/oral route, they are very stable in the environment, including counter tops and door knobs, and a sick child will typically produce and excrete so many rotavirus particles during the course of an illness that if each was worth a dollar, a single illness would pay off our national debt. Since no adults are expected to be free of rotavirus antibody, our plan was to identify those for our study who had the least amount of this antibody with the hope that they would be the most susceptible to another rotavirus infection.

As expected, none of the volunteers we screened for this minimum infectious dose study lacked rotavirus antibodies, so once the volunteers with the lowest rotavirus antibody concentrations were identified, the challenge study was begun by having them consume specified quantities of rotaviruses in drinking water. Only four subjects were enrolled in the first arm of the study to limit the potential damage if our stool material caused some unexpected adverse reaction. Once these four experienced no visible side effects, we then challenged several larger groups of subjects, decreasing the amounts of virus used as we went from group to group with the goal of finding the lowest number that was needed to cause an infection. In the final analysis, extrapolation of our results suggested that swallowing only one live rotavirus particle could produce an infection. Based on this, we revised the conclusion drawn from the echovirus-12 study to now say that a very low level of fecal contamination in drinking water could be sufficient to cause a viral infection.

Probably the most important outcome of these first challenge studies, by my criteria, was the finding that a low percentage of the challenged subjects did not get infected with rotavirus, even when they consumed very large numbers of live viruses. This suggested that these subjects had immunity against rotavirus infection. By this time, I had developed more than a passing interest in identifying what might be responsible for preventing rotavirus disease. Based on most studies with other viruses, the popular choice for this "protector" was antibody. Taking it a step further, this protector was not expected to be just any antibody, but was likely to be antibody that could prevent an infection by neutralizing or disabling the virus. Such antibody is fittingly designated as "neutralizing antibody."

Neutralizing antibodies are known to function by binding directly to specific sites on proteins that reside on the surfaces of virus particles and, through this interaction, somehow prevent the virus from reproducing in an infected cell, thus preventing disease. One mechanism used by these antibodies to block virus reproduction is to bind to a specific site on a virus surface protein that is involved in viral attachment to a target cell, thus preventing the attachment process. This is not the only mechanism of viral neutralization. However, a virus must infect a cell in order to reproduce itself, and it is not difficult to envision that if it cannot attach to a cell, its ability to reproduce will be blocked. The possible importance of neutralizing antibodies in prevention of rotavirus disease was to become a major topic in my research.

In order to determine whether antibodies might be the protectors in our adult subjects who did not become infected, even when administered large numbers of rotaviruses, we conducted a new series of studies, this time challenging subjects who had both low and high levels of rotavirus antibodies. Rotaviruses cause disease (diarrhea and vomiting) after they are swallowed only when they infect the cells that line the small intestine. Therefore, it had been generally accepted that if antibodies prevent rotavirus illnesses, they must find their way into the intestine to accomplish this feat. Consequently, we not only measured the quantities of rotavirus antibodies in the blood of our volunteers, but also in their small intestines. The latter was a heroic and costly effort requiring the endoscopic acquisition of intestinal aspirates from every subject in the study.

In the end, we observed that protection against rotavirus infection and mild illnesses did correlate with higher concentrations of rotavirus antibody in both the blood and intestine, and in some cases the correlation was improved if the analysis was restricted to neutralizing antibody. Although suspected, these results provided the first direct evidence that antibody, and more specifically neutralizing antibody, might play a role in protection against rotavirus illness.

There were a lot of weaknesses with our antibody study, and like most scientific undertakings, it produced more questions than answers. Probably the biggest question concerned the applicability of these results to infants and young children who are the primary targets of severe rotavirus disease. The answer to this question could be obtained only through studies with this younger population, but it would have been unethical to challenge these subjects with any virus, let alone a virulent rotavirus. Therefore, we needed to find another approach to answer questions on the importance of antibody in prevention of rotavirus illnesses in children.

By the time we started our second set of rotavirus challenge studies, our little Institute was joined by a new member who was not only a researcher, but also a pediatrician. Up to this time, the clinical portion of our rotavirus studies had been overseen by the Institute's Director, the only MD on the staff, whose specialty was Internal Medicine. However, studies in children needed the guiding hand of a pediatrician. Our new member was to be that person.

David Bernstein and I became a rotavirus team, the outcome of which had substantial significance in both of our lives Our histories didn't have a lot of commonality when we hooked up, although we did share one experience; we both received herpes virus training at UCLA. That was where the obvious similarities ended. David was Jewish, was born and raised in the Bronx, lived in a high rise apartment building until he left home for college, never had an opportunity to participate in extramural sports, and became an MD. I, on the other hand, grew up on a farm in Montana, was raised in a Catholic household, sports were my life, and I was a PhD. Our demeanors reflect our origins. Although we both have type A personalities, you have to be around me longer than David to recognize this fact. He has been known to inflict severe damage to doors while at work when he gets angry; I have generally spared the workplace doors and, instead, have typically transferred my frustrations to the home front. I think David may have had the better method for pressure release. Regardless of the differences in our personalities, we were to eventually work successfully together, side-by-side, for nearly 30 years.

When David and I began to direct our collective attention toward the pediatric population to answer immunological questions about rotaviruses, it was already known that children who became naturally infected with rotaviruses were often protected against subsequent rotavirus illnesses. However, the nature of the actual protector was unknown. Was it antibody, or more specifically, was it neutralizing antibody?

The proteins on the surfaces of rotavirus particles are not identical between one rotavirus strain and the next. Because of this, antibodies made against these proteins on one strain do not necessarily recognize the proteins on the surface of another strain of rotavirus. Similarly, if the antibodies in question are capable of neutralizing rotaviruses belonging to one strain, they may not neutralize rotaviruses belonging to another strain. If this is the case, the two rotavirus strains, by definition, belong to different serotypes.

To begin to answer questions about immunity to rotavirus, we proposed to determine whether young children who had experienced natural infection were protected against disease caused by all human rotavirus strains, or were they protected only against those strains that were neutralized by the antibodies made against the original infecting strain or serotype. If protection was serotype-specific, it would suggest that neutralizing antibody was the primary protector.

Our initial attempt to get this research funded was through a grant request to the National Institutes of Health. During the next months, we performed the footwork needed to make the study happen, including recruiting several pediatric practices located around Cincinnati where the subjects could be seen as patients, and blood and stool samples could be collected for analyses. During the following months, we wrote the grant. Finally, after several more months, we learned that our request had been nixed by the Study Section that reviewed it. Their main objection was that, in America, children are naturally exposed to a very limited number of rotavirus serotypes during a typical rotavirus season. Therefore, exposure to multiple serotypes, as needed to provide a complete answer to our primary question, was not likely to happen in American children.

Since I still believed in the importance of the project, this setback didn't dissuade me from continuing the search for funding which was moved to another front, this time to the US Agency for International Development. The mission of USAID is to provide support to developing nations at multiple levels. My logic was that if we could determine what might protect developing world children from a virus that was killing over half million each year, this activity would fall within the boundaries of that mission. Our Director was an experienced politician, and more often than not knew the right person to contact. In this case, the right person was the manager for these types of studies at USAID. Thus, we met in this fellow's office to spring our ideas and develop a battle plan. At least that was my goal.

Mostly what happened that day at the USAID Headquarters in Northern Virginia was a lot of arm waving and hem-hawing as I told my story to the USAID manager. His actions and words were clearly just a diversion to get us safely out of his office. Even so, he provided enough of a glimmer of hope that I wasn't yet willing to give up on this funding source. Instead, I continued to pester this guy and his staff on a regular basis for the coming weeks, always attempting to get some remnant of a firm decision regarding the funding for our proposal. Weeks turned into months, during which time vague promises were made, but nothing conclusive came from USAID.

Mentally, I had finally checked this one off when, out of nowhere, the manager actually called me to declare that USAID would fund the entire study we had proposed. My euphoria at receiving this long-awaited news lasted only about a week. Then I again began to realize that evidence of dollars coming my way was not materializing. Several more weeks and multiple phone calls later, the manager again agreed to support our study, but this time the offer was accompanied with the bombshell that the study would have to be performed in Bangladesh, wherever that was. Admittedly, this made more sense for USAID because Bangladesh is one of the world's poorest countries, and USAID had been supporting clinical studies there for years. It also made more technical sense because exposure to rotaviruses representative of multiple serotypes was much more probable in Bangladesh than in America. But traveling to Bangladesh to conduct a study was not high on my list of things to do before I encountered the Grim Reaper. However, if I really wanted the study funded, there was no obvious alternative. Thus began my foray into international medicine.

The plan arranged by USAID was for somebody in our group to make an initial visit to a research center identified in Bangladesh. From there, a research plan would either be shaped or it wouldn't. The name of the center selected had no meaning to me, and the USAID manager's description didn't provide much clarification. It even required several conversations for me to understand that the place was called the International Center for Diarrheal Diseases Research, Bangladesh, since every time he would say the name he would slur I-C-D-D-R-B into one syllable. Later, I knew I had arrived when I could do the same.

As soon as our study site got shifted, my colleague David immediately announced "this leaves me out." Visiting a developing country to conduct research was not high on his priority list. Since our Director had made the first contact that got us into this situation, he felt more of an obligation to make the trip with me. But, in reality, it was my deal to make or break, so I had to lead the charge. Thus, with much trepidation, the two of us set off, neither having any notion of what we were going to experience. In the airport on our way out of town, the Director's wife forced him to purchase an extra $500,000 worth of trip insurance. Then Shirley suggested the same to me. With that done, I was sure we were goners. The last advice provided by the Director's wife before we boarded the plane was "if you come back, leave everything in your suitcase behind."

As we landed in Dhaka in mid-afternoon a couple of days later, my first impression was that people were swarming like ants. Everywhere I looked, there were little brown people. Even the banks of the water-filled ditches next to the airport runway seemed to be crawling with human activity. As we entered the century-old debarkation area, we were confronted with another swarm of humanity, every member of which was grabbing for our bags, presumably with the intention of toting them somewhere for a tip. Fortunately, we were quickly collared and removed from the line of fire by an ICDDR,B representative.

My first order of business on entering any country since my time in Europe was to obtain local currency. To make this exchange in Bangladesh, our escort ushered me into a tiny alcove inside the airport, but the instant the transaction was completed, even before I could get the money into my wallet, he was pushing us toward his waiting car.

As we emerged from the airport door into the parking lot, I encountered my first beggar, an emaciated woman carrying an equally emaciated child on her hip. As her hand passed in front of me, I deposited the equivalent of about $2 from what I still had in my fist. That was my first mistake. Out of the pavement, trees and heavens, at least 50 pathetic individuals of all sizes and descriptions descended on us, screaming and crying for money. We all ran for the car, jumped in and locked the door. In the blink of an eye, all 50 of our new-found friends were banging and scratching at the windows, most with tears streaming down their faces. One mother kept shoving her blind, deformed child in front of the window where I sat as she pushed away a leper whose begging hand was missing several fingers. Our driver immediately commenced honking and moving forward, plowing through the throng of beggars as he pulled away.

In my naivety, I had nearly caused a riot before I had even left the airport. My first two lessons in Bangladesh were: don't make eye contact with street people and never give them money unless you are already moving away fast.

As we pulled out of the airport and onto what was considered to be a main thoroughfare, the driver sped up to over 60 mph. At that moment, I regretted not having given away all my money in the parking lot because we were about to die anyway. Every motorized vehicle we encountered was traveling at comparable speeds, and those approaching us were coming straight at us. There were no real lanes, and our driver, or the drivers of the oncoming vehicles, would repeatedly duck away just before we met head-on. When I came up for air after several minutes, I began to realize that I was not yet dead and there really was some order to this madness. The rule was that the biggest vehicle had the right of way. It was just necessary to determine whether it was you or the other guy in the split second before you crashed. Eventually the traffic slowed to a snail's pace when we approached the inner city. I was never so thankful to be in the middle of a traffic jam in my life.

Eventually we crawled through the locked and guarded front gate of what appeared to be a five-star hotel, fronted by a chaotic scene of pedestrians, ox carts, bicycle taxis, and large dilapidated buses with passengers hanging one-handed on all sides or perched on the roofs where there was standing room only. They apparently had great balance. As we alighted, we were met by a group of exquisitely-dressed porters who swished our luggage in one direction and us in another. By the time we checked in and arrived at our spacious, perfectly furnished rooms on the 19th floor, our luggage was already there. The curtains, however, were drawn, perhaps to help the guests ignore what was occurring outside their windows.

Regardless of the reason, when I pulled open the curtains, the reality was there. My window opened to the backside of the hotel. Directly below was a pond that, even viewed from the 19th floor, was clearly more a cesspool than a pond. On its opposite shore was a sprawl of open lean-tos massed together where, after dark, a series of miniature fires could be seen as the inhabitants prepared their evening meals. Later I learned that the fuel used for these fires was dried cow dung, standard fare for much the developing world where real firewood is only a distant memory.

During the daytime, I observed the activities of the folks below as if it was all part of some scientific experiment. The most discernible were those that revolved around the pond. It was evident that this was the wash tub for the locals, both for clothing and themselves. However, only yards from where these functions were performed, the adult population used an enclosed box, positioned on wobbly stilts over the edge of the pond, for defecation. It was unclear from my vantage point whether the pond was also used as their source of drinking water, but since there seemed to be no other possibilities, I assumed it was. This pond gave new meaning to the term, "a multiuse resource." It also elicited a new definition for "inner city living."

A couple of hours after our arrival while still in obvious jet lag, we were driven to a social gathering which was to be our introductory meeting with ICDDR,B personnel. Our contact, the USAID manager that we had met several months earlier in Northern Virginia, had made the arrangements, and he would be present to grease the skids for us. He was a 50-something bureaucrat with seemingly limitless energy which sometimes worked against him. On one of his earlier visits to a field site in Bangladesh, he was in a hurry as was typically the case, and took a shortcut through an open field to traverse between points A and B. It was nighttime, and this guy was not familiar with the specific terrain. As he marched determinedly onward, brushing aside weeds and knocking over bushes in his headlong rush, he catapulted head first into a pond filled with human waste. After he surfaced and was pulled onto shore, feces matted his entire body. He survived and so did the story which became a classic at the ICDDR,B.

As the driver approached the site of our evening gathering with ICDDR,B personnel, Dhaka took on a very different flavor. The garbage piled on the roadsides dwindled to almost nothing and the wall-enclosed homes lining the streets mimicked those found in an upscale American suburb. The gate through which we passed on entering the compound where the party was being hosted was serviced by two guards, one whose function was to ask who we were and a second whose job was to open the gate. After we stepped out of the car and through the surrounding lush gardens, we entered the air-conditioned, marble-floored interior of our host's home. There we were met by a doorman who proudly escorted us to the party inside. It was a grand celebration being held in our honor with about 50 guests, most of whom we would never see again. In the confusion associated with multiple introductions by our escort, it became less and less evident who we would really be dealing with in this venture, if there really was to be a venture.

Toward the end of the evening and several wine-coolers later, however, this particular bit of confusion began to be sorted out when a visiting investigator from Johns Hopkins University asked "when would be a good time to meet tomorrow." His name was David Sack and he had been in Dhaka off and on for many years, conducting clinical studies with a variety of enteric pathogens. David then introduced me to another American who had also been in Bangladesh for years as part of international studies. This second

American lacked the enthusiasm shown by David, and even displayed some reticence to carry on a conversation with me at all. It later became evident why. Regardless, by the time we left that evening, it was at least clear that those two Americans would be the key players if we were going to establish any type of collaboration.

We met with David early the next morning, and he proceeded to fill in the history and mission of the ICDDR,B. It had started as a regional cholera hospital/research center, but had evolved into an international center for studies on all diarrheal diseases. I only later realized, due to my ignorance, that it was ranked number one in the world in that category. Almost every scientist who had made a reputation in international studies with enteric pathogens had at least visited, if not worked several years, in this facility. Our USAID contact had actually done me a great service in getting me there.

One of the unique features of the ICDDR,B was its field site in a district called Matlab, located about three hours south of Dhaka. This was a region in the Bangladesh delta interlaced with waterways and, as I was soon to learn, was accessible only by boat. Matlab contained nearly 200,000 inhabitants which were scattered within primitive villages along the banks of its several rivers. The study clinic, a modified paddle boat anchored on one of the river banks, served as the medical center for the entire region. From this site, field workers were launched for weekly visits to every home in the district, thus maintaining continuous health records on all its inhabitants. With this handle on the demographics of the area, and the fact that enteric pathogens have been a staple of the diet in Matlab for millennia, the site had provided an opulent reservoir for continuous studies on diarrheal diseases for several decades.

David quickly realized that neither of his Cincinnati visitors was planning to move to Bangladesh any time soon, but he also realized that USAID had deposited some potentially useful talent on his doorstep. Although the ICDDR,B, had multiple investigators that were highly skilled in studying enteric pathogens, none of the present group were rotavirus specialists. Taking all this into account, David concluded that initiating a collaborative study with us could provide a valuable addition to their present arsenal of activities, but the success of this venture would depend on his ability to attach it to an ongoing study. No one from our Cincinnati group was going to take the extended leave in Bangladesh that would be required to initiate a new study.

The second American we met during our first evening in Dhaka was leading an investigation of a new cholera vaccine, and had by then enrolled nearly the entire population of Matlab. When we arrived, his massive walk-in freezer at the ICDDR,B was overflowing with serum and stool specimens collected and cataloged as part of this study. David's suggestion was that we piggyback onto this study by examining stool specimens collected from study subjects with severe diarrhea for the presence of rotavirus. Since blood specimens had also been collected as part of this study from each subject at the time of their illness, we could examine these to determine whether rotavirus antibody was present, at the time of their infection, in subjects whose illnesses were later found to be caused by rotavirus. The presence or absence of this antibody would reveal whether or not they had been infected with rotavirus sometime in the past. If rotavirus antibody was on board, it could be examined for neutralizing antibodies to determine what serotype of rotavirus was responsible for the previous infection. In this way, we could determine whether, in this developing nation setting, a previous rotavirus infection protected against a subsequent rotavirus illness. If this was found to be the case as predicted, we could then ascertain whether or not this protection was serotype-specific. The project would entail a massive amount of work on our part, but it was doable, and the outcome could potentially answer the question I was attempting to ask before coming to Bangladesh, i.e., was neutralizing antibody the protector stimulated by a rotavirus infection?

When the leader of the cholera study was approached with the plan, he was less than enthusiastic. The specimens to be used were his, and he was guarding them carefully. He gradually explained, over a series of several days of drawn out discussions, that when he had shared specimens in the past, the so-called collaborators had on occasion sequestered them in their own laboratories. To exacerbate the situation, it had sometimes happened that the next report he received on the progress of the collaboration was a published manuscript, and little mention was made of his role in the project. I could understand why he was reluctant to trust me, some unknown out of the hinterlands of Ohio. We eventually got past this sufficiently, using David Sack's feather-gloved guidance, to at least agree to discuss the project further after I returned home.

In the meantime, we were given the Matlab tour which consisted of a two hour van ride on a narrow road shared by every description of vehicle and animal life, followed by another hour on a speed boat while sucking in polluted mist from the river. I attributed my bout of diarrhea, which began a day later and persisted for several months, to my exposure during the last leg of this journey. My Director, who sat in the back of the boat and inhaled less river water, never got sick. In fact, he left Bangladesh majorly constipated. I would guess the quart of Pepto-Bismol and pound of peanut butter he consumed every day during our stay may also have contributed to his intestinal status.

Part of the trip to Matlab was a combination of van/boat transportation in that the van had to be transported by ferry across a small river at about the mid-point on the trip. The ferries made the round trip only once each hour, thus providing ample time for the locals to solicit the ferry customers for cash. As my Director and I waited outside the van for the ferry to arrive, two girls about five years of age cautiously approached and began quietly speaking to us in their native tongue. What they were saying required no explanation since one of the pair kept pushing a small coin, worth about two cents, across her palms directly in front of our faces. She kept smiling and repeating her little phrase, each time with twinkling eyes radiating a hopeful plea. I had already trained myself to avoid eye contact with beggars, but this training disintegrated in the presence of this tiny girl. I didn't give her any money on that trip because I knew I had no escape route, and the airport experience was still flashing through my head. However, I knew that when we made the return trip later that afternoon, I would donate to her cause if she was still there. When our van was unloaded from the ferry several hours later, she spotted me immediately. It was as if she had been waiting all day for my return. I rewarded her persistence. It was probably a stupid thing to do, but this might have been all her family had to live on for the month. As soon as I handed her the cash out the window of the moving van, she evaporated. I guess that was her only chance to avoid having her money taken by a larger and stronger entrepreneur.

Matlab was as described, an area of islands and peninsulas containing large numbers of people living together with their animals in rickety shacks along the river banks. Some villages had pump wells to replace the river water, but if the pump-handle pins fell out, as they sometimes did, the pumps could remain unused for weeks until some trained passer-by replaced the pins. The folks living in those villages were not technological geniuses. We visited during low water season, but during the monsoon season, half of the country goes underwater. I was told that sometimes during a typhoon, the only survivors in some of these areas were those who were capable of attaching themselves to the trunks of palm trees and hanging on, literally for days. These individuals would often carry scars developed from wounds left by the embedded tree trunk. So if the diseases and starvation didn't get you, the typhoons would. It isn't a country filled with an abundance of old people.

The ICDDR,B in Dhaka is not only a research facility but also has an associated hospital where literally thousands of patients with diarrheal diseases are treated each year. During the last day of our visit, we were introduced to the cholera ward, a room the size of a large gymnasium filled to capacity. In that one viewing, we saw more cholera patients than the average doctor in a developed country could hope to see in a lifetime. Most were lying face up on cots wearing nothing but loose shirts. Their butts were positioned over holes sewn in the centers of the cots, below which were buckets used not only to collect what was being purged but also to measure its quantity. Each patient had a family member attending them whose responsibility it was to determine how much came out and replace it by oral rehydration. David assured us that if a patient with cholera made it to their hospital before they were already flaccid, they invariably survived, typically requiring only the treatment just described. With this simple, low-tech procedure being so effective, I wondered why cholera is so lethal in most settings, especially during epidemics. Apparently the afflicted aren't kept properly hydrated.

After we returned to Cincinnati, with my Director's wardrobe still intact in spite of his wife's request, I began the process of making the Bangladesh study happen. It was decided that if anything were to be done, I would be required to return to Dhaka and bring the technology for detecting rotaviruses with me. This meant assembling the reagents to be used for this assay and packing them into two massive containers filled with dry ice. Thus, about six months after returning from my first visit to Bangladesh, I was off again, this time for a planned two-week stay.

I was wiser when I arrived in Dhaka the second time, and had trained myself to ignore the beggars. In fact, I also ignored what was on the mind of the local airport agent who was responsible for releasing my two boxes of supplies. After my arrival, he met me at the gate along with an ICDDR,B representative, and we adjourned to his office. There we commenced to stare at one another for about ten minutes, neither of us showing any signs of relenting. He never really asked for a bribe, but after my experience with the apartment superintendents in New Jersey 18 years earlier, I recognized what he wanted. He finally determined that I was a hopeless case, I collected my boxes, and the driver deposited me at the ICDDR,B, where my part of the study commenced.

During this two-week visit, I taught several lab personnel how to conduct the rotavirus detection assay using the reagents I had transported, and at the same time, personally tested multiple stool samples from diarrheal patients in the cholera vaccine trial for the presence of rotavirus. Before this effort was launched, however, the American leading the cholera trial discussed with me the potential manuscripts that could come from our joint project, and in what order the authors would be listed. This may not strike a novice as important, but you don't have to be at the laboratory bench long before you recognize that the only important authors on a manuscript are those listed first, last and second, in that order. Anyone else may as well be chopped liver.

The discussion was launched with an announcement from my new colleague, asserting "I will be first author on all publications involving clinical aspects of this study. If you don't agree to this arrangement, you may as well go home now."

That left me no real choice since he held every card in the deck. He then moved on to recite the list of authors that would be included on the manuscripts, some of which had left Bangladesh years earlier and I would never even meet. He was hard-nosed, but he was also loyal to persons who had worked with him. In the end, he didn't even enforce his side of our bargain.

Those two weeks constituted one of the most productive in my career. I didn't have anything else to do but work all day and assemble the results at night. By the time I left Dhaka, I had identified 461 subjects who had experienced a severe rotavirus infection during the two-year period of the cholera vaccine study. This time I returned home to Cincinnati with 461 stool specimens stored on dry ice as part of my luggage.

The acute blood specimens collected in association with the illnesses of those 461 subjects, along with blood specimens from age-matched healthy controls, were eventually delivered on my doorstep at the Christ Hospital Institute. The entire study took nearly three years to complete, but the results were remarkably clear. The subjects who experienced severe rotavirus illnesses were all children less than five years of age, and they were usually free of rotavirus antibody in the blood specimens collected at the start of their rotavirus illnesses, at least significantly more often than the age-matched controls. Thus, a prior rotavirus infection, even in this setting, did provide some measure of protection against a subsequent severe rotavirus illness.

This protection was not perfect, however, and when a subject experienced a rotavirus illness after a previous rotavirus infection, these illnesses were often with the same serotype of rotavirus that caused their first illness. Thus, the protection we observed after a natural rotavirus infection was not serotype-specific. Since there are multiple serotypes of human rotavirus, this meant that something other than, or in addition to neutralizing antibody may be responsible for protection against rotavirus disease. This finding flew in the face of current dogma regarding the importance of neutralizing antibodies in protection against viral diseases. It also set the stage for the next segment of my rotavirus career.

During the same time frame that the Bangladesh studies were being performed, our group in Cincinnati, led by David Bernstein, was conducting a clinical trial of our own with rotavirus. Human rotavirus was discovered in 1973 and within a short time became recognized as the primary cause of severe diarrhea in young children worldwide. Because preventing exposure to this virus, either early in life or multiple times thereafter, is virtually impossible, the only realistic way to prevent rotavirus illness is by vaccination. This is something that needs to be accomplished early in life to prevent rotavirus illnesses in infants. Recognizing this situation, a rotavirus vaccine had already been developed and was being tested in infants by the early 1980's. This vaccine, like all rotavirus vaccines that have been evaluated in humans, was composed of live rotaviruses that were delivered orally to mimic natural rotavirus infection.

The first rotavirus vaccine was composed of a calf rotavirus. The logic was that humans could probably be infected with an animal rotavirus, but these infections in a different species were expected to be without symptoms. This is called the Jennerian approach to vaccine development based on Edward Jenner's use of a cowpox virus to prevent the deadly human illness, smallpox. Even though the calf rotavirus was expected to be attenuated for humans, i.e. not cause human disease, it was still passed multiple times in cell culture to insure that this was the case. This method of attenuation was first employed by Albert Sabin who developed the live poliovirus vaccine about 25 years earlier at Children's Hospital in Cincinnati, a vaccine that is still being used in much of the world today. Although the first rotavirus vaccine provided good protection against rotavirus illness in vaccinated infants when tested in Finland, it elicited little or no protection when later tested in Africa, one of the settings where a rotavirus vaccine is most needed due to the high mortality caused by the virus in the developing world.

During the time the first rotavirus vaccine was being tested, two additional animal rotaviruses were also being groomed as candidate vaccines. One was another calf rotavirus and the second was obtained from a monkey. The logic employed to develop these candidate vaccines was the same as that used for the first calf rotavirus vaccine.

The second calf-derived vaccine was found to elicit quite good protection against rotavirus illness when tested in a small trial in Philadelphia, so the pharmaceutical company that had licensed this vaccine was anxious to test it in additional settings. Since our group had established a reputation as a center to conduct clinical studies with rotaviruses as a result of our adult challenge studies, we were asked to be one of those settings.

In the winter of 1988-89, we conducted the first rotavirus vaccine trial in Cincinnati children using the new calf rotavirus vaccine. The results were that this vaccine provided little or no protection to our vaccinees. Interestingly, however, only one strain of human rotavirus circulated in Cincinnati during the 1988-89 rotavirus season, and subjects that became ill due to natural rotavirus infection with this virus during that season were fully protected against subsequent rotavirus disease for at least the following two years. Based on its remarkable ability to elicit protection, this circulating rotavirus strain had the earmark of a potentially effective vaccine.

At nearly the same time David Bernstein and I completed this vaccine trial, we obtained the results of the Bangladesh study which suggested that protection after natural rotavirus infection was not serotype-specific. Coupling these two findings, logic dictated that if our protective circulating strain could be developed into an effective, single strain vaccine, it might protect against human rotavirus illnesses caused by all serotypes. Unfortunately, the strains that circulated in Cincinnati during the two-year study were all found to belong to the same serotype as the original circulating strain. Thus, this vaccine trial provided no useful information concerning my prediction of cross-serotype protection following vaccination with a single strain of human rotavirus.

To develop the virulent 1988-89 Cincinnati rotavirus strain into a vaccine, we needed both to eliminate its virulence (attenuate it) and find someone to pay for its development as a vaccine candidate. The first task seemed to have only one logical method of attack. This was to pass the virus multiple times in cell culture, anticipating mutations (i.e. genetic changes) would be selected that would allow the virus to grow better in the cultured cells and less well in the human gut. This was the method utilized by Albert Sabin when he developed his attenuated, live poliovirus vaccine.

I set about accomplishing this task almost immediately, using a human rotavirus obtained from the stool of one of the placebo controls that became ill during our 1988-89 vaccine trial. Since the subject was #12 in that study, we called the virus strain, and subsequently also the vaccine, 89-12.

The second task, to identify a source of monies to pay for the vaccine trials, was more daunting. David Bernstein and I reasoned that we could apply for a government grant, but the likelihood of being awarded a grant for such a technically mundane activity was miniscule. Therefore, we went after sponsors that were the most likely to financially benefit if the vaccine was successful. These were the pharmaceutical companies. During the subsequent months, I attempted to sell the idea of a single strain human rotavirus vaccine to the giants in the vaccine industry, and eventually was invited to present my case at two of these companies. Disappointingly, there were no takers.

During my time on the money trail, I grew the 89-12 rotavirus strain passage after passage in cell culture, and multiple vials of the 33rd passage were prepared as a vaccine by a contractor to the National Institutes of Health. Again, our Director had the right contacts, and one of them was the manager of the Enteric Diseases Program at the National Institutes of Health. Once the contact was made, this manager made the final arrangement to have our new rotavirus strain bottled as a vaccine and safety-tested for microbial contaminants by the NIH contractor. Thus, the stage was set to test the new vaccine if I could obtain a sponsor to fund the study.

By the time I had been shown the door by the major vaccine manufacturers, David Sack, my advocate and collaborator in Bangladesh, had returned to his old job at Johns Hopkins University. Within a short time, he had also become a consultant to a small Boston biotech company called Virus Research Inc (VRI). Since one of his responsibilities with VRI was to identify promising new and inexpensive technologies for them to acquire, he strongly suggested that they contact me. He was clearly a believer in the approach we were using for our new rotavirus vaccine, and sold the idea to VRI.

Within weeks after David suggested my name to VRI, his urgings resulted in our first meeting with VRI personnel. A short time later, they made the decision to license our vaccine and pay for its development during early clinical testing.

So, the stage was finally set. Through luck, persistence, and blue collar science, I had developed a vaccine that was about to be tested in humans. This second chance to do something practical with my life as a scientist was beginning to pay off.

15 Never Say Die

The rotavirus vaccine field was not crowded when David Bernstein and I jumped into it in the early 1990's, but we were also not alone. The original calf rotavirus vaccine had come and gone, and our results in Cincinnati with the second calf-derived vaccine provided one of the outcomes that led to its demise. In fact, the developer of this vaccine exasperatingly informed me that "you have set the world of rotavirus vaccines back by at least five years by your findings." I don't think it was our fault, and besides, I'm sure it wasn't anywhere near that dramatic, but the conclusions stemming from our trial did not help.

The other major candidate vaccine for rotavirus being evaluated during that period was derived from a rhesus monkey and was, accordingly, called rhesus rotavirus or RRV. The developers of this vaccine clearly had the greatest name recognition and connections of those in the field. The group was led by a pioneer in enteric viral diseases whose laboratory was at the National Institutes of Health, one of the most renowned centers for biomedical studies in the world. By the late 1980's, the NIH had cornered almost the entire world market on funding for rotavirus vaccine trials through both industry and government sponsorships. They even had monies from the World Health Organization, an honor that provided a special blessing on any vaccine candidate. Because they had the money, the RRV vaccine was tested across the globe, over and over again, before it was finally abandoned due to lack of consistent protection.

The downfalls of both the RRV and second calf rotavirus vaccines were perceived by their respective developers to be due to the lack of ability of their candidates to stimulate neutralizing antibodies against the various serotypes of human rotavirus. Consequently, both developers concluded that to alter this situation, they needed to humanize their animal rotavirus strains. Thus, both created a series of new rotavirus strains with the primary genetic makeup of their parent RRV or calf rotavirus strains. However, each new virus contained one gene derived from a different serotype of human rotavirus. In every case, the gene in question had the ability to be decoded into one of the two neutralization proteins of rotavirus. The end result was that their new vaccines no longer contained a single rotavirus strain, but instead, were composed of either four or five rotavirus strains representing each of the dominant human rotavirus serotypes. With their four-virus RRV vaccine in hand, the NIH convinced the pharmaceutical giant Wyeth to license their product that was subsequently named Rotashield. At about the same time, Merck licensed the five-virus, calf-derived rotavirus vaccine, and eventually assigned it the trade name RotaTeq. Thus, when I presented our story on the 89-12 vaccine to these two companies, it was already a case of too little, too late.

The guiding theory behind the development of these two multi-strain rotavirus vaccines was that protection was due solely to neutralizing antibodies. Regardless of the reason, both multi-strain vaccines were eventually shown to consistently provide high levels of protection, at least against severe, potentially fatal, rotavirus illnesses. Based on these results, it became universally accepted, except in small pockets of the world such as our tiny institute in Cincinnati and in our equally miniscule sponsor's headquarters in Boston, that neutralizing antibodies were the sole protectors after rotavirus vaccination with a live rotavirus.

What did all this mean to me, an unknown entity who had just uncovered evidence that something other than neutralizing antibodies played a role in protection and, based on this finding, was in the process of attempting to test a vaccine composed of only a single rotavirus strain? It meant that my competitive juices had better get flowing once again if I was going to convert a world of nonbelievers. Of course, if we didn't lose our sponsor and could take the evaluation of our vaccine to completion, the validity or proof of my hypothesis would eventually show up "in the pudding."

Clinical evaluation of a vaccine is a slow, grinding process driven by caution. This is good if you are a vaccinee, but being a vaccine inventor, it seemed like it would have been quicker to tear down Mt. Everest with a teaspoon than get through our early evaluation steps. The initial human trials, called Phase I, were conducted simply to test the safety of the 89-12 vaccine. These studies were started in adults, and when these were completed, the vaccine was tested in children who had experienced a previous rotavirus infection. In order to err on the side of caution, the bar in these trials was set at the top of the pole. If even one vaccinee developed gas within a week after receiving the vaccine, the study would have to be repeated. As might be expected, one of our first ten adult subjects did just that. Thus, another six months were required to test the vaccine on a second set of ten adult subjects. Once we finally got past this hurdle, the same anomaly occurred in the first trial with children, so that study also had to be repeated with a second set of subjects. By the time they were finished, the first safety trials had eaten up nearly three years.

Now we were at the point when the evaluation of our vaccine became dicey. Until this moment, we had administered 89-12 only to subjects who had had previous rotavirus infections. It was now time to take the leap into the true target population, i.e. previously uninfected infants. Although it was extremely unlikely that our vaccine would cause anything more dastardly than would happen after a natural rotavirus infection, you can never be sure, and this was the time for bravery, both for us and especially for the parents who were the first to allow their children to be administered our experimental vaccine. In the end, these parents were our greatest advocates. Many had an older child who had been hospitalized with severe rotavirus illnesses and each of these provided a detailed description of the horrific experience it had been. They would say, "My child seemed to be well one minute and on death's door in the next, and the diarrhea just kept coming and coming. I would give almost anything to have my new baby not have the same experience."

This Phase I safety and immunogenicity study started with six infants who were administered our new vaccine, and when all went well, we added 21 more. For each set of subjects who received the vaccine, a comparable number of placebo recipients were also included in a blinded fashion. This was done to insure that if some nasty bug was passing through Cincinnati at the time, its effects would be detected in the placebo recipients as well as the vaccinees. In addition to the safety concerns in infants, we also needed to show the vaccine stimulated immune responses in these subjects. If that did not occur, the vaccine was dead in the starting gate. Fortunately, we got past both hurdles, at least as well as one could hope with only a few subjects.

By now we had put nearly four years into our clinical studies with the 89-12 vaccine. That was the bad news. The good news was that no show-stoppers had reared their ugly heads. We did, however, have some indication that our vaccine was not completely without side effects and might produce mild fevers, but with the small number of subjects tested, the results were inconclusive. Therefore, we and VRI plodded on into the first efficacy trial.

When this trial was finally ready to be conducted, we had lost our home at The Christ Hospital due to insufficient funding by several of the investigators, and those of us with funding had become part of Cincinnati Children's Hospital Medical Center. Thus, our first Phase II efficacy trial was conducted in our new home. This was a four-center study that included Cincinnati, but also incorporated study sites in Pittsburgh, Philadelphia and Baltimore, the latter of which was managed by my colleague David Sack. He was still a believer in our vaccine, and was there to again encourage us in its development.

The results of the efficacy trial took nearly two years to generate, but they were worth the wait. Although the vaccine still showed evidence of a side effect, its efficacy was quite remarkable. Protection against rotavirus disease was the best for any rotavirus vaccine tested in a multicenter study. The safety concern continued to center on excess low grade fevers in the vaccinees, something that was not likely to kill a vaccine outright, but could in the long run.

Our results were published in The Lancet in July of 1999, the outcome of which was that David Bernstein and I became instant, albeit temporary, celebrities. We were interviewed by over a dozen newspaper and radio reporters as the news of our trial was relayed across the globe. This recognition had little to do with our new publication and much to do with the fact that the one licensed rotavirus vaccine was withdrawn from the market in America the same week our manuscript was released. This was Rotashield, the four-virus, RRV-derived vaccine developed at the NIH and manufactured by Wyeth. It had taken nearly a decade and multiple vaccine trials between its licensure by Wyeth and its approval by the FDA for inclusion in the infant vaccination series. However, it took only nine months for the vaccine to be eliminated in America. During this nine-month period, the Centers for Disease Control had monitored vaccinees for any potential adverse reactions, and had observed that several more vaccinees than expected developed intussusception during the week after receiving their first dose of Rotashield. The indication of a problem was subtle in that only about 1 in 10,000 vaccinees developed the complication, but this was sufficient to get the product taken off the market.

Intussusception is the name assigned to a blockage condition of the small intestine that is initiated by closure of unknown origin, and is exacerbated by the telescoping of the intestine due to its peristaltic action. It is extremely painful, and of course, fatal if uncorrected. Sometimes the blockage self-resolves, but normally it requires intervention consisting of an air enema (blowing air up the child's anus), or an operation in which the surgeon attempts to manually dislodge the blockage. If this is not successful, a section of the child's intestine must be removed to eliminate the problem. Thus, intussusception is not a trivial condition. In America, an average of about 1 in 2,000 children develop intussusception during their first two years of life from natural causes. Even though the incidence associated with Rotashield vaccination was five-fold less than that which occurs naturally, even a small excess number of cases during the week after receiving the vaccine was not acceptable.

This intussusception crisis created "decision time" regarding further development of live rotavirus vaccines. Was there something unusual about Rotashield that would not be applicable to other live rotavirus vaccines or, when evaluated in a sufficiently large number of subjects, were they all going to trigger intussusception? Would any company be willing to spend the billion dollars needed to bring a new rotavirus vaccine to market with the cloud of Rotashield hanging over its head?

Once the encouraging results of the first 89-12 efficacy trial were deciphered, nearly two years before the Rotashield implosion and our publication in The Lancet appeared, it was time for VRI to pass the baton to a larger company with deeper pockets. They had never planned to take the vaccine to completion, but had only hoped to get it successfully over the first few hurdles before they passed it on. Somehow, the billion dollars needed to bring a vaccine to market was not congruent with their budget. So who were the big dogs in the vaccine business? The main ones in America at the time were Wyeth and Merck, but they were spoken for. Beyond our borders, there was also a very short list of big pharmaceutical companies interested in vaccine development. Which should be the target?

The project manager for the 89-12 vaccine at VRI, a former Cincinnatian named Dale Spriggs, recognized that VRI had almost no in-house rotavirus experience. Thus, he knew it was imperative that he get our input into every major decision made during the development of the vaccine. This included even finding a new partner. David Bernstein had, at that time, been working with the British pharmaceutical company SmithKline (SK) for nearly a decade in pre-clinical (animal) studies with a new herpes virus vaccine. SK had also briefly expressed an interest in licensing a different strain of human rotavirus that I had developed as a potential vaccine. Whether or not these were the driving forces, VRI concluded that the 89-12 baton should be passed to SK. Therefore, Dale, David and I scheduled a trip to the headquarters of the SK Biologicals Division in Rixensart, Belgium, to make our case.

Immediately before this visit in January of 1997, the three of us attended a rotavirus meeting at the home of the World Health Organization in Geneva, the primary purpose of which was to heap praise on the Rotashield vaccine and its developers. There were other related topics discussed, such as how to get Rotashield quickly evaluated and utilized in developing countries, but what I remember most was the praise. Perhaps too much praise can be a bad omen because, less than three years later, intussusception took out this vaccine.

One evening at dinner during the time of this meeting, Dale explained to David and me how we should approach SK to sell our product. He sternly preached that we first needed to block from our minds the accolades that were coming to Rotashield, and once this was accomplished, we should dwell only on the positives of our product. His speech rattled on for some time before he finally concluded that his love affair with the 89-12 vaccine, nourished over the past several years, was not being properly appreciated by David and me, even if we were the inventors. It was his responsibility to get our attention on this issue so that we would show no reservations when we made our presentation to SK. In his mind, it was a critical situation that called for extreme measures.

After nearly a full minute of silence and deep thought, Dale finally burst forth with, "Hey guys, you have to get on board with this right now, once and for all. You have no choice. You have to throw yourselves on the hand grenade."

I don't know whether we threw ourselves on the hand grenade as Dale intended, but between the three of us, we convinced SK to sub-license the 89-12 vaccine. I think the vaccine sold itself, and we were just there to deliver the specifics. Regardless, the tactics worked. By the end of 1997, VRI had negotiated a contract for further development of the 89-12 vaccine with SK.

Once the vaccine was in the hands of a big pharmaceutical company, our input took a sharp turn downward, something we had not envisioned but should have expected. Dale explained to SK that they needed us, and should seek our advice as he had done. They listened a little, but didn't hear a whole lot. They did, however, realize there was no in-house rotavirus experience at SK, so they at least asked me to teach a SK investigator the basic principles of rotavirus biology that I had acquired over the past 16 years. Thus, within months after the contract between SK and VRI was signed, my lab hosted a single, six-day visit by what I came to recognize as one of SK's finest. Admittedly, we had everything in place to help our visitor master the essential ingredients of years of rotavirus knowledge in one week, but she actually succeeded. She departed not only with all the information we could stuff into her head, but also with all the supplies she could carry in her pockets, specifically our lab methods and reagents.

Several weeks after returning to her lab in Rixensart, our visitor had grown the 89-12 vaccine strain, and was attempting to develop a new vaccine lot. When I had performed the multiple passages of the 89-12 virus in cultured cells, and prepared a vaccine directly from the passage 33 material, no attempt was made to isolate a single live rotavirus particle from the mixture in order to develop a homogeneous vaccine. Genetic mutations occur constantly in living organisms, but they are especially common in RNA viruses that lack the repair mechanisms available to other biological entities whose genes are composed of DNA rather than RNA. Even rotaviruses in the stool of an infected child are never homogeneous. Thus, when I began passing the rotaviruses from the stool of one infected child in cultured cells, the selection process used to attenuate the virulent viruses present in this stool was, by definition, destined to create greater genetic diversity in the progeny viruses.

The end result of all this was that when we administered the 89-12 vaccine to our subjects, we inoculated them with viruses containing an array of genetic differences. SK knew this would not be acceptable for a vaccine that was to be marketed. One important reason was that any differences in responses from one subject to the next after vaccination had to be due to differences in the vaccinees and not to inconsistencies in the vaccine. At the same time, however, SK did not want to select a virus from our 89-12 stew that was inferior as a vaccine to the stew itself.

In an attempt to bridge both needs, SK randomly selected ten viruses from our 89-12 preparation, and the genes of each virus were compared to the viral genes in our vaccine stew. The plan was to select the rotavirus that most closely resembled the viruses that dominated our vaccine preparation, and use it to create a new product. Fortunately, all ten rotaviruses selected from the 89-12 vaccine were genetically similar, so selection of a single rotavirus that was representative of the others was not difficult. SK named the virus they selected RIX4414 in honor of their Rixensart facility in Belgium, and the trade name for the vaccine became Rotarix.

The first Phase II efficacy trial of Rotarix in infants got underway in Finland in 2000, about two years after SK sent a visitor to our lab in Cincinnati. Fortunately for us, when Rotashield collapsed a year before the study in Finland was scheduled to begin, SK never seemed to flinch in their mission to develop a new rotavirus vaccine. Later I learned that this was a myth, and SK did flinch, so much so that the company almost ceased development of Rotarix. This wouldn't be the last time SK would flinch.

The results obtained during this first Rotarix trial in Finland, published in 2004, confirmed what we had learned about the efficacy of its parent, the 89-12 vaccine. There were also suggestions of something equally important but entirely unexpected; the vaccine appeared to be fully attenuated in that fevers developed by the vaccinees were no more common than in placebo recipients. Thus, selection of a single virus from the myriad of potential virus strains in our 89-12 vaccine may have gotten the vaccine over another major hurdle.

Based on the successes found in Finland, Phase II evaluations of Rotarix were initiated almost immediately in Singapore and in three countries in Latin America, including Mexico, Brazil and Venezuela. By this time, Glaxo had become part of SmithKline. The new company, GSK, stayed on course with Rotarix development but, based on negative comments by American pediatricians because of the Rotashield debacle, concluded that it would not be prudent to immediately test the waters with another rotavirus vaccine in the USA. This fact, and the recognition that few of the greater than 500,000 deaths due to rotavirus in the world each year occur in the more affluent countries, caused GSK to activate a new paradigm in vaccine development, i.e., the evaluation of Rotarix was performed in less-developed countries in parallel with developed countries. Prior to this time, vaccines had always been introduced into the world's most wealthy countries, and only when the markets there were firmly established were they released into poorer nations at lower prices. Enactment of this new paradigm also permitted the vaccine to be evaluated up-front in more challenging environments, knowing it would eventually have to work well in less affluent countries if it was to significantly affect the mortality figures due to rotavirus infections.

The Rotarix trial conducted in Singapore provided the next reason for GSK to flinch. Rotarix had been administered to only a few infants when one developed intussusception within days of vaccination, the very outcome that killed Rotashield. This could have occurred only by chance, but it also could have foretold the demise of the vaccine. I later learned that GSK had serious in-house disagreement about whether to proceed with Rotarix development or to cut their losses early. In the end, they decided to carry on, at least until another case of intussusception was detected. With that decision, we had dodged another bullet.

Then the flinching really began. The initial results obtained in the three Latin American countries concerned the safety and immunogenicity of Rotarix, the latter being determined by the abilities of vaccinees to mount antibody responses against the vaccine virus as determined through analyses of blood specimens. Although no significant safety concerns were uncovered during this trial, including excess fevers in vaccinees, the immunogenicity results were bleak.

In Finland, the percentage of subjects protected by the vaccine had mimicked their abilities to mount immune responses. Furthermore, it was generally accepted that protection after vaccination would be no better, and probably worse, than measurable immune responses to the vaccine. Thus, when only 60% of the Latin American infants produced detectable rotavirus antibody responses after receiving two doses of Rotarix, GSK was ready to trash the vaccine. These less than sterling results were learned only days before GSK held a "partners" meeting in Rixensart. I attended the meeting, but my clear perception was that I would soon become an ex-partner. During the course of this three-day event, GSK highlighted every product they had in development, including some that were only in the planning stages, but Rotarix was never even mentioned.

I returned from the meeting totally dejected, holding little hope that the efficacy results would alter the inevitable. Months went by without any word on the level of protection against rotavirus disease elicited by Rotarix in Latin America. During that period, all manner of career changes came to mind. Finally, I was casually informed that an abstract on the efficacy results had been submitted as a "late-breaker" to the major clinical meeting on infectious diseases held annually in the USA. This message provided only enough information to know that we were on again. This tidbit of knowledge restored my sanity, but it also made me aware that I didn't hold any special status in the eyes of GSK. I guess they felt that the investigators presenting the results deserved the opportunity to surprise their audience, and I couldn't be trusted to keep their findings to myself. In the final analysis, protection against severe rotavirus disease in Latin America came in at an acceptable 83%, and was bumped up to 97% against very severe rotavirus illnesses.

One caveat amongst these highly encouraging results was that the rotavirus strains against which the vaccine provided protection in Latin America all shared some serotypic relationship with Rotarix. Thus, nothing was learned about how protective the vaccine would be against rotaviruses with no serotypic similarity to the vaccine strain. In addition, the number of subjects enrolled was too few to get any real assurance that the vaccine would not trigger intussusception in a low percentage of infants. This paucity of information needed to be rectified.

My primary role during these Rotarix trials was to provide a central laboratory for specimen analyses. My group examined blood specimens collected after vaccination to quantify rotavirus antibodies as a measure of vaccine responsiveness, and stool specimens collected during any episode of gastroenteritis during the follow-up efficacy evaluation period to determine if rotavirus was the cause of the illness. These activities had been initiated in my lab as a service to Wyeth during their development of Rotashield and the same were being performed for Merck during the development of the RotaTeq vaccine. Some of the funds I received for this work were used to support my other studies which were primarily associated with deciphering immunological mechanisms of protection against rotavirus. I also used these monies to develop a second rotavirus vaccine whose main ingredient was a single rotavirus protein. This was the back-up candidate in case 89-12 development was torpedoed by an adverse response such as intussusception, or vaccination with 89-12 provided insufficient protection against rotavirus disease.

Since I was an inventor of a vaccine that competed with both Rotashield and RotaTeq, these arrangements with Wyeth and Merck were rather unique. Maybe the decision makers in these companies felt confident that I could not manipulate the results of the tests performed in my lab because the identities of the specimens were fully blinded, but I instead hope it was their faith in my integrity that permitted me to wear two hats.

With the outcome of the three-country, Latin American trial in hand, GSK was ready to begin Phase III trials. The first was conducted in 11 Latin American countries and Finland. It was to be one of the two largest pre-licensure vaccine trials ever sponsored by a pharmaceutical company. The other, which was being conducted primarily in America and Finland, was with Merck's rotavirus vaccine candidate. Both studies enrolled over 60,000 infants each, half of which received the respective vaccines and half were administered a placebo. Such massive studies were done to insure that the risk of developing intussusception after vaccination was less than had been found after administration of Rotashield. That vaccine did not have lasting success, but its demise had a lasting effect on the development of future rotavirus vaccines.

The outcomes of these two monumental rotavirus vaccine trials were published in tandem in January, 2006, in The New England Journal of Medicine, and were recognized as the premier clinical publications of the year. As reported, neither group of vaccinees experienced more intussusception than the respective placebo recipients in these trials, and both vaccines provided more than 85% protection against severe rotavirus disease.

During the large Rotarix trial, rotaviruses that were serotypically dissimilar from the vaccine strain were found to have circulated in Latin America. There weren't a large number of children infected with these strains, so the results were inconclusive, but the vaccine did provide some level of protection against rotaviruses belonging to a serotype not contained in the vaccine. This was the first time Rotarix had been put to this test, but more information needed to be collected before my prediction concerning cross-serotype protection after infection with a single strain of rotavirus could be confirmed.

The next Rotarix trial was conducted in six countries in Europe where nearly 4,000 infants were administered two doses of Rotarix. Two of the most important outcomes of this trial were that the vaccine provided 96% protection against severe rotavirus disease, and astonishingly, 75% protection against hospital admissions due to gastroenteritis of any cause. This was remarkable, but would be much more remarkable if these results were translatable into the developing world setting. A third important outcome of this European study was that the vaccine provided 75% protection against a rotavirus serotype not represented in Rotarix, and the numbers of illnesses due to this serotype were sufficient to make the results statistically significant. Perhaps my hypothesis concerning the adequacy of a single-strain rotavirus vaccine would now be credible to a larger audience.

Based on the results of the large Latin American study, Rotarix was licensed in Mexico in August, 2004, and the product was launched in the Mexican private market in January, 2005. Shortly thereafter, the vaccine was licensed in multiple countries in Latin America and became part of the routine immunization series in several, the largest of which was Brazil.

By 2006, the World Health Organization was sufficiently impressed with the results of Rotarix trials that they recommended the vaccine for universal use in the most economically-deprived countries in Latin America and Europe. They, however, withheld their recommendation for the world's poorest countries in Asia and Africa until the vaccine was shown to be effective in those settings.

In the meantime, the Rotarix vaccine continued to be licensed throughout the world including, among other places, Europe and Australia in 2006 and finally in America in 2008. By the time it was available in the USA, the vaccine had been licensed in over 110 countries. Merck's rotavirus vaccine was launched in America in 2006 and also continued to be licensed around the world.

Even though the large majority of the deaths due to rotavirus occur in the world's poorest countries, there had been no efficacy trials with either of the new rotavirus vaccines completed in any of these settings by the end of 2007. This left a gaping hole that had to be plugged before the overall value of these new vaccines could be evaluated. To understand the potential pitfalls associated with the effectiveness of these vaccines in the least developed nations, one only had to recall the fate of the first calf rotavirus vaccine. When tested in Finland, it provided excellent protection, but in Africa it was deemed a failure, and further evaluation was halted.

In 2005, efficacy trials with Rotarix were begun in Africa, first in South Africa and later in Malawi, but subject follow-up was not completed until July, 2008. Overall efficacy against severe rotavirus disease was 61% during these trials, less than had been found in previous studies conducted in more affluent countries. Importantly, it was shown that multiple illnesses occurred in the African trial that were due to rotaviruses belonging to serotypes not represented in Rotarix, and protection against these strains was at least as effective as against rotavirus strains that did share a serotype relationship with the vaccine virus. Thus, the reduced efficacy of Rotarix found in this developing world setting was not due to lack of cross-serotype protection.

Even though protection was less in Africa than it had been elsewhere, the numbers of severe rotavirus illnesses in countries where Rotarix was tested were so large that even a vaccine that provided only 61 percent protection would still save many thousands of lives each year. For this reason, the World Health Organization recommended universal use of Rotarix in all the world's poorest countries in April, 2009, thus providing the key to unlock the door leading to benefactor funding for the distribution of the vaccine in these settings.

At this brief moment in time, it appeared that Rotarix had successfully evaded every booby trap in the mine field of vaccine extinction, and all that remained was to get it distributed and used in the world's poorest nations. At least, that was how it appeared. However, on March 22, 2010, the FDA announced a temporary halt in the use of the Rotarix vaccine in America. This set off a minor chain reaction across the globe as Hong Kong, Israel, Switzerland and Panama, to name a few, swiftly followed suit. The reason given for the action by the FDA was that DNA of a pig virus had been found in the vaccine. This discovery was made by a group of investigators at the University of California, San Francisco, who were randomly evaluating vaccines for the possible presence of extraneous viruses using new DNA amplification techniques. The contaminant was from a porcine virus called PCV-1. This virus is shed in large quantities in pig feces but causes no illness. Furthermore, it is believed that humans are regularly exposed to this virus through consumption of pork, and pass-through PCV-1 DNA is regularly found in human stools in the absence of disease.

By the time of the FDA announcement, it was estimated that over 30 million doses of Rotarix had been distributed worldwide without evidence of any adverse effects. Even with this colossal amount of information, the FDA still reacted, thus creating a domino effect around the world. Fortunately, the EMEA, Europe's equivalent of the FDA, considered it a non-event, as did the World Health Organization. Thus, the use of Rotarix was continued in most nations where the lives of many young children would have been lost in its absence.

Once PCV-1 was discovered in Rotarix, the source of the contamination was quickly identified by GSK in the seed stock of the cells in which the vaccine virus was grown. It was then determined that the likely origin of PCV-1 in these cells was the enzyme trypsin which is obtained from pancreatic juices of pigs and is added to cultured cells during routine maintenance.

On May 7, less than two months after Rotarix was recommended for removal in America, GSK representatives testified before a panel of experts assembled by the FDA to evaluate whether its earlier recommendation to remove Rotarix from use in America should be maintained. During the six week interlude, GSK scientists had examined the stools of vaccinated children and on May 7 testified that there was no evidence that the PCV-1 virus in the vaccine had infected intestinal cells of the vaccinees. Further support that PCV-1 was not infectious in these subjects was provided by the lack of detectable immune responses to the pig virus in these vaccinees. These data were presented along with evidence accumulated by the Centers for Disease Control that the use of Rotarix had already saved multiple lives worldwide, and routine immunization with the two rotavirus vaccines had almost eliminated hospitalizations due to rotavirus in America.

Even with these data, it was doubtful that the ban on Rotarix distribution in America would be lifted by the FDA. That is, not until another bombshell was dropped. During the meeting, it was revealed that RotaTeq, the other rotavirus vaccine used in America, was also contaminated with PCV-1 as well as with a second porcine virus called PCV-2. These discoveries were made shortly after the March 22 recommendation was issued on Rotarix but had not been shared with the news media until just prior to this meeting held nearly two months later. With this new finding, it was apparent the FDA either had to recommend that both vaccines be removed in America or that the use of both should be continued. Since the use of neither rotavirus vaccine had been associated with adverse responses after vaccination of millions of children, the benefits of their usage far outweighed the unidentified risks. Therefore, on May 14, the FDA reversed their earlier recommendation for Rotarix, and stated that vaccination with both rotavirus vaccines should be continued in America.

This setback with Rotarix was just the most recent hurdle in the development and distribution of a vaccine that could save hundreds of thousands of lives across the world. Today, the increase in the use of Rotarix has finally begun to make a dent in the numbers of child deaths due to rotavirus, but only when this and other rotavirus vaccines are routinely administered to infants in all of the world's poorest nations will their full impact be realized.

Epilogue

After the dust settled on the latest problem with Rotarix, it became time to reflect on what my life has meant. Hopefully it is more than being the inventor of a vaccine that may be off the shelves tomorrow. During the multiple times when the 89-12 vaccine, and then Rotarix, seemed destined to be discarded, the temptation was always to consider all I had worked for to be a failure. On each of these occasions, after I had told myself to get a grip, taken several deep breaths, and was once again ready to move on, I realized that all anyone can do is try, and I certainly had done that. Even when I made career decisions over the years that seemingly resulted in dead ends, I know now that I had acted on the knowledge I had at the time. And there is no way of knowing whether what appeared in hindsight to have been a better decision might have eventually landed me in a worse spot.

Now, as an inventor of a vaccine that is being used to save the lives of young children each day, I rationally understand I am fortunate to have been in the right spot this particular time; at some point I will probably even emotionally appreciate that fact, as well as the fact that I was able to contribute to the world of virology in other significant ways as witnessed by nearly 200 scientific publications. As with everyone who is entering their Golden Years, I need to recognize that my contributions and, thereby, sense of self-worth, are determined by a lifetime of actions, no one of which can be used as the measure of success or failure. However, this must be understood and accepted before it can be appreciated. Perhaps someday I will.

ABOUT THE AUTHOR

Richard Ward was raised in Bozeman, Montana, where he graduated from Montana State College. He received a PhD degree in biochemistry from the University of California in Berkeley and became a Member of the Technical Staff at Sandia National Laboratories in Albuquerque, NM. He served as a Virology Section Chief at the Environmental Protection Agency in Cincinnati, Ohio and later joined the Gamble Institute of Medical Research in Cincinnati where he eventually became the Director of Clinical Virology. He joined Cincinnati Children's Hospital Medical Center as a Professor of Pediatrics in 1995. He is the author of nearly 200 scientific publications on viral biology and immunology.